Viennawalks

This is the
Henry Holt Walks Series
which originated with
PARISWALKS *by Alison and Sonia Landes.*
Other titles in the series include:

LONDONWALKS *by Anton Powell*
JERUSALEMWALKS *by Nitza Rosovsky*
ROMEWALKS *by Anya M. Shetterly*
RUSSIAWALKS *by David and Valeria Matlock*
VENICEWALKS *by Chas Carner and Alessandro Giannatasio*
BARCELONAWALKS *by George Semler*
BEIJINGWALKS *by Don J. Cohn and Zhang Jingqing*
NEW YORKWALKS *by The 92nd Street Y*
MADRIDWALKS *by George Semler*
BERLINWALKS *by Peter Fritzsche and Karen Hewitt*
FLORENCEWALKS *by Anne Holler*
PRAGUEWALKS *by Ivana Edwards*

VIENNAWALKS

REVISED EDITION

J. Sydney Jones

Photographs by
J. Sydney Jones

An Owl Book

Henry Holt and Company • New York

Henry Holt and Company, Inc.
Publishers since 1866
115 West 18th Street
New York, New York 10011

Henry Holt® is a registered
trademark of Henry Holt and Company, Inc.

Library of Congress Cataloging-in-Publication Data

Jones, J. Sydney.
Viennawalks / J. Sydney Jones; photographs by J. Sydney Jones.
p.   cm.—(The Henry Holt walks series)
"An Owl book."
Includes bibliographical references and index.
1. Vienna (Austria)—Tours.   2. Walking—Austria—Vienna—
Guidebooks.   I. Title.   II. Series.
DB849.J665   1993   93-30360
914.36'130453—dc20   CIP

ISBN 0-8050-2385-2

Henry Holt books are available for special promotions
and premiums. For details contact:
Director, Special Markets.

First Owl Book Edition—1985

Designed by Claire Vaccaro
Maps by David Lindroth

Printed in the United States of America
All first editions are printed on acid-free paper. ∞

1   3   5   7   9   10   8   6   4   2

For Tess
A born Viennese

Contents

Acknowledgments

Thanks again to the city of Vienna and my friends there who make it always feel like home, no matter how many years transpire between visits. Special thanks to Lonnie Johnson for his insightful comments and beer evenings.

Gratitude and *Danke* also for this second edition to my editor at Holt, Theresa Burns, for whom no telephone query was too silly. Her enthusiasm for the Walks Series is infectious.

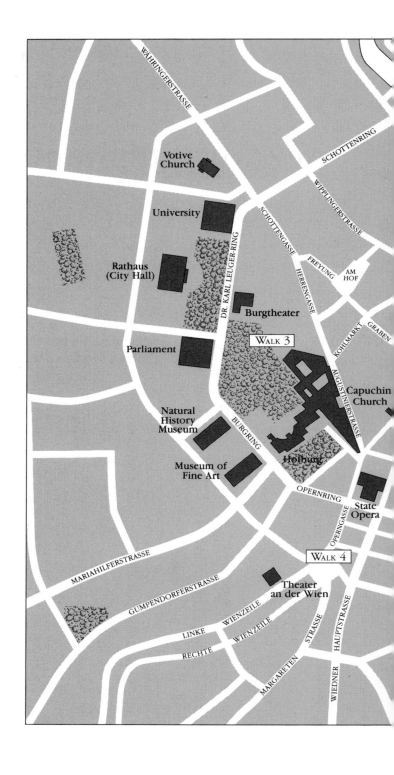

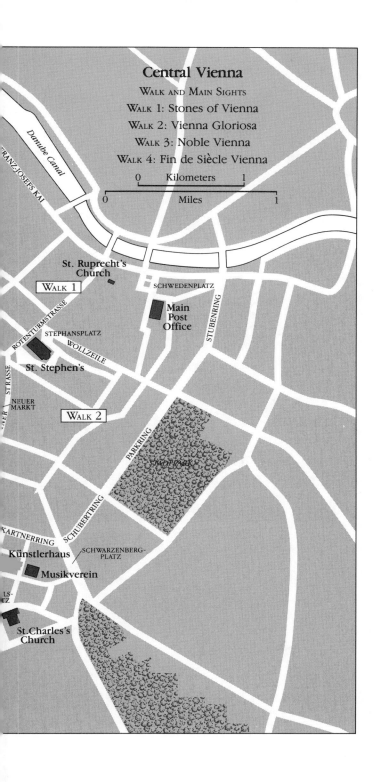

Central Vienna

WALK AND MAIN SIGHTS

WALK 1: Stones of Vienna

WALK 2: Vienna Gloriosa

WALK 3: Noble Vienna

WALK 4: Fin de Siècle Vienna

0 — Kilometers — 1

0 — Miles — 1

Danube Canal

FRANZ-JOSEFS KAI

St. Ruprecht's Church

WALK 1

SCHWEDENPLATZ

Main Post Office

ROTENTURMSTRASSE

STUBENRING

STEPHANSPLATZ

WOLLZEILE

St. Stephen's

STRASSE

NEUER MARKT

WALK 2

PARKRING

STADTPARK

SCHUBERTRING

KÄRTNERRING

Künstlerhaus

SCHWARZENBERG-PLATZ

Musikverein

LS-TZ

St. Charles's Church

Introduction

When I was in college and was force-fed the masters of literature, I used to groan to myself when confronted with the inevitable Foreword or Author's Note.

"Oh, come off it, mate," I used to say to myself. "A book worth its salt has no need of an introduction. Do get on with the business at hand of telling a story or informing, whatever your purpose may be."

Hardy comes especially to mind: the grand old master compelled, in his old age, to write foreword after foreword to his collected works—the early stories of which, had they been penned by another, would never again have seen the light of day. All those jejune stories and novels from the time when this great storyteller had been learning his craft; all those prefaces-as-apologies, excusing youthful excess, amateurish construction.

Now I am confronted with the distasteful task of putting forth my own preface; granted, it is more explanation than apologia. My sophomoric scorn has been since tempered with fortyish compassion, yet still I blanch at the thought of having to beg my readers' indulgence. But get on with it, man, I should tell myself; make a clean breast of things. . . .

Vienna is a city built in concentric rings about itself, like a tree grown ungainly from sapling to granddaddy of the forest. A Roman and medieval core, protected by a wall, sprouted baroque suburban appendages that were, in turn, bordered by the outer Line Wall in the eighteenth century. These two walls were razed in the mid-nineteenth century; boulevards replaced them and an urban renewal project out-Haussmanning Paris's Baron Haussmann took place. Yet still there is this concentric-ring construction to Vienna, the rings created by the Ringstrasse and the Gürtel. The medieval core—the Inner City, Old City, or First District as it is variously known—is still the center of Vienna, practically as well as geographically and metaphorically. Not even the most chauvinistic of Viennese would try to convince a visitor that Vienna has anything comparable to Chelsea or the Left Bank outside of the Inner City. There are neighborhoods of distinction in the outer districts (outside of the Ring) and chic addresses and in spots. Some districts are more chic than others, some more neighborhoodlike, some filled with historical importance. None, however, provides the variety, history, continuity, and centeredness (in the physical sense of the word) that Vienna's First District does.

That the tours in this guide focus on the Inner City then, as most other guides to Vienna do, is not an indication of staleness or lack of imagination on this writer's part. I could very well have led you on a merry chase to some of the lovely streets outside of the old city: rambling along the streets that Freud frequented, for example, or where the aristocracy settled near Schönbrunn in the lovely greenery of Hietzing, or among the fortresslike housing developments that "Red Vienna" of the 1920s and 1930s created. But such excursions in a walking guide like this one would be disastrous, for once the major sight has been visited, what is the walker to do? Hop on a tram and head back to a more walkable area where more variety exists? Or grin and bear it and wander for block after block through outer-district neighborhoods that might prove a fascinating diversion for the native Viennese, but might amount to too much knowledge about too little for the visitor or traveler?

Decisions have been made then initially, long before the walking or writing began on this guide. I had to choose areas for walking that not only were manageable by foot but illustrated aspects of Viennese life I found most fascinating, rewarding, historically informative, bizarre—whatever adjective I took at the time as my operative motto.

Arbitrary, if you will. But arbitrary only within the confines of considered opinion. Time after time I came back to the realization that Vienna does exist in a miniaturized, contiguous nutshell in the First District. Palaces and Gothic churches, but also neighborhoods and the vagaries of daily life are all to be seen and experienced here in one walkable area. Although the final walk in this book does veer out of the Inner City into the neighborhoods of the Sixth District, near Vienna's outdoor market, I have not attempted to denigrate other districts by this choice, but rather to tantalize you with the possibilities that lie outside the Ringstrasse. It is—to revert to Victorian custom now—this author's fervent wish that this book will act as a catalyst and introduction to Vienna and will guide you to an understanding and recognition of the layer upon layer of life still to be uncovered after these four tours are completed. This is a starter, then, an hors d'oeuvre. I leave it to you, the intrepid traveler, to discover the main course.

About the actual tours themselves: there are four, and each attempts an excursion in time as well as space. Taken in numerical order, these four tours will provide a historical primer for the visitor to Vienna. Taken all at once, however, they might prove to be too much. These are ambitious walking tours, each taking about four hours. I suggest a thorough reading of the tour the night before setting out, so as to digest the historical bits. That way you won't forever have your nose in the book as you are walking. Each tour could easily be broken in half, thus providing eight shorter walks.

One final thing before we get on with it. I recently returned to Vienna after an eight-year absence, in part to do the updating for the second edition of this book, in part out of nostalgia. I was prepared for the worst—after all, everything changes. And change in the late twentieth century usually means degradation when it comes to an urban environment.

I was happily surprised. If anything, Vienna is more beautiful and "European" than I remember it being. The monuments have had recent face-lifts, open space has been made into intimate little parks at every turn, and new artists and architects with a new vision have helped to bring Vienna quite gracefully and elegantly into the modern age. Unlike most European cities, fast food has not taken over. The car has made greater incursions, but Vienna is still blessed with one of the finest public transit systems in the world, and the air is still breathable, the water cool and sparkling as always.

With the breakup of the Eastern Bloc there has been, however, a perceptible shift in the openness of the Viennese. With a new influx of immigration from the East, Austria has new problems as well as opportunities, for it is the eternal buffer state. Neutral in the Cold War, it must now learn to take sides, and it is not yet clear where the country is headed: back into an Austria-first mentality or forward into a new internationalism.

Politics and philosophy aside, it *is* clear that Vienna has come into the European family in one respect: cost. No longer is Vienna the inexpensive capital of faded elegance. Expect to pay typical international prices at hotels and restaurants. The upper end of costs is still reasonable compared to New York, London, or Paris, but overall prices have increased greatly since the first edition of this book.

But I cannot end this introduction on a sour note:

Vienna is still suspended somehow out of time, like one of those fragile moments in a Vermeer painting. For anyone wanting to experience what life is like in a truly great European city, Vienna is a must. I do not say this out of some kitsch idea of Euro-Disney but out of a profound respect and love for a city that was for many years my home and refuge and that continues to be for many a refuge in a world at times out of touch with the human dimension.

Information
and Advice

BEFORE YOU GO

As the most important thing you could do for yourself before traveling to Vienna is to read about the city, I shall cover the most mechanical, general tourist information first and quickly. Then we can get to the reading material.

No tourist visa is needed for a stay of up to three months in Austria for those holding U.S., Canadian, or British Commonwealth passports. Your passport will merely be stamped at the border or at the airport. Your place of residence is responsible for filling out the police registration forms for you. As in most European countries, the authorities in Austria like to keep track of its population, both native and foreign. If you stay in private lodgings, the host or hostess may ask you to fill out the police registration forms yourself; if you stay in a hotel or pension, this matter will be taken care of for you. Let us only hope that you need not, in the former case, have to go personally to the nearest police station with forms in hand—in quintuplicate, of course. Such bureaucratic engagements can provide a miniseminar in the Kafkian psyche. If you are planning a stay longer than three months, it is advisable to apply for a visa from the Austrian embassy or consulate closest to you before departure. By the way, I can recommend no better airline for flights into Austria than Austrian Air, one of the only commercial liners left to serve its admirable food and coffee off porcelain.

The best times to visit Vienna are autumn and spring. But I am biased. Summer is a bit of a bore in Vienna as not only can the city be humid and less than fresh-smelling, but also this is the season when most of the attractions that travelers associate with Vienna are closed down. The Lipizzaners go out to well-deserved pasture as do the members of the Philharmonic and the State Opera. Theaters and concert halls shut their doors for vacation, and what is left for musical sampling is mostly imported mediocrity at outdoor performances. The Salzburg Festival steals the cultural limelight in the Austrian summer.

Winter is not a bad season to travel to Vienna, with off-season prices, uncrowded museums, and all cultural life going at full steam. But winters can be cold, and the winds here chill to the bone. A motherly bit of advice to those of you traveling from the more temperate climes to Vienna in the winter: do not expect to walk into a centrally heated world here. The Viennese still do, by and large, try to heat their bodies with clothing rather than their environment. If accustomed to the ease of jumping from one acclimatized environment to the other, rethink your categories for Vienna. A warm coat, sweaters, and warm (fur-lined) walking shoes are all a must for a Vienna winter.

Now for the important stuff: books. A lot of drivel has of course been written about the Habsburgs (all but synonymous with Vienna, "their" imperial city for centuries) and more especially about the Mayerling tragedy and the sad life of Empress "Sissy." But for every bit of historical pulp churned out about the city there are corresponding fine, informative, historically accurate, and entertaining books of merit that act as a counterbalance. See the Selected Bibliography for the complete list of my personally recommended books and authors. For now I shall go through a short list of books that no thoughtful traveler can afford to miss.

Taking precedence on anybody's list of Vienna books must be the works of Edward Crankshaw. This English historian has written about most aspects of Austrian history, focusing, however, on the lives and the reigns of the Habsburgs. Crankshaw's books should be your constant companions in the months before departure.

There are a couple of good histories of the city: one by Ilsa Barea, *Vienna, Legend and Reality*, and another by Lonnie Johnson, co-authored with Inge Lehne, *Vienna, The Past in the Present*. Johnson has also written an excellent primer to Austria in general, *Introducing Austria*.

Another popular history, this time of the Habsburgs themselves and thus, tangentially, of Vienna as well, is *The Habsburgs* by Dorothy Gies McGuigan. Out of print in English though the German paperback edition is available in Vienna, this provides a fine anecdotal outline of the lives of that family of kings and queens.

The nineteenth century, and in particular fin de siècle Vienna, has become something of a cottage industry for historians and popular writers alike. This epoch before World War I has been researched and written about to the point of something like nausea. I must myself confess to being among that legion of eager writers who has added his or her two cents' worth to the general discussion. My *Hitler in Vienna 1907–1913* is both a primer to Vienna's turn-of-the-century renaissance and a brief biography of the most important developmental years of Hitler, an inmate of fin de siècle Vienna. On a more intellectual scale—that is, a book of essays rather than a narrative history—is Carl Schorske's *Fin-de-Siècle Vienna*. Several art books, in particular Peter Vergo's, deal with the artistic revolution, *Jugendstil*, at the turn of the century. (See the Selected Bibliography for a detailed listing of books.)

GENERAL INFORMATION

For the best pamphlets in all the minutiae I broadly label General Information, contact the Austrian National Tourist Office, at any one of four North American locations: 500 Fifth Avenue, Suite 2009-2022, New York, NY 10110, (212) 944-6880; 11601 Wilshire Boulevard, Suite 2480, Los Angeles, CA 90025, (310) 477-3332; 500 North Michigan Avenue, Suite 1950, Chicago, IL 60611, (312) 644-8029; or 2 Bloor Street, Suite 3330, Toronto, Ontario, M4W 1A8, (416) 967-3381. The London offices are at 30 St. George Street, London W1R OAL, (071) 62 90 461.

Once in Vienna, all sorts of useful pamphlets and maps can be had free of charge from the Vienna Tourist Board, Obere Augartenstrasse 40, A-1025 Vienna, or at a handy downtown location, Kaerntnerstrasse 38, open from 9:00 A.M. to 7:00 P.M. daily.

Arriving in Vienna is a rather painless experience. By train you'll come in at either the west or south train stations (Westbahnhof and Sudbahnhof), both of which are just a tram or subway ride away from the center of the city. Arriving at the airport at Schwechat, you're only a twenty-minute trip to the center by express bus, available from 6:00 A.M. to midnight and caught just outside the main terminal building; or by train, which you can catch in the subbasement of the airport and which goes every hour. Both take you to just near the Ringstrasse at Wien-Mitte, Landstrasse. These means of transportation are well under ten dollars.

When first arriving in Vienna, you may want to orientate yourself in the city with a general sightseeing tour before setting out on these more specialized walks. There are two major sightseeing companies: Cityrama Sightseeing Tours and Vienna Sightseeing Tours. Both of these provide reasonably priced minitours of the city. Cityrama Tours depart from Stephansplatz and Vienna Tours from the Opera. (More information on times can be had from your hotel or pension.)

About times and time in general: Vienna is on Central European time (six hours ahead of New York, nine ahead of San Francisco) and goes on daylight savings time between late March and late September of each year. Shops are generally open from 9:00 A.M. to 6:00 P.M., Monday through Friday, with a half-day opening on Saturday. Sunday the city closes down. Food shops (and many other service shops as well) may open earlier—some as early as 6:00 A.M.—and also close at midday for a Central European siesta of up to two hours. Food shops at the West and South train stations have longer opening hours and, if you find yourself caught in a pinch, are open on Sunday. Maddening to most travelers, these business hours are—once one learns how to work around them—part of Vienna's peculiar old-world charm. One quickly learns that, in Vienna, shopping is not one of those freedoms listed in the constitution.

But all of the above information is useless if you cannot read time, European and Austrian style. No A.M., P.M. goofiness here. The twenty-four-hour clock is used, as in the military. Midnight is 24:00; noon is 12:00. The short-hand form of writing times, as for the theater or movies, is confusing in the extreme, however. A fraction is used with the full hour to indicate how much of the preceding hour has been used up. The only thing that saves this bizarre situation is that the fraction comes before the hour in the written form. Thus, $1/47$ is 6:15 or, literally, one-quarter into the hour before seven; $1/27$ is 6:30, etc.

Another numbering difference occurs with floor numbers in buildings. Since the bottom or ground floor is called just that in German, it follows that the first floor must be above it. *Sometimes* this is true. I emphasize the "sometimes" because often there are intervening floors—as many as three—between the ground floor and the "first" floor. As you climb the endless flights of dimly lit stairs, keep looking for the wall signs to find out just what floor you are really on.

ACCOMMODATIONS

I once knew a traveling couple who were gemütlichkeit fetishists. They brought with them not only their own wineglasses, but also a few odds and ends to hang on the walls of hotels and pensions where they stayed. With this traveling household, they managed to sink roots in any room in a matter of minutes. Why I bring this up is that Vienna can do all this for you: many of the pensions in the city have these homely little odds and ends already scattered about. It is not uncommon to stay in rooms with molded ceilings, parquet floors, Persian carpets, and solid oak tables and chairs. Depending on your budget and taste, any kind of atmosphere can be found in Vienna. Stick to the more modest pensions rather than hotels; do not stay near the train stations no matter how plentiful the pensions are there or what the travel-on-the-cheap books say. Best bets for pensions outside of the First District are in the Seventh, Eighth, and Ninth districts. Some good Inner City pensions just on or off Graben are Pertschy, Aclon, and Nossek. Rooms in private houses are also available; for these, go to the office of the Vienna Tourist Board at the Kaerntnerstrasse location near the Opera.

But, as stated in the introduction, there are no real bargains anymore in Vienna; expect typical Northern European prices in all classes of pensions and hotels. There are hotels aplenty for those who want to splurge. One of the best hotels in the world, with a very colorful history, lies just behind the State Opera, the Hotel Sacher. On a corner opposite the Opera is the Bristol, still the smart place for five o'clock tea, and down the Ringstrasse toward Schwarzenbergplatz is the lovely and elegant Imperial. You want to stay in a hotel that is still a palace? Fine. Try the Hotel in Palais Schwarzenberg and be prepared to pay palatial sums as well.

For the purely adventurous there are always the youth hostels, one of which is situated in the cellars of a flak tower. These flak towers, left behind by the Third Reich, look as surreal as the events of the years in which they were built and cannot be easily destroyed, since their walls are too thick.

The best starting point for making reservations is to request a hotel and pension list from the Austrian National Tourist Office. Be sure to write the hotel or pension you select well ahead of time (with self-addressed envelope and international reply coupons). If you care to, you can take potluck most of the year and travel without reservations, but specially difficult times (outside of the summer months) are September, when the trade fair is on, and May, when the Vienna Festival is held.

TRANSPORTATION

It should be obvious that the major form of transport I am encouraging is of the self-propelled variety. The walking tours in this book have, to a large extent, been limited to the Inner City, just so they would be eminently walkable. If, then, you choose a pension or hotel that is not located on the far side of Madagascar, you will be able to stick to your own two feet. But for those spots farther afield you have an excellent (though not terribly logical) transport system at your command. The first thing you need is a ticket (*Fahrschein*), which can be purchased in advance in books of five from the tobacconists (*Tabak-Trafik*) by asking for a *Vorverkauf Fahrschein*. If these tickets are purchased on the tram or bus not only is the price higher, but you must also have exact change to feed the machines. Beware: There are no such machines on the subways. Tickets must be purchased before entering the turnstiles. Controllers do spot-checks on the transport system and can issue fines that will put a damper on anybody's fun.

An excellent choice for the short-term visitor is the twenty-four-hour or seventy-two-hour pass, also available at the tobacconists, which allows unlimited use of Viennese public transport for either span of time. There is also a weekly card that requires a photo and is valid for seven consecutive days. The eight-day card, which is a better bargain, allows you to select any eight days of unlimited travel.

Trips on Vienna's transport system are on a one-fare basis: it is the same fare for two stops as for ten miles. There are special short-trip tickets, but these are too complicated to explain because they are not valid for a set number of stops, but only for certain zones on each of the different lines. Another thing about fares: One ticket is valid for as many transfers as are necessary to get from point A to point B, with as many carriers of the system as are needed (subway, tram, *and* bus).

There are buses, trams, and subways in Vienna, and the city is definitely committed to public transport. It is happily reported that all of Vienna's public transport system, if laid out in a straight line, would cover the distance between Vienna and Venice. The Vienna subway, or U-Bahn, is speedy and efficient. So far it has five lines: the U1, between the north side of the Danube and Reumannplatz in the south; the U2, which goes back and forth between Karlsplatz and Schottenring, roughly following the western edge of the Ringstrasse; the U3, traveling between the Volkstheater and Erdberg in the Third District and going under the First District; the U4, between Karlsplatz and Hutteldorf in the west; and the U6, going north and south from Heiligenstadt to Meidling.

Trams and buses have numbers clearly posted on them and their destinations as well. Purchase a transport map from any of the tourist information offices in town or from the Transport Authority in the underground passage at Karlsplatz to find exactly which tram, bus, or subway line you should take to reach your destination. (There are almost three dozen different tram lines that spider-web the city and another seventy-five bus lines covering those areas missed by tram and subway.) In general, most destinations are easily reached from city center as this is the terminus of many lines.

For those of you wanting to take taxis, they are omnipresent in Vienna except, of course, when you need one. Fares are controlled up until midnight, after which it is a sellers' market, but still within controlled outer limits. Taxis can be found at taxi stands all over the city, hailed in the street, or ordered by phone (look under "Taxi" in the white—not yellow—pages).

ENTERTAINMENT

Once known only as the "capital of music," Vienna has expanded its entertainment profile in recent years to include avant-garde theater, mime, and arty film houses. But unless (with the exception of mime) you have a good command of German, your experiences are going to center on those traditional music houses the city has to offer. The first thing to remember about these concert halls, as mentioned earlier, is that they are closed during the summer months, from July through September.

Of all Vienna's musical treats, the State Opera is perhaps the best known in the world. This is not simply a matter of promotion, either, for Vienna's Opera still does rank in the top five in Europe. And it is not only opera that plays here, but also ballet with guest artists appearing regularly. Compared to the costs in the rest of the world, tickets to the State Opera are quite reasonable: one can sit in a moderately good gallery seat for prices beginning at under twenty dollars. These tickets, however, are not easy to come by, and there are many Byzantine ways to secure tickets with which the Viennese alone are familiar. Ticket agencies—often allied with travel agencies—do of course sell tickets. But it behooves these agencies to sell the more expensive tickets, as their profit is a cut of the ticket price. One can try the *Abendkasse* (box office) on the day of the performance at the Opera (or other theaters, for that matter), but do not expect great success there. Only the seats with high prices and poor views will be left at the Opera box office. The usual practice for tickets for the federal theaters (State Opera, Volkstheater, Volksoper, Burgtheater, and Akademietheater) is to go to their central ticket agency, the Bundestheaterverband, Goethegasse 1, just in back of the Opera. There you can purchase tickets one week in advance of the performance date. However, go early in the morning of the first sales date. When there is a particularly good performance at the Opera with world-famous singers, the Viennese will begin lining up at night for the next day's opening. By midweek, you can assume that most of the good tickets, if not all, have been purchased for an Opera performance. By lining up at six or seven in the morning at the federal ticket office one week before performance, however, you should be able to get a moderately priced ticket with no problem.

A cheaper alternative for operagoers is *Stehplatz*, or standing room. But this also involves the inevitable lining-up process. For this you go to the Operngasse side of the Opera, to the door marked *Abendkasse*. Be sure to be there by at least 4:00 P.M. the day of the performance. Overzealous Opera ushers will shepherd you until about 6:00 P.M. when you are allowed to buy standing room tickets. The best of these are in the parterre or, if that is sold out, in the *Galerie*. Both types of tickets are sold for under two dollars. And be sure to bring a handkerchief or scarf with you so that you can mark your place on the railing of the standing room. Once you reserve your place in this manner, you can slip out for a cup of coffee or a snack before the performance begins.

I imagine you are all wondering just how anybody has time for work in Vienna what with lining up at all hours of the day and night to hear a bunch of nuts bellowing about unrequited love and lost gold. Students, retired people, and intrepid travelers are the ones who primarily use the *Stehplatz* gimmick; their primary resource is time rather than money. Quite egalitarian when you stop to think of it.

Now you know how to get a ticket; what about where and for what? There is enough music outside the walls of the Opera to satisfy the greediest pair of ears. On any given night during the season, there may be as many as seven different classical music events going on. (This is not counting modern musicals at Theater an der Wien and operetta at the Volksoper.) The two main concert halls, the Konzerthaus and Musikverein, alone have five different performing halls between them, and they are all usually in use at the same time. Tickets can be purchased in advance directly at the house in question. The *Stehplatz* trick holds true for the main, large halls of both the Konzerthaus and Musikverein, but it is nothing like the torturous process at the Opera. Usually you can just show up a half hour before performance time and get one of these greatly reduced tickets.

However, tickets for the Vienna Philharmonic, which plays on Sunday mornings at the Musikverein, are all but impossible to get. Seats are grabbed up in subscriptions, and there is even a subscription for the *Stehplatz*, which is done on strict *Stehplatz* rules at the beginning of each season. If you want to hear the Philharmonic (truly one of the great orchestras of the world), listen to them at the Opera, where they play nightly.

Besides music, there are twenty-eight theaters in Vienna, where you can see everything from Schiller to Pinter and beyond. The best way to find out what is happening at all these places of entertainment is to stop at the Vienna Tourist Board in the Kaerntnerstrasse and pick up the current *Wien Programm*, a monthly schedule of music and theater.

The daily papers also have listings of concerts and theaters as well as movies. Of the theaters in Vienna, two do plays in English: the English Theater, Josefgasse 12, and the International Theater, Porzellangasse 8. Of the movie houses in Vienna, two specialize in English-language films: the Burg Kino on the Opernring and the Schotten Kino on Schottenring. The Albertina Film Museum in back of the Opera also plays retrospectives from all over the world, often of the masters of Hollywood. One must join the Film Archive (part of the Albertina Museum itself) for a nominal yearly subscription to be entitled to purchase very reasonable tickets to these film showings.

There are also plenty of English-language publications to be purchased from the kiosks all over Vienna: the homegrown varieties of these publications come and go as finances dwindle, but there is usually at any given time some four-color magazine and a tabloid newspaper printed in Vienna. Two bookshops in town specialize in English-language books (with a bias, however, on British as the American editions are so expensive to import): the British Bookshop on Blumenstockgasse near St. Stephen's Cathedral and Shakespeare and Company on Sterngasse in the First District near the old Jewish ghetto.

One other fine institution long-term visitors to Vienna should know about is the British Council Library on Schenkengasse in the First District just off Herrengasse. Yearly membership here entitles you to the loan of four books, four records or tapes, and four films or videocassettes. You can browse through newspapers and magazines as well.

As for the museums, there are well over a hundred state, city, and private ones spread throughout Vienna. You could spend half a lifetime just seeing all these. I mention some on the course of the walks, but must-sees are the *Kunsthistorisches* on the Burgring with its incredible collection of Breughel paintings; the Austrian Gallery in the Upper Belvedere on Prinz Eugen Strasse with its Klimts, Schieles, and Kokoschkas; and the Historical Museum of the City of Vienna on Karlsplatz for its historical introduction to the place. State museums cost over five dollars and the city museums are from one to three dollars. (The latter are free on Friday mornings.) A list of museums and special exhibits is available through the tourist board.

FOOD AND DRINK

No one would try to push Vienna and Austria as culinary-rich places. But there is one great thing to be said in favor of eating in Vienna: seldom will you be terribly disappointed here, as you can be elsewhere in the world where expectations are raised for taste treats. A left-handed compliment, perhaps, but the food in Vienna is hearty rather than refined, stick-to-the-ribs rather than elegant. And if it is thus, it is consistently so. Soups, some type of pork and kraut or potatoes, and easy on the green vegetables, as if they were some sort of luxury crop (and they were for centuries).

Breakfast in Vienna is continental: coffee and rolls. Lunch is a large meal and can be a good bargain if you take what is called the *Menü*, or special of the day. This usually includes soup, main course, and dessert. Dinners are lighter affairs, but of course all this depends upon individual preference.

Pork, as mentioned above, is the mainstay of every meal, whether in the form of *Wurst* or fresh meats. The Austrians are terribly inventive with meat won from swine: there must be a good twenty varieties of *Wurst* alone. Stop at a good deli to educate yourself about all these varieties, which can help to make great picnic lunches in one of the city's numerous parks. Cooking *Wursts* are as numerous as the smoked or dried variety. To try out some of these, stop at one of the *Wurstelstands* to be found around the Ring and in the heart of the city. Most popular are the *Bürenwurst* and *Bratwurst*, but even

Weine
aus den besten
Rieden.

a simple frankfurter can be a taste experience here. It is interesting to note that in Frankfurt a hot dog is called a Wienerwurst, while in Vienna (Wien) they are called Frankfurter. Americans pay homage to both varieties with our "wienies and franks." Fresh pork can be served up in a multitude of ways, the most common being the Wiener schnitzel fried in a golden flour shell, or the *Schweinsbraten* (roast pork). Pork in Austria is very good—corn on the cob is intended for hogs here, not humans.

Breads and pastries in Vienna are also superb. It is not uncommon for one bakery to turn out ten different kinds of bread and rolls a day, six days a week. To live in an apartment building above such a bakery is pure delight (and quite possibly hell for those conscious about their figures, for the tempting smells begin wafting up the stairs in the middle of the night—bakers start their work at 1:00 A.M.). A Viennese tradition is the *Semmel*, something resembling a hot cross bun in shape and in texture. Ask for *Handsemmeln* at the bakeries, for they are hand-formed and have a better texture than machine-rolled ones.

Another bread-related Viennese idiosyncrasy is the *Knödel*, an oversized dumpling made of either *Semmel* crumbs or potato dough. At first sight a rather grotesque and gross accompaniment to roast pork or when found swimming in a soup, these *Knödeln* can slowly become great friends; once taken seriously, they can prove to have an amazing degree of subtlety to them. The one true test for tenderness of a *Knödel* is if they can be cut with a fork, without the aid of a knife. In fact, it is considered an insult to attack one of these minicannonballs with a knife edge, implying that the cook boiled them too long.

Of pastries, the less I say now, the better. You will discover the sinful world of them soon enough for yourself. Suffice to say that the chocolate is very chocolate, the whipped cream (*Schlagobers*) very creamy. You can take it from there.

Imbibing in Vienna is all that it should be. Austrian beer is quite good, of a class with its German cousin.

Some of the best beer comes from small, independent breweries that do not "export" their stock—that is, they do not ship it outside of small regional areas. The big beer concerns, as those the world over, use the old brewing techniques, but now buy hops, malt, and other ingredients from the cheapest rather than best sources. Still, the beer is relatively free of additives, hearty, and well aged. Two times a year, at Christmas and Easter, there is a special *Bock* beer brewed, as strong as wine and full-bodied as you would expect such a brew to be. In general, some of the best beers in Austria come from the provinces of Salzburg and Styria.

Wine here is synonymous with tart and white. The Vetliner is the major varietal: fruity yet strangely dry and tart. The Wachau region of the Danube Valley produces some of the best samplings of this wine. Gumpoldskirchen, just to the south of Vienna, also produces a world-class wine. *Heurige* is a word that you will encounter repeatedly in Vienna: it refers both to the Austrian "beaujolais," or current year's wine (white), and to the simple inns where these are served in the outskirts of Vienna. Some of the best of these wine taverns are in Perchtoldsdorf and Stammersdorf across the Danube. Avoid Grinzing wine—the atmosphere is nice but the wine is terrible and will severely hurt your gray matter.

Schnapps—a magic word. They make it here from anything they can get their hands on, it would seem. *Slivowitz* is a fiery plum variety; *Obstler* is made from apples and pears; *Enzian*, from the delicate alpine flower of the same name. Schnapps is not made for sipping; these drinks, taken straight, are best thrown down with a beer chaser on a cold winter's day.

Coffee is excellent in Vienna and served in dozens of ways. See Walk 4 for a complete description of the wonders of the coffee bean, Viennese-style.

Where to buy food and drink? The most basic option is the grocery shop, or *Lebensmittel*, where you can find the makings for an at home or alfresco meal. Simple food prepared for hearty tastes can be found at the *Gasthaus* or *Beisl*, usually cozy places with wooden floors and a coal stove humming in the corner. There will be good tap beer and a few varieties of open wine to choose from. No mixed drinks. Though there has recently been a spate of new American-type bars opening in town, which specialize in "long drinks" as they are called here, and though the large international hotel bars do lean toward the dark-and-morbid bar atmosphere, most of Vienna still eschews that scene. Beer, wine, and schnapps in warmly lit, cozy nooks is the rule here: conversation rather than pickups.

Restaurants tend, by their very name, to cater to more exotic culinary art forms. There are the usual smattering of international restaurants and even specialty Austrian ones serving regional dishes from the provinces. Prices go up accordingly as you graduate from *Gasthaus* to restaurant.

The *Heurige* also provide good and wholesome fare, which you select yourself directly from the kitchen.

The coffeehouses of Vienna, besides serving the famous Vienna roast, may also provide some food, especially a lunch *Menü*. For samplings of all the above, see the recommendations at the end of the book.

TIPPING

Service is normally included with the food and drink bill, but it is still customary to tip from 10 to 15 percent, if you enjoyed the service. If you have been treated shabbily—and this will seldom happen in a town of professional waiters and waitresses—there is absolutely no need to tip. On the contrary, there is no reason to reinforce bad manners. You will find that at most places you are permitted to give the reckoning of what you have consumed; but fear not, the waiter has his own tally running in his head. At some beer houses the *Ober*, or headwaiter, marks beers drunk by a slash on the *Deckel*, or cardboard coaster, under your beer mug.

TELEPHONE, TELEGRAPH, AND POST OFFICE

The major post office is at Barbaragasse 2 in the First District and is open twenty-four hours a day (as are those at the major train stations). From here you can place long-distance calls. Telegrams can be sent from the above post offices as well. Operators speak English and calls may be placed in English. Remember, however, that calls originating *from* Europe are more expensive than those originating from North America. Phone booths can also be found at every post office in each district and at fairly regular intervals along the street. A one-schilling piece is needed for these booths: insert the schilling, listen for the dial tone, dial the number, and when the other party answers, press the *red* button to make the connection. You have about three minutes to speak. When the call is nearing completion, there will be a beeping tone after which you can insert another schilling to continue. If there is no answer, press the black button for the coin return.

Stamps for letters (*Briefmarken*) can be purchased at tobacconists and letters mailed at mail drops (orange-yellow boxes) on the streets. *Aerogrammes* can also be purchased at the tobacconist's and simplify matters somewhat for they are envelope, stamp, and letter all in one and you need not worry about the weight of the letter when buying stamps. Post offices near you can be found by looking under "Post" in the telephone directory. Their normal hours are from 8:00 A.M. to 6:00 P.M., Monday through Friday.

MONEY AND BANKING

Austrian currency is the schilling, which has varied in value against the U.S. dollar between five and ten cents over the last decade. The basic coins are the groschen, of which there are 100 in a schilling. Groschen pieces include the two-, five-, and ten-groschen coins, all made out of aluminum (the metal of which must be worth more than the monetary value of the coin). Schilling coins come in one-, five-, ten-, and twenty-schilling pieces. Paper money is in the following denominations: 20, 50, 100, 500, and 1,000 schillings.

Banks are open Monday through Friday from 8:00 A.M. to 3:00 P.M. with a 12:30 to 1:30 midday closing and a long day (till 5:30 P.M.) on Thursdays. Banks give pretty much the same rates all over the city. Travel bureaus and hotels also change money—but the exchange rates go down accordingly. On weekends you can change money at the West and South train stations, the airport, or the tourist information office in the Opernpassage. Exchange rates at these locations are roughly the same as the bank rate.

SHOPPING

Antiques (*Altwaren*, or used goods, as much of it is called here) are still an excellent bargain, even though containers of the stuff are sent out of the city for North America every day. Because of the distinction between antiques and *Altwaren*, you can buy furniture and all sorts of household items and clothing that are not quite old enough to be officially antique, at fair prices. Look for the *Altwaren* signs and just browse.

Trachten, or traditional Austrian dress, is one of Vienna's finer offerings. Everything from lederhosen to loden coats can be found here, with samplings such as hunting hats, fine sweaters, and knee britches to be found in between.

Among the fine porcelain and ceramic to be had here, some of the best and most unique everyday ware is called *Gmunden*, after the town where it is produced. Very rustic and charming in design. Petit point is another old-time though somewhat kitsch Viennese specialty. It can be found at most souvenir shops in the city center.

A minispecialty of the city is its wrought-iron ware,

done in every form from candelabra to pots. Wineglasses in the interesting *achtel* (1/8 liter) and *viertel* (1/4 liter) sizes can also be found at kitchenware shops.

And you must never forget the old standby, the Sacher Torte, which can be purchased directly from the hotel outlet and shipped all over the world in custom-made wooden boxes. So filled with eggs is this cake that it stays relatively fresh for weeks.

DRESS

At the risk of sounding terribly clubby and fusty, I broach this silly subject. Vienna is a city in the old-fashioned meaning of the word. While modern casual attire (everything from see-through T-shirts to jeans) is worn and considered appropriate almost anywhere, you may want to have one snazzy change of clothes just for those occasions when you feel like it. Most Viennese dress for the Opera, concerts, and the theater. But then they would dress to go to the bakery as well. You cannot take them as your standard. Ties are no longer obligatory at the Opera, as they were not so many years ago. Basically it is up to you, but it can be fun to dress to the teeth here, in one of the few cities of the world where it is still done. You can feel wonderfully dramatic here in all sorts of attire without calling overmuch attention to yourself.

SAFETY IN THE STREETS

For Vienna street safety is not a course in karate but in watching the traffic signals. In this newly mechanized society enamored with techno-living, pedestrians come second. More than any other urban dwellers, the Viennese have been wounded by the car. It gives them far too much opportunity to insulate themselves from humanity in their steel coffins, and there appears to be no such thing as pedestrian right-of-way here, at least in practice.

But all this is somewhat refreshing. If cars are the only thing one has to be cautious of in Vienna, then at least it is an improvement on walking in other cities, where it is two-legged animals rather than four-wheeled machines that must be guarded against. Weirdly enough, Austria has one of the highest homicide rates in Europe (though still infinitesimal when compared to North American cities). But these homicides are almost exclusively limited to gangster versus gangster, and the city itself is as safe as you could want it to be. There is hardly a district or neighborhood where one cannot safely walk at any time of the day or night. Parts of the Second District in the neighborhood of the Prater amusement park are somewhat unsavory, since this is one of the centers of the skin trade; even this is not to be termed unsafe in the mugging meaning of the word. Unwholesome would be more apposite. Parts of the Gürtel also are unpleasant for walkers, but this is as much because of the heavily trafficked nature of the avenue as it is because of its nighttime skin trade. And if you have any nose at all for low-life locales, you will have no trouble avoiding the rough inns and taverns of the city, which are relatively few at any rate.

The tours provided in this book can be taken at any time of the day or night (indeed, some are better after dark with all the public buildings alight, especially in the summer months) without giving a second thought to muggers and the like.

EMERGENCIES

Austria is an orderly country; there are enough policemen to go around. In the First District, many of them wear shields that state which languages they speak. There are police stations in every district as well; they can be found by looking under "*Polizei*" in the phone book. The emergency number for the police is 133; for the fire department, 122; and for an ambulance, 144.

For medical or dental care you might want to contact

the Amerika Haus at Friederich-Schmidt-Platz 2, just in back of the Rathaus on Dr. Karl Lueger Ring, telephone 31 55 11. They maintain a list of referred doctors and dentists. If you want to take potluck, *Praktische Arzt* means a GP and *Zahnarzt* is a dentist, and you can find one of these in almost any street by the bronze shields on house doors (or ask the advice of the people with whom you are lodging). For medical emergencies there are many hospitals in town: the Hospital of the Barmherzigen Brüder, Grosse Mohrengasse 9; Universitätsklinik in the Vienna General Hospital, Alser Strasse 4; and for children the Santa Anna Children's Hospital on Kinderspitalgasse, telephone 48 35 77. Medicine is socialized to a degree in Vienna, but that does not mean it is free. For emergencies, be prepared to pay at least the initial handling charges of admission and a physician's visit. But the charges are nowhere near as steep as those found in North America.

Pharmacies are called *Apotheken* and can be found on every other block, it seems. They are open Monday through Friday from 8:00 A.M. to 12:00 noon and again from 2:00 to 6:00 P.M. They have half-day openings on Saturdays and are closed Sundays. For night or Sunday service simply check the *Apotheke* nearest you, which may or may not have night service; if it does not it will list the nearest pharmacy that does.

OTHER SIGHTS OF INTEREST

There was just no way to include all the Viennese sights that one should see in the course of four walking tours. Some obvious "musts" have not been included in the tours. You *must* visit the Belvedere (take the D tram from the Ring up Prinz Eugen Strasse to the stop called Belvedere), which was the residence of Prince Eugene of Savoy built in the grand manner by Hildebrandt. There are Lower and Upper palaces with magnificent grounds in between. Art museums are housed in both: in the

A view of Vienna from the Upper Belvedere

Lower is the Baroque Museum and in the Upper is nineteenth- and twentieth-century Austrian art—Klimt, Schiele, Kokoschka, and the Fantastic Realists. This is a three-star attraction that I just could not fit into the scheme of the tours.

Another palace farther afield is that at Schönbrunn. (Take the U4 subway to either the Schönbrunn or Hietzing stops.) Magnificent rooms to visit; grounds that go on for acres all clipped and coiffed like the finest hairdo. See especially the Wagenburg museum of carriages just in front of the palace itself. Also the zoo—the only baroque one in the world (and it looks very pretty but pity the poor animals there)—can provide a pleasant half-day stroll. John Irving's bears were set free from here.

The Prater in the Second District (take the U1 for

this) is a huge amusement park with the giant Ferris wheel that is as much a symbol of the city as is St. Stephen's. A good view of the city can be had from atop this wheel. A bit hectic, but the kids love it.

For *Jugendstil* fans, there are more Wagner houses and buildings to be seen. (See Walk 4 for these addresses.)

Sadly missing from these walking tours are some of the monster apartment-house complexes erected in the interwar years and associated with "Red Vienna," the first socialist government. These experiments in total living—all services and parks included within the blocks-long complexes—are worthy of a visit just for the sociological import. You come away from these utopian projects with a new understanding of the depth of European socialism. The easiest of these to visit is the Karl Marx-Hof (the name tells it all); take the U4 subway to the end of the line at Heiligenstadt and the monster is just across the street from the subway station.

Entire districts have also been excluded from the light of day in these tours. Most of the inner ring of districts—that is, those inside the Gürtel—could be explored in a morning's walk. The Seventh and Eighth are among the loveliest. In the Seventh you can find the renovated baroque area known as the Spittelberg, with narrow, cobbled streets and newly renovated apartment houses. Now an area of high rents, the Spittelberg was once Vienna's most notorious red-light district.

In the Ninth District there are lots of attractions: the General Hospital at Alser Strasse 4 is a product of the Josephinium era, and its several courtyards lead through medical history; Freud's old apartment at Berggasse 19 has been turned into a small Freud museum (the Viennese have finally got around to claiming this Moravian Jew as a native son) chockablock full of Freudiana. Not far afield from this is the Liechtenstein Palace, at Fürstengasse 1, which now houses the Museum of Modern Art, and nearby is the Strudlhofstiege, with associations with that great Austrian novelist Heimito von Doderer, some-

A detail of Hundertwasser's KunstHausWien
façade

thing of a Viennese interwar James Joyce (memorial
rooms at Strudlhofgasse 43).

A couple of recent additions to Vienna's skyline are
well worth a visit to the Third District. There the artist
Hundertwasser has been given a free hand in the design
of a municipal housing project on Hetzgasse, four stops
from Schwedenplatz on the O tram line. You cannot visit
the interior of these apartment houses, but you can get
an idea of the fanciful nature from postcards in the main
shop on the Kegelgasse side. Not to worry: these buildings you literally cannot miss; they jump out at you on
a street of somber buildings. There is not a straight line
in the place. Hundertwasser has created a pastiche of his
painting style in mortar and brick—lovely, fanciful, architectural mosaics. Just a couple of blocks away, at Untere
Weisbergerstrasse 13, is the KunstHausWien, a recondi-
tioned furniture factory (Thonet) with the Hundertwasser

31

stamp to it as well. A permanent collection of Hundert-wasser's art is housed here as well as revolving exhibitions of modern and avant-garde art.

Another recent addition is the Museum Quarter, housed in the former Messepalast where trade fairs have been traditionally held. This huge architectural undertaking is just behind the twin museums on the Burgring and, when completed, will contain the Museum of Modern Art, the Art Hall, and the Leopold Museum.

And there are always the Vienna Woods, that green belt surrounding the city saved from urban development only in the eleventh hour last century. Only a tram ride away, these woods are crisscrossed by thousands of kilometers of paths leading from wine houses to *Gasthäuser* between the little villages ringing the metropolis. To explore the woods all you need is a copy of *Wienerwald Atlas*, published by Freytag-Berndt und Artaria. The maps included in this book are finely detailed and show, in a variety of colors, all the trails of the woods. Some easy walks are in the Lainzer Tiergarten, where you can walk among the wild boars; up the Cobenzl or Leopoldsberg above Grinzing through the vineyards. Many more possibilities are also listed in the back of this atlas.

And, though hardly a part of the woods, the Zentral Friedhof, Vienna's central cemetery, is something to see. The greats are buried here as well as the near greats and those who wished to be great but had only enough money to display such fabled greatness in the bizarre panoply of mausoleums and headstones to be seen here. Take the number 71 tram from Schwarzenbergplatz to the end of the line for this one.

And while out in this neck of the woods, you may also want to avail yourself of the curative hot mineral baths at the Oberlaa Spa Center, one of Europe's hottest natural sulfur springs. You can swim or just relax in the heated pools located at Kurbadstrasse 10, in the Tenth District. Take the 67 tram from the city center.

GLOSSARY

Mark Twain claimed that he got through the rigors of a walking tour in Germany with only four German words: *Danke*, *Bitte*, *Bier*, and *Kuss*. What more could anyone want? Using the language in Vienna will be more difficult for those who know German than for those who know none: Viennese dialect and German are all but two languages. Food especially has bizarre Viennese variants to standard German, mainly because of the richly textured ethnic mix in the city. The following is a ground-zero vocabulary to help you get along:

Excuse me	*Verzeihung*
Please	*Bitte*
Thank you	*Danke*
You're welcome	*Bitte*
Where is . . . ?	*Wo ist . . . ?*
How much is . . . ?	*Wievel ist . . . ?*
Yes	*Ja*
No	*Nein*
Right	*Rechts*
Left	*Links*
Straight ahead	*Geradeaus*
Good	*Gut*
Hello	*Grüss Gott*
Good-bye	*Auf Wiedersehen*

Remember that the German *w* is pronounced like the English *v* and the German *j* like an English *y*.

CHRONOLOGY

As Vienna's history dovetails so with that of the house of Habsburg and of its empire, this chronology is not only confined to the history of the city, but also includes those events that helped shape it as capital of an empire. If one looked for the preponderant theme throughout the history of Vienna, it would, in fact, be this dual—some might say schizoid—nature of the city: both a metropolis and capital of an empire. To this day Vienna cannot decide which it would rather be and to whom it owes its allegiance.

6000 B.C.	The first lasting settlement in the Vienna area.
3000 B.C.	Danubian culture identified in the Vienna area.
1800–800 B.C.	Bronze Age settlements in the immediate area of modern Vienna.
400 B.C.	The Celts settle in the Vienna area and build an *Oppidum* on the Leopoldsberg above the Danube.
A.D. 8	The Vienna area becomes part of the Roman province of Pannonia.
c. A.D. 100	Roman encampment built on the Celtic Vindobona.
433	The Huns invade the area now known as Austria.
500–700	Avars and Slavs settle in the area.
c. 800	Charlemagne conquers the Avars and brings Austria within the boundaries of the Holy Roman Empire.
881	"Wenia" first mentioned in the *Salzburg Annals*.
c. 1000	First reference to medieval settlement in Vienna after the "lost" centuries.
1137–1156	Babenbergs, rulers of the Eastern march for more than 150 years, move their seat to Vienna, and Duke Heinrich II, "Jasomirgott," begins the city's first court life.
1147	St. Stephen's Cathedral is consecrated.
c. 1200	The center of Vienna reaches the limits of expansion, which it will maintain until the nineteenth century.

1221	Municipal and trading privileges granted to Vienna by Duke Leopold VI of Babenberg.
1246	Frederick the Bellicose of Babenberg dies and Babenberg rule comes to an end. Ottokar II of Bohemia succeeds the Babenbergs and begins construction of Hofburg.
1276	Rudolf of Habsburg, newly elected king of the Germans, takes Vienna and Ottokar II dies two years later at the Battle of the Marchfeld.
1359	Cornerstone of the south tower of St. Stephen's laid.
1365	University of Vienna founded by Duke Rudolf IV.
1421	Jewish pogrom.
1433	South tower of St. Stephen's completed.
1469	Vienna becomes seat of a bishop.
1477	Archduke Maximilian of Habsburg marries Mary, heiress to Burgundy.
1485–1490	Vienna under Hungarian rule.
1493	Maximilian elected Holy Roman Emperor.
1496	Philip, son of Emperor Maximilian I, marries "Mad" Joanna of Castille, heiress to Spain, thus doubling the size of the Habsburg domains.
1498	Maximilian I founds the court choir and orchestra, forerunners of not only the Vienna Choir Boys but also the tradition of musical Vienna.
1526	Archduke Ferdinand of Austria is elected king of Bohemia and Hungary, marking the beginnings of Habsburg dominion in Central Europe.
1529	First Turkish siege of Vienna repulsed.

1551	Jesuits come to Vienna to reinforce the Counter-Reformation.
1572	Emperor Maximilian II founds Spanish Riding School.
1620	Battle of White Mountain near Prague confirms Habsburg hegemony in Central Europe.
1645	Swedes threaten Vienna toward end of Thirty Years War.
1679	Plague epidemic.
1683	Second Turkish siege under Grand Vizier Kara Mustapha ends in rout of Turks by combined German and Polish armies. Eugene of Savoy begins long and glorious military-political career with the reconquering of Hungary.
1683–1740	The great age of baroque palace building.
1704	Line Wall erected as second ring of fortifications.
1718	Vienna becomes seat of an archbishop; beginnings of the Viennese porcelain industry.
1740	Maria Theresa, the first female successor, ascends the Habsburg throne through Pragmatic Sanction; there follow twenty years of European wars as surrounding states attempt to bite away at the Habsburg Empire.
1749	Schönbrunn Palace completed.
1766	Opening of the former game reserve the Prater to the public.
1780–1790	Josephinium era, named after the reforming Emperor Joseph II, who granted a patent of religious tolerance, among other enlightened reforms.
1791	Mozart dies in Vienna.

1805	French troops occupy Vienna after Battle of Austerlitz.
1809	Vienna again occupied by French forces; Battles of Aspern and Deutsch-Wagram; Haydn dies in Vienna during this second occupation.
1814–1815	Congress of Vienna in which Austrian, Russian, British, and Prussian statesmen redraw the map of Europe after the disturbances of the Napoleonic Wars.
1815–1848	*Vormärz*, pre-March (1848), the politically repressive era of Metternich and his police state, and the cultural epic known as Biedermeier, when the homely virtues came to the fore.
1848	The March revolution is of a limited nature at first; later, however, the Habsburgs and Metternich flee the city and in the autumn Habsburg forces storm the city. Franz Joseph assumes the throne.
1857	Franz Joseph orders the destruction of the city walls.
1865	The Ringstrasse partly opened.
1867	Austrian Empire becomes a dual monarchy, the Austro-Hungarian Empire.
1869	Opera House opens.
1871–1875	The Danube is regulated by means of canals.
1873	World Exhibition in Vienna; stock market crash.
1881	Tragic fire at the Ringtheater; construction begins on new wing of Hofburg.

37

1889	Archduke Rudolf, son of Franz Josef and Elisabeth and heir to the Habsburg throne, dies at Mayerling under still-to-be-explained circumstances; Hitler born in Braunau am Inn.
1897	Mahler takes over direction of Vienna Opera; Karl Lueger begins his thirteen-year term as mayor of Vienna.
1900	Sigmund Freud's *Interpretation of Dreams* published; *Jugendstil* reigns supreme in Vienna.
1907–1913	Hitler lives in Vienna as down-and-out aspiring artist.
1908	Annexation of Bosnia-Herzegovina and beginning of the end for the Habsburg monarchy.
1914	Assassination of Austrian Archduke Franz Ferdinand, heir to the throne, and his wife in Sarajevo, which precipitates World War I.
1918	End of World War I and declaration of the Republic of Austria with the socialist Karl Renner as first chancellor. The painters Klimt and Schiele, the Austro-socialist Viktor Adler, and the architect Otto Wagner die. End of more than six hundred years' reign by the Habsburgs.
1920–1934	Era of "Red Vienna," when some 64,000 apartments for workers are constructed by the municipality.
1934	Civil war between Right and Left in Vienna; Chancellor Dollfuss suppresses socialists and is later assassinated by Nazis in unsuccessful putsch attempt.
1938	Anschluss, annexation to Germany, accomplished; beginning of new Jewish pogrom on a grand scale and of Hitler's "revenge."

1944	Beginning of Allied bombing of Vienna.
1945	Austria occupied by Allies at the end of World War II. Second Republic established.
1945–1955	Time of "four-in-a-jeep" occupation by French, Russians, British, and U.S. Vienna divided into four zones, with First District shared communally among the Allies.
1955	State treaty signed in Upper Belvedere establishing permanent Austrian neutrality. Opera House reopens shortly after the last of the Russian troops leave.
1956	Vienna becomes the seat of the International Atomic Energy Agency.
1965	OPEC takes Vienna as its seat.
1967	United Nations Industrial Development Organization has its headquarters in Vienna.
1969	Socialist Bruno Kreisky becomes chancellor of Austria; beginning of subway system construction; Strategic Arms Limitation Talks (SALT) open in Vienna.
1975	Beginning of construction on United Nations City on the banks of the Danube.
1978	Opening of the subway system.
1979	Opening of UN City.
1983	Bruno Kreisky's thirteen-year chancellorship ends; a new socialist-liberal coalition takes power.
1984	Referendum narrowly defeats the proposal to put a nuclear reactor at Zwentendorf, near Vienna, on line. Austria remains nuclear free.
1985–1994	Era of new building and urban renewal.

Walk · 1

The Stones of Vienna

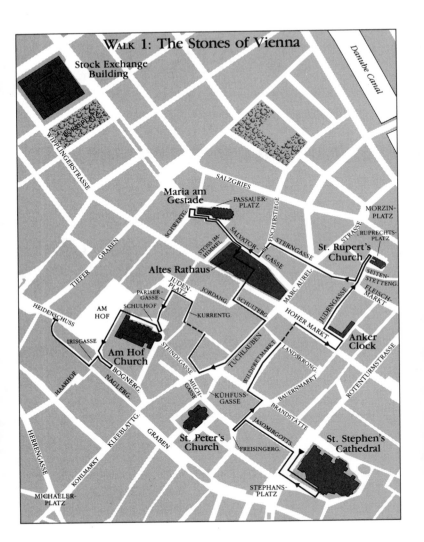

WALK 1: The Stones of Vienna

Stock Exchange
Building

Danube Canal

Maria am
Gestade

PASSAUER-
PLATZ

MORZIN-
PLATZ

St. Rupert's
Church

RUPRECHTS-
PLATZ

SEITEN-
STETTENG.

FLEISCH-
MARKT

Altes Rathaus

AM
HOF

Anker
Clock

Am Hof
Church

St. Peter's
Church

St. Stephen's
Cathedral

STEPHANS-
PLATZ

MICHAELER-
PLATZ

Starting Point: Stephansplatz (St. Stephen's Square)
Public Transport: U1 subway to Stephansplatz

Vienna is a crazy quilt of history. Entire epochs are de-lineated by building styles from the baroque to the concrete-and-glass towers of modern times, and these styles may well be sewn together to form the fabric of one city block. This may be confusing at first for the visitor, but once the pattern is understood, these blocks become a walk through time.

Vienna is also an archaeological tell awaiting exca-vation. Walking Vienna is as much a vertical as it is a horizontal pursuit, from church steeples towering above the city to excavations and catacombs under the streets.

Ruskin told the story of Venice through its stones. A similar tale is to be gleaned from Vienna's stones, both above- and belowground. During the course of this first tour we will uncover the origins of Vienna, from its be-ginnings two thousand years ago as the Roman outpost Vindobona (remains of which are to be found under the Hoher Markt) through the turbulent and very dark Dark Ages to the Middle Ages.

But at the same time, this and the other walks in this

book are much more than a walk through time. We will be walking as well through the byways of a vibrant and thriving European city, one of the last truly European cities on this excessively Americanized continent. There is an entire way of life to experience on these walks, a way of life that is not a museum piece or a quaint stage-setting for tourists. Vienna is its citizens and their daily routines as much as it is its fine buildings and ornate history. A student of life as much as I am a student of history and architecture, I will try always to keep each aspect in proper perspective, hoping sometimes even to successfully blend them into the amazing mélange that a day in the life of Vienna always is. The qualities of the grapes grown in the vicinity of Vienna take on as much importance as the human qualities of the men and women who have played decisive roles in the city's de-velopment; the shop front of a corner grocery can be as engrossing as a Gothic steeple.

This first tour begins at the Stephansplatz in front of the cathedral, **St. Stephen's** (Stephansdom, Stephans-kirche, St. Stephans, or simply *"der Steffl,"* as the Vien-nese refer to both their cathedral and its staggering southern tower). For the 1.7 million-plus inhabitants of Vienna, this of all sights is considered the center of the city, both spiritually and geographically. Since construc-tion originally began in the twelfth century, St. Stephen's has been completely rebuilt three times, the last after its destruction by German artillery in 1945. Architectural styles from the Romanesque to baroque are incorporated in the cathedral as are stones from the old Roman wall and wood from the forests of the Vienna Woods. St. Ste-phen's has witnessed marriages—such as the famous double wedding in 1515 that won for the Habsburgs both Hungary and Bohemia, and Haydn's, Mozart's, and Jo-hann Strauss's—as well as burials. Until the eighteenth century, thousands of Viennese were buried in the cata-combs under the church in the days when Stephansplatz was the churchyard-cemetery. Inside the catacombs, which are open to the public, piles of bones provide a chilling physical testament to the history of Vienna. The viscera of the Habsburgs are still stored there in simple urns. (Their hearts are in St. Augustine's Church, and their wax-filled corpses are to be found in the crypt of the Kapuzinerkirche, the Capuchin Church.)

St. Stephen's has survived invasion, plague, and occupation. Bullet scars from the 1848 revolution and fire damage from the 1945 conflagration are both visible on the inside walls.

It is not then a matter of arbitrary guidebook kitsch that prompts me to begin these walking tours of Vienna in front of a cathedral. St. Stephen's is a metaphor, in sandstone, of Vienna and the Viennese. Just as St. Stephen's is a mishmash of architectural styles that oddly blend into a harmonious whole, so the Viennese themselves are a jumble of races and peoples, a true melting pot of Europe. Just as the cathedral has managed to survive the centuries, carrying an air of grace into a largely graceless century, so too have the Viennese *fortwurstelt* (muddled through) the changing times with a surprising degree of elegance.

Facing the cathedral we go around the right side, the southern side. Just past the side door we come to the base of the tower. For a nominal fee you can climb up 343 of its 418 steps to the observation tower, but I advise against counting each step. There are some excellent views to be had on the way up through the slit windows. Such windows, so reminiscent of those in a fortress, tell the story of the medieval church, which was as much fortress as place of worship.

Near the top we come to the belfry, now empty, which before 1945 held the Pummerin, or Boomer (its real name was Josephine, after Emperor Joseph I, but the Viennese are quite nickname-happy and generally are stubborn about any sobriquets they may have created). At 37,000 pounds, the Pummerin was one of the largest bells in the world; it was cast in 1711 from Turkish cannon captured in the siege of 1683. Eight men were needed to pull its 1,800-pound clapper. It fell in the 1945 fire and was destroyed, but a new monster bell weighing more than 44,000 pounds was cast from parts of it and other bells damaged in the flames and now hangs in the lower northern tower on the other side of the cathedral. One other difference as well: This new bell is electrically rung.

So, not many more steps and we are up in the observation room of the southern tower. (We could have taken the easy way up and used the elevator on the northern tower, but we would have only a 180-degree view of the city; the view from the southeast to southwest is blocked by the roof of the cathedral.)

On this observation floor there are four windows, one for each direction of the compass. First, go to the *Ostfenster* (east window) to the immediate left of the stairs. This isn't necessarily the best view of the city, but it affords a fine peek at this city of contrasts. Prominent in the distance are the smokestacks of the oil-refining yards near the airport at Schwechat. And in the middle distance is the greenery of Stadtpark, one of the city's many internal greenbelts. Industry and love of nature: they are not necessarily mutually exclusive. The city limits of Vienna encompass an area (granted it is a large area, stretching outside of the built-up areas) consisting of a startling two-thirds portion set aside as open space. Half of this greenery is actually used agriculturally (think of the vineyards circling the city) and the other half has been set aside as woods and gardens for recreational purposes. The Vienna Woods fall into this second category.

To the far left from this east window, at about ten o'clock, is another long strip of green: the Prater, formerly an imperial hunting refuge, now an amusement park and public gardens.

Keeping to the middle distance, track across the view to the right to about one o'clock to the green dome (corroded copper) of the Salesianerkirche; behind this church Prince Metternich, that nineteenth-century precursor of

Kissinger, built his palace. This area is still known as Embassy Row. Just to the right of this point, at two o'clock, is the beginning of the long expanse of lawn leading up to the Oberes (Upper) Belvedere—as opposed to the Unteres (Lower). Eugene of Savoy, one of the saviors of Vienna during the seventeenth-century Turkish siege, commissioned the famous baroque architect Hildebrandt to design this summer seat. The lower tract was a residence, the magnificent upper building that we see at the end of the lawns was the reception hall. (Just to be fair to the most famous architect of his day, Eugene's city palace was built by Hildebrandt's rival, Johann Bernhard Fischer von Erlach, on the Himmelpfortgasse.)

The composer Bruckner died in the gatehouse of the Upper Belvedere; Archduke Ferdinand and his morganatic wife Sophie departed from it on their (and the world's) fateful journey to Sarajevo. The Upper Belvedere is now used as a museum of nineteenth- and twentieth-century Austrian painting, housing such greats as Waldmüller, Klimt, Schiele, and Kokoschka.

Now follow the warren of chimneys, red-tiled roofs, and courtyards toward the foreground, into the Inner City, or First District. The streets curve pleasantly and unexpectedly in baroque and Renaissance fancy: no right angles here. These are streets that were laid out for pedestrians and horse-drawn carriages and not for the automobile.

At about two o'clock in the foreground is the green cupola of the steeple of the Franciscan Church, Franziskanerkirche, on the intimate square of the same name. Then, closer to Stephansdom itself, at three o'clock in the extreme foreground, is the steeple of the Deutschordenskirche and the peaceful courtyard of this military and Hospitaler order. Both Mozart and Brahms lived here for short times.

Looking closer to the foreground now, all around the rear of Stephansplatz we can see the baroque and Renaissance houses of this quiet quarter. We can also see

47

part of the east roof of the church of St. Stephen's and the ornate scalloping of the roof tiles.

The next window on your right as you face the east window is the *Südfenster*, the "south window." Immediately the eye travels to the biggest object in sight, the green dome and twin pillars of the Karlskirche, St. Charles's Church, a huge and ornate gift of the Baroque age.

To the right of this church, at twelve o'clock in the middle distance, is the oblong green roof of the Vienna State Opera, Staatsoper, which is as much a symbol of Vienna as is St. Stephen's. Ironically enough, the Opera too was destroyed in 1945 during Allied bombing raids on the city.

Out in the distance now we can see the rolling hills of the Wienerwald, Vienna Woods (or, more properly, Wold). The woods ring the city from the southwest to the northwest, ending at the Danube, providing the green lungs of Vienna. Saved from development in the late nineteenth century, they are Vienna's greenbelt.

In the middle distance, at two o'clock, are two strange reminders of World War II. What look like ungainly water towers or concrete building blocks laid down by a giant are *Flaktürme*, flak towers left over from insane Nazi "fortress Vienna" thinking. Thick, ten-foot walls would protect the last-ditch fighters of the Third Reich. They were built to last, at any rate. Blasts strong enough to demolish them would also destroy surrounding buildings. So here they still stand, grim reminders of a world out of joint. The one farther to the left is known as Das Haus des Meeres: an aquarium has been built into its walls, utilizing their thickness for something other than air-raid protection.

Just in front of these twin flak towers, like bizarre clones (though actually almost a century older), are the twin brownish domes of the Museum of Fine Art and Natural History Museum on the Burgring. And just in front of these museums, closer to the foreground, is the great green expanse of the roofs of the Hofburg, the city palace-fortress of the Habsburgs for more than six centuries. A minicity in itself, the Hofburg was built in stages through all those centuries.

Just to the right of the roofs of the Hofburg we can see the graceful spire of the Michaelerkirche, St. Michael's Church, facing the main entrance to the Hofburg. And in the extreme right foreground just beneath us is the street known as Graben running off its short distance to the right. Once part of the western defenses of the Roman fortress of Vindobona, which was built on this site in the first century A.D., the street was a moat in the Middle Ages. (*Graben* means moat or ditch.) The street leading off to the left from the base of Graben is Kärntnerstrasse, the Broadway of Vienna, the ancient route to Corinthia.

The next window going clockwise is the *Westfenster*, from which you look directly out over the twin western Pagan Towers (which you will have the chance to examine in detail in Walk 2) and the ornately tiled roof of St. Stephen's to the oldest quarter of Vienna, site of the Roman camp of Vindobona. In the middle ground at eleven o'clock is the stump of the tower of the Minoritenkirche, Church of the Minorites; in the center of the middle ground is the green dome of Peterskirche and just beyond that are the tall spires of the Rathaus, built by the same architect who restored the southern tower we are now standing in, both done during the nineteenth century. These spires lumber heavenward with the heavy burden of city government. In front of the Rathaus we can just make out the peaked roof and rounded window of the Burgtheater, one of the premier stages of the German-speaking world.

Both of these last two buildings are on the Ringstrasse, itself the product of that same mid-nineteenth-century building boom that created the Opera, Stadtpark, and other monumental projects when the old city walls were destroyed. To the left of the Rathaus, just behind the steeple of St. Michael's and a dome of the Hofburg, is the Hellenic Parliament building, also on the Ring.

In the middle ground at twelve o'clock are the twin

The view from the south tower of St. Stephen's

neo-Gothic spires of the Votivkirche, Votive Church, built
to celebrate Kaiser Franz Joseph's survival of a clumsy
assassination attempt. Beyond these spires the huge glass-
and-concrete home of the new General Hospital are to be
glimpsed, and directly to the right is the ultramodern
glass shell of a new municipal building. The contrast here
could not be greater between Alt Wein, the old "charming" picture of Vienna (even though, as with the Votivkirche, it is only a nineteenth-century legacy) and
modern-day Vienna, both striving for pride of place. And

50

in the distance, on the slopes of the Vienna Woods, we can make out the plots of vineyards that have been here for thousands of years, dwarfing by their subtlety all these grandiose architectural statements.

Now look over the right-hand Pagan Tower to the delicately filigreed steeple in the middle ground. This is the steeple of Maria am Gestade, the Church of Our Lady of the Riverbank, actually situated on what used to be an arm of the Danube that at one time formed a natural defense to the northwest. The steeples of Vienna are not just handy landmarks; they are symbols of the history of the city writ in miniature. With Maria am Gestade, for example, we have a church that was built on the foundations of an old Roman temple. The roots of this church come from the earliest beginnings, then, of Vienna as a city. Its steeple, defiant in its ornate design, was destroyed in both Turkish sieges and in the Napoleonic Wars. The Viennese rebuilt it each time. In 1945 it fell victim again and was once more rebuilt.

Another bearer of history is far out the right-hand side of the window in the middle ground (or in the far left-hand side of the next window): the stocky, square tower of Ruprechtskirche, St. Rupert's Church, built on a little knoll over the Danube Canal, Vienna's oldest church, and built on Vienna's oldest square.

Moving to the north and last window, we can see clearly now to the far left in the distance the last slopes of the foothills of the Alps (locally known as the Vienna Woods) as they are terminated by the Danube River. We can just make out the white outlines of the Josefskirche on the right-hand slope, the Kahlenberg. It was on this slope that the Celts, masters of this area for seven centuries before the advent of the Romans in the first century, built their *Oppida*, or hilltop fortress-town. Before the Celts there were other Stone Age peoples. Settlements have surely been there since the days of the Neanderthals. The Stone Age peoples came first as nomadic hunters and later settled to farm the fertile land near the river. These early Stone Age peoples must have attained a high level of culture, if we judge by grave findings alone. The amazing *Venus of Willendorf*, which is now to be seen in all her full-breasted and full-thighed glory at the Natural History Museum, was a product of these 30,000-year-old settlements. And it is amazing—if indeed we take the Venus as a mother-goddess figure—how long this one "Viennese" impulse has lasted: down until today with the cult of the Madonna of Catholic Vienna.

But the Celts were the first known inhabitants of what

we now know of as the Vienna area. To them we owe the name: from the Celtish *Vindobona* (white place: most probably referring to the manner in which the waters of the Danube churned at this spot) the Romans adopted this name (accenting it on the second syllable, Celtic style), which later generations made Wien (or its Latinization as we in English know the name, Vienna). The Celts mined iron ore in the mountains to the south and salt in the mountains to the west, in the Salzkammergut (salt crown land). Salzburg (salt castle) owes its name to this ancient salt trade.

After this last slope of the Alps ends at the river, notice how the land lies flat and unbroken as far as the eye can see to the right, or north and east. This is the Pannonian Plain, the steppes. It is this landscape that determined the future importance of Vienna. Vienna was and is a meeting place between east and west, an exchange depot between the Occident and Orient, the gateway to the southwest. Situated on the river highway of the Danube as well as on the old Amber Road from Jutland to Italy via the Semmering Pass, Vienna was destined from the outset to become an important trading center.

The Celts dealt in one of the most highly prized commodities of all in the prehistoric world: salt, the symbol of perpetuity and incorruption. They mined it and shipped it. They were one of the most powerful of the early inhabitants of the Danube basin, but their days were numbered with the advent of the Roman Empire. Fairly peacefully, the Romans acquired the whole of the province of Pannonia in the first century A.D. and built a fortress here by the century's end.

The Romans were in turn displaced by the migrations of the early Dark Ages: first came the German tribes; then, out of the flat landscape to the east, the Huns and the Slavs; and finally the Avars and Magyars. For a good five centuries the site of Vienna was lost to history. During the Early Middle Ages of Merovingian and Carolingian

development in the rest of Europe, Vienna was a waste-
land of warring tribes, crude huts, and a long, interminable historical silence. This was truly a dark Dark Age.
The standards of daily life were drastically retarded compared to the rest of Europe. This condition would remain
for centuries. No buildings survive from this period and
there are few historical records. But it is now generally
accepted, from the archaeological evidence, that Vindobona was continuously settled during the early Middle
Ages.

The flat, elongated plateau just across the river from
the Kahlenberg is the Bisamberg, a fine wine-growing region with a tart, fresh white wine. At its foot and to the
center of vision, where modern housing developments
now sprout up, is the scene of two famous battles of the
Napoleonic Wars: Aspern and Deutsch-Wagram, the first
an Austrian victory—Napoleon's first defeat—and the second, not long after, a French victory. It was on this
Marchfeld as well, in 1276, that Rudolf I of Habsburg
defeated the Bohemian King Ottokar II to win Vienna for
his family.

At eleven o'clock in the middle distance is the green
expanse of the Augarten, once a royal estate and now a
public garden and home of the Vienna Choir Boys. Two
more of those surreal flak towers can be seen in the Augarten. These gardens are across the Danube Canal, a
canal that was only developed in the sixteenth century
to prevent flooding. Until that time, the Danube, in several different arms, flowed directly by the medieval center
of the city.

In the middle distance at one o'clock is the Donau-
turm (Danube Tower)—every European city *has* to have
one of these steel erections, it seems. Very Freudian in
this city of Freud. Good views can be had from atop the
tower. Nearby at about two o'clock is the new complex
of United Nations City, built on the banks of the Danube.
Austria's status as a result of World War II—permanently
neutral yet a member of the United Nations—made it a
logical meeting ground and home for UN agencies.

Farther to the right, at three o'clock, is the huge Ferris wheel in the Prater amusement park, the *Riesenrad*, and closer to us in the foreground are two churches: the Jesuitenkirche, Jesuit Church, to the left, and the Dominikanerkirche, Dominican Church, to the right. The Jesuits in particular did more to determine the city's character than any other religious order. Summoned during the Counter-Reformation from Italy by Ferdinand, the brother of Emperor Charles V, the Jesuits have been in Vienna since 1551. Many historians credit their introduction of miracle plays as the basis for Vienna's perpetual love of theater.

Just to the rear of the second church, the Dominikanerkirche, are parts of the old city fortification wall (*Bastei*). The section of the city from center foreground to the two churches was an important medieval core of Vienna, and even in the days of Roman hegemony the mercantile center was established outside the walls here in the narrow alleyways.

That large building in the foreground at three o'clock with the mass of green roof reminiscent of the Hofburg's is the War Ministry. How symbolic that it was built here, as if defending against those open plains to the east.

So, after this lengthy introduction to the layout of the city in general, we can proceed back down to Stephansplatz.

Before leaving St. Stephen's square, check out two things: One is the postmodern glass-and-aluminum façade of **Hass Haus**, designed by Hans Hollein, directly across from the cathedral. Lovely reflections of the church's spire are to be seen in the glass. Its construction, in such close proximity to the church, caused quite a stink with architectural conservatives. Second, you should go down the entrance to the U1 directly in front of the cathedral. At the foot of the steps (and just to the left of the handily placed rest rooms) is the entrance to the **Virgilkapelle**, the Chapel of St. Virgil, a recently unearthed Romanesque gem, which now serves as a museum. You can get a glimpse of this subterranean chapel from the viewing window next to the entrance in case the museum itself is closed during the hours of your visit. This is one of the newest and most mysterious of Vienna's system of city museums. This underground chapel was chanced upon only in the early 1970s with the construction of the subway system. After the damages suffered by the Cologne Cathedral during the construction of that city's subway, the Viennese engineers were extremely careful in the construction of their subway system. There was to be no sinking cathedral in Vienna, and indeed the planners were most successful. The care they took with the excavations paid off in a double sense, for this lovely Romanesque chapel was discovered and excavated at the same time. What was uncovered is a rectangular room about 35 feet long and 18 feet wide, laid out in an east–west orientation. The floor of the so-called chapel lies 40 feet below the level of modern-day Stephansplatz. The vaulting that can be seen on the ceiling is a later addition—the building actually stems from the early thirteenth century. Originally, so the archaeologists tell us, the room reached a height of 43 to 46 feet—thus its ceiling rose to about 5 feet aboveground. Windows on the east and west sides faintly illuminated the chapel, and six recesses—two on each side and one on each end—divided the room. Each of the recesses was decorated with the lovely red wheel crosses that you see today, except that immediately following excavation these were much more vividly red than they are now, having been treated with a preservative fluid. This was done because shortly after excavation and their exposure to air the mortar and paint began to peel.

In old records historians found that the chapel was actually the crypt of a family known as the Chrannests, the elder of whom was a finance minister to one of the early Habsburgs. It was located under the charnel house, known as the Chapel of Maria Magdalene, which was destroyed in 1781; at that time the Chapel of St. Virgil

On Jasomirgottstrasse

(so named after the statuary found here) also fell into disuse. One sticky question remains. The Chrannest family arrived in Vienna many generations after the supposed building of this crypt. What was its former function? One Stonehenge-like theory has it that the sun on October 13 (calculated by computers making corrections for the shift of the axes since the Middle Ages) rose to shine directly through the western window of the crypt. Who then might the crypt be connected with? October 13 happens to be the name day of Saint Koloman, a name that means little to the rest of the world but who was a very important saint in the nearby countryside during the Middle Ages. The Babenbergs, rulers of Vienna before the Habsburgs, proposed Koloman to Rome as a saint after whom their church (ultimately St. Stephen's) could be named in honor of to achieve a bishopric and thus end their obeisance to the bishopric of Passau. This project amounted to nothing with the untimely end of the Babenberg line, but Koloman and the proposal to Rome are historical fact. Whether the rising sun on October 13 can be tied to this bid for ecclesiastical (and tithing) independence is still a matter for debate, but it remains a fascinating conjecture.

Returning aboveground, we exit Stephansplatz by the street to the immediate left, Jasomirgottstrasse. Look to the corner building on your right, the **Meinl Bank**, and you'll see one of Vienna's oldest mercantile trademarks on the façade: the statue of a boy holding coffee beans. Meinl's, an upgraded Viennese version of the A&P, started its financial life as a tea and coffee importer.

Jasomirgottstrasse takes its name from Duke Heinrich II of Babenberg, a far-seeing member of that rather conservative, myopically monarchical tribe who were the first Germans to be ceded the duchy of Austria by the Holy Roman Emperor. Duke Heinrich II—or Jasomirgott, as the Viennese were fond of calling him because of his habit of ending each pronouncement with *"ja, so mir Gott helfe"* ("so help me God")—was the first of his family to move the seat to Vienna. It was during his reign in the twelfth century that Vienna was elevated to an independent dukedom, that St. Stephen's was consecrated, and that "Wien" was first mentioned in historical records as a *civitas*.

Jasomirgottstrasse is chockablock full of the spirit and history of the city. To the right, at **Jasomirgottstrasse 4**, is a modernish apartment house that no one would ever accuse of grace or historical import. It has one of those faceless 1950s' façades that so often resulted from those impoverished postwar years of economical rebuilding. One wonders if future travelers will find the charm in such buildings that we twentieth-century travelers find in baroque and Biedermeier buildings. Yet on this façade is a mosaic celebrating the life and deeds of Duke Heinrich II of Babenberg, "Jasomirgott." The topmost picture represents a scene from the royal household on Am Hof, a lavish rather cosmopolitan court as compared to its contemporaries. It was during Jasomirgott's reign that the minnesinger tradition was born in Vienna. Such notables as Walther von der Vogelweide and Reinmar of Hagenau were drawn to Vienna for the patronage to be found here (as happened in the eighteenth and nineteenth centuries, when musicians from Haydn to Mozart to Beethoven were also drawn to Vienna for the same reason). Jasomirgott laid the foundations for a center of the arts that were to last for centuries.

The second illustration in this façade is the presentation of the monastic charter to the Schottenkloster, the Scottish monastery, whose church, Schottenkirche, is still to be seen on Freyung in the western region of the Inner City. Duke Heinrich II summoned Irish monks (not Scots) from his hometown, Regensburg, to set up the first of Vienna's great monasteries, which were to play an important role in the economic and artistic life of the growing city.

The third scene shows his marriage with Theodora, a Byzantine princess, at which time Vienna took on a

Greek name in some histories, Windopolis. In the fourth scene the Second Crusade is represented. The soldiers of this crusade camped at the gates of Vienna.

A different type of building is to be seen directly across the street, **Jasomirgottstrasse 5**, the **Stephanshof**. Here is a typical late–nineteenth century building full of façade decoration. Take a look way up to the top floor to the atelier, which must have fantastic views of Vienna. Only in the last decade have these attic spaces been developed into huge apartments. (One quick lesson—keep your eyes turned upward in Vienna, regardless of dog droppings you might step into and parking meters that might neuter. Vienna's Inner City streets are narrow, crowded, and bursting with visuals. If you are always keeping your eyes at street level you'll be blinded by shop fronts and never see the buildings and city for what they are.)

Continue up the Jasomirgottstrasse to its intersection with Bauernmarkt, so named after the fifteenth-century farmers' market (*Bauer* means farmer) that was located here. The house at the top of Jasomirgottstrasse, **Bauern-markt 1**, has some particularly lovely lintel decoration as well as a courtyard that is an oasis in the midst of the noisy city. Enter the courtyard by the small entrance just under the street number. The *Hof*, as these interior courts are called, could almost be in the country, allowing in light and fresh air but protecting the inside windows from the street noise. To the immediate right upon entering is the oldest statue of the saint Johann Nepomuk in all of Vienna, from 1694. And it still stands, unguarded, in a private building. Churches, streets, and shrines named in honor of this fourteenth-century saint are to be found all over the city. See also the railed arcades that give onto the individual flats known as *Pawlatschen*. This is a particularly Viennese form of eighteenth- and nineteenth-century courtyard construction. For the Viennese, this garbled, glottal-sounding (to our ears) word is synonymous with charm and gemütlichkeit, a cozy comfortableness. These types of *Höfe* bespeak a more open-air and idyllic life—whether it really was or not—of a different century. We will come across many such tranquil inner courtyards in our walks.

Go back out of this court onto Bauernmarkt and you will have a fine view back down Jasomirgottstrasse to Stephansdom. Our path leads to the left, but we'll take a quick and short detour to the right for a moment, about ten paces to Freisingergasse, a street that has nothing to do with singing or freedom, but that was, in the twelfth century, the location of the court of the bishop of Freising. At **Freisingergasse 1** is a little shop, symbolic of Vienna's ancient specializing tendencies, that sells only buttons. At the **Knopfkönig** (Button King), you will find anything you need, from horn buttons to leather buttons. It is worth a visit just to see that such specialty shops can still exist in the days of shopping malls and supermarkets.

Opposite the button shop, on the corner of Bauernmarkt 1 and **Freisingergasse 4**, is a little framed relief of the Annunciation from the seventeenth century (on the second-floor level). The work on this is nothing to write home about, but the care with which this three-hundred-year-old stone relief was placed into the façade of a much younger building is.

Let's continue back on Bauernmarkt in the direction of the street named Brandstätte. At their intersection, **Brandstätte 6**, is the **Haus Zacherl**, built in 1905 by Josef Plecnik, a student of the famous Viennese architect Otto Wagner, whose work we will look at in the second and fourth tours in this book. This building is an amazing *Jugendstil* tour de force in the middle of classicist and baroque architecture and serves as a fine introduction to Secessionist architecture. Notice especially the bronze reliefs on the top story: they are a pastiche of the caryatids used on the aristocratic palaces of Vienna, those nameless Amazons who function as ersatz pillars holding up lintels and entire stories. The embossed metal

statue on the second floor facing Brandstätte is of Archangel Michael.

Turn left here onto Brandstätte, a street that takes its name after the fire of 1276 that destroyed much of Vienna. Ironically, another fire, that resulting from the bombings of 1945, destroyed most of the older buildings in this street, leaving it bereft of the feeling of tradition it should have. Up until 1444 this area was the scene of jousting tournaments on *Fasching* Tuesday in the carnival season.

Continue alongside the block-long Haus Zacherl to the intersection with Wildpretmarkt, where we turn right. Wildpretmarkt was one of the many market areas surrounding the ancient city center, already well known in the fourteenth century. In the mid-nineteenth century it became a market for *Wildpret*, or game. Traditions die hard in Vienna, and the city is still an excellent place to find game meat. During the late summer and early fall months especially, chalkboards on the sidewalks outside many of Vienna's restaurants will announce *Wildpretwohen*, or game-meat weeks. Deer (*Reh*), wild boar (*Wildschwein*), and, for the lucky, the tender chamois (*Gemse*) can all be found.

The Wildpretmarkt is a conglomeration of building styles from classicism through art deco to modern chrome and glass. Follow its course to the intersection with Landskrongasse. As with most of the streets of this quarter, this street's name comes from the Middle Ages, when two of the houses (no longer standing) bore signs: *"Zur grossen Landeskrone"* and *"Zur kleinen Landeskrone"* ("At the Sign of the Big [or Little] National Crown"). These medieval signs or shields hanging on a house are not comparable to our present-day Bide-a-Wee, etc., which announce weekend houses. In those centuries before town planning and the advent of consecutive numbering of houses (in the eighteenth century), the names actually acted as the addresses of houses. Some of these signs are

A Pawlatschen *courtyard*

still to be seen, in their more kitsch aspect, in front of *Gasthäuser* and restaurants.

Now buildings in Vienna clearly bear their numbers in white lettering against a blue background displayed over the main door. Sometimes this numbering is to be found on either side of the door with older signs of German-lettering style in black against a white back- ground. And sometimes, just to confuse you, the old German-lettering style and the new blue signs are to be found on the same house but with different numbers. Go by the blue sign; it is the twentieth-century updating of the house number. Perhaps it would have been easier if we'd stayed with "At the Sign of . . ." after all?

Facing Wildpretmarkt, at **Landskrongasse 8**, is a *Durchhaus*, literally a through-house or passage connect- ing one street with another by going "through" the build- ing. But unlike passageways in other cities that were set aside specifically for shops and show windows, these Vi- ennese *Durchhäuser* result from tradition rather than con- scious plan. In the days of the walled city, when the gates were securely closed at nightfall, the narrow lanes were heavily traveled by horse-drawn vehicles. Pedestrians took to using courtyards of apartment houses as much as possible to avoid the noise and jostle of the streets. These connecting courtyards became well-known shortcuts for the Viennese, and use was allowed by each of the private owners. At the entrance to many of these you will still see the rusted signs proclaiming the right of the owner to deny passage whenever he or she pleases: *"Bis auf Wi- derruf freiwillig gestatteter Durchgang"* ("Passage is volun- tarily permitted until further notice").

The *Durchhäuser* of Vienna, as with the courtyards of the city, provide a quiet and sometimes romantic refuge from the hurly-burly of urban life. Some, especially in the districts outside of the Inner City, can also be just down- right dark and dank.

The *Durchhaus* at Landskrongasse 8 is of an in- between sort: Built into a modern apartment building, it is part shortcut and part shop area; part romantic and part dark and crusty. You take this *Durchhaus* through to the **Hoher Markt**, the oldest square in Vienna and, approximately, the center of the old Roman camp, Vindobona.

Before entering the passage, however, note first the stone relief over the portal representing fishermen at work. A modern sculpture, this relief recalls the importance of the fish trade in Vienna of the Middle Ages and that this area (specifically, the Hoher Markt itself, by 1317) was the location of several fish markets. Also, this scene serves to remind us of an important fact that is easily forgotten by visitors and inhabitants of Vienna alike: Vienna is a river city. Before the controlling of the Danube, Vienna lay on the main current of the several arms of that river. Now the Danube Canal (we'll see it later in this walk) flows quite uneventfully through the middle of the city while the main body of water is far removed from city center.

As you walk through the *Durchhaus*, you will come across two marble plaques on the wall to the right. The first explains that this present *Durchhaus* and building stand on the site of one of the main roads of the Roman camp—hardly an insignificant reason to have a passageway over the same spot today. In the second plaque a more detailed history of the area is given with reliefs of the high-peaked roofs of medieval houses—study them carefully, for there are almost none to be seen in the flesh in Vienna. From the fifteenth century, both a linen exchange and cobblers' guildhouse stood to the left. A building named the Schranne stood to the right; it was the urban law court and insane asylum, with gallows and pillory in front on Hoher Markt. A small lane, the Linnengäschen, ran between these buildings. Later in the fifteenth century, the guildhalls were incorporated into the Schranne. Vienna's law courts were located here from the fourteenth until the mid–nineteenth century, when that function was moved to Landesgerichtsstrasse.

The remaining late-Gothic gem of a building complex was, unbelievably, torn down. A new building was built and shortly thereafter taken over by one of the first of the Austrian national banks. This building was subsequently destroyed in 1945, when much of the Hoher Markt was also destroyed. The building encircling us now comes from 1949–1950, impoverished years both economically and architecturally.

So, let's get out into the daylight on the Hoher Markt. The first thing you'll notice about this square is that it does not seem very squarelike. It is more a wide spot in the road with some sort of ornate fountain to your right, which formerly gave the square some cohesion but now is all but dwarfed by new construction.

The one aspect that gives this major traffic artery any resemblance to its medieval counterpart is the plethora of shopping possibilities. There is everything here from clothing stores to stationery shops, from grocery stores to bookshops, with even a cookware shop thrown in for good measure. The Hoher Markt is still a marketplace, for all its renovations.

The huge apartment house across the square is, if you can use your imagination, the location of the oldest medieval fortifications of Vienna, the Berghof. But we'll come to that later. For now, go to your right about thirty steps to **Hoher Markt 3**, where you will find the entrance to another bit of vertical Vienna.

Entering through a café in another passage at number 3, you will find steps leading down to the old **Roman ruins** uncovered after World War II. It is now part of the city museums of Vienna and is open daily (except Monday) from 9:00 A.M. to 12:15 P.M. and from 1:00 P.M. to 4:30 P.M.

The showroom itself, below the street noises of the Hoher Markt, is only a tiny fraction of the ruins of Roman Vienna, most of which are yet to be excavated. What is to be seen below is simply the corners of two houses inhabited by Roman cadet officers. But what is to be experienced under the earth here is well worth the few steps underground.

The area to the east of the Alps, including the Danube basin, was gradually brought into the Roman orbit, from the first century B.C. until the first A.D. Friendly alliances with the Celts and with some of the German tribes, who were beginning their southward migration that would alter the face of the ancient world, slowly changed into military necessities. By A.D. 8 the Romans had simply annexed the Vienna area into the province of Pannonia as a bulwark on the Danube against future incursions of German *Völker*. Friends and allies became subjects; to the east of Vienna, Carnuntum (Roman ruins to be seen) became the center of a system of *limes*, or forts, built along the Danube.

It was not until the reign of Trajan (98–117) that the first fortress was built at Vindobona to protect the western flank of Pannonia, for it was here that the natural obstacles to attack, such as river and mountains, gave way.

Once you get belowground to the showroom, look at the map on the wall to the immediate right of the entrance and you will see how the position for the *Lager*, or fortified encampment, of Vindobona was well chosen. Built on a rise overlooking the Danube, the fortress had natural lines of protection on three sides: to the north the banks fell away sharply to the Danube, and to the east and west smaller streams bounded it. Only to the south was there open country, and this was fortified with several towers and a moat (which in the Middle Ages became known as the Graben). The parameters of the Roman encampment are now occupied by the modern streets of Salzgries to the north, Tiefer Graben to the west, Naglergasse and Graben to the south, and by a line just inside Stephansplatz and Rotenturmstrasse to the east. The camp was cut in quarters by two main roads leading between four main gates in the walls. The east-west road, Via principalis, separated the six cadet officers' houses to the north from the military head-quarters (*Praetorium*).

It was this original Roman encampment that deter-mined the future growth of Vienna in so many ways: not only were its bricks and stones to be used in later build-ings and protective walls, but also the boundaries of the encampment set the shape and dimension of medieval Vienna.

Both the Thirteenth and Fourteenth legions served initially in Vienna, but after A.D. 114, the local legion became the Tenth, or Victorious, Legion. They were to remain in Vindobona for the next three hundred years while mercantile "suburbs" grew up around the southern and eastern fringes of the encampment, populated by the indigenous population as well as by Roman and eastern traders.

Vindobona was destroyed during the Germanic in-vasions of the latter part of the second century and was rebuilt after those invasions were finally repelled, but the Roman era had had its peak. The emperor Marcus Au-relius spent almost a decade in the Danube province driving back the German tribes and at the same time setting down his code for living well in the *Meditations*. Some historians say that this emperor was a much better philosopher than general and that it was his generally lackadaisical policy toward the German tribes that al-lowed their breakthrough across the Danube in the first place. But whatever the case, by 180 Marcus Aurelius was dead (tradition has it that he died in Vienna or nearby) and Roman order was restored to Pannonia. But it was a tenuous order, holding doggedly on for another two cen-turies until the final withdrawal of the Roman troops and destruction of Vindobona in the early fifth century.

The aisle in this subterranean museum, which goes by the attendant's desk, represents the alley between the two corners of two officers' houses. These are known to be officers' houses because fragments of both the eastern and western gates have been unearthed farther afield; the layout of all Roman encampments was so precise and is so well known that a few surveyor's calculations were all that were needed to determine what these fragments of ruins *had* to be.

Vindobona was an important outpost; the youngsters (from thirteen to sixteen years old) who were sent as officers to learn their trade had plush housing and very special treatment. Their houses were palatial: 2,000 square yards. They had 150 men of the contingent set aside just to serve them. From the best families of Rome, these unknown six cadet officers are symbolic of the oligarchy that the empire protected.

Also to be seen underground is an example of the absolutely sinful wastefulness of the Romans: their floor and wall heating. Like modern Western societies, they chose to heat their total environment rather than their bodies. Ironic to note is the attempted copying of this heating system by the Germanic tribes that settled on top of the Roman ruins. Above the right-hand officer's house are ruins from that later Dark Age. Archaeologists reckon that this attempt at copying the Roman floor-heating system was unsuccessful, ending in a fire that destroyed this fifth-century house.

Let's go aboveground. The fountain across the road from this point is the **Nuptial Fountain**, Vermählungs-brunnen, from the early eighteenth century. During the War of the Spanish Succession, Emperor Leopold I vowed to erect a memorial column to St. Joseph if his son, later to become Emperor Joseph I (after whom the original Pummerin bell in St. Stephen's was named), returned safely home from lifting the siege of Landau. Return the son did and Leopold's bluff was called: he commissioned Johann Bernhard Fischer von Erlach (the Elder) to erect a wooden column. But this impermanent wooden one was replaced not long after by a marble monument designed by his son, Joseph Emanuel Fischer von Erlach. The Viennese are fond of calling this little baroque jewel the Josefsbrunnen, and Joseph and Mary are depicted atop the fountain with a priest marrying them. The three are roofed by a bronze cupola, and biblical scenes of the life of Mary and Joseph are shown in relief on the main body of the fountain.

Just to the right of the Nuptial Fountain, on an archway connecting two buildings of the **Anker Insurance Company** at **Hoher Markt 10 and 11**, is the **Anker Clock**. This is a musical clock with historical figures that march along the archway as the minutes of the hour tick off. The *Jugendstil* artist and sculptor Franz Matsch spent six years, from 1911 to 1917, building the clock, but it was silent for many years after completion—midway through construction it was decided that the clock should be unveiled as a monument to the Austro-Hungarian victory in World War I. History saw it otherwise. But the clock performs splendidly for us now, and each day at noon all twelve of the hours march by accompanied by their special theme music. This clock actually is a mini-history lesson: Starting at one o'clock there is Emperor Marcus Aurelius, followed by Karl the Great, better known to us as Charlemagne. Next comes Duke Leopold the Glorious of Babenberg with his wife. (It was Leopold who gave Vienna its first charter.) Next is the minnesinger Walther von der Vogelweide. Duke Rudolf IV of Habsburg the "Founder," who began building both the university and the southern tower of St. Stephen's, is at five o'clock, with his cathedral architect Hans Puchsbaum at six o'clock. Emperor Maximilian I (1459–1519), who so expanded the Habsburg realms by the lovely ploy of marriage, is at seven o'clock. Andreas von Liebenberg (eight o'clock) was the mayor of Vienna at the time of the 1683 Turkish siege and died defending the city; Count von Starhemberg (nine o'clock) was the military commander inside the walls during that same siege, and at ten o'clock is Prince Eugene of Savoy. Maria Theresa, empress of Austria, and her consort, Franz Stefan of Lorraine, hold the eleven o'clock position, and the final place of honor is given to Papa Haydn. One wonders, however, in the light of the fact that Haydn's first names were Franz Joseph and because the clock was intended as a war memorial, whether this final figure was planned to be Emperor Franz Joseph who died in 1916 after a sixty-eight-year reign.

Beyond the Anker Clock is the street known as the Fischhof. A fish market existed here as early as the thirteenth century. During the times of the Roman encampment, such markets were kept outside the walls, especially on the far side of Rotenturmstrasse in what is now the Fleischmarkt area that we will be visiting later in this walk. (The civilian area of the Roman settlement was actually farther afield, in the area encompassed now by the Rennweg in the Third District, built on an earlier Celtic settlement.)

The Danube has had, of course, more importance for Vienna than its being a supplier of fish. Vienna is at the confluence of trade routes, both ancient and modern. Besides the river traffic of the Danube and the Amber Road from the Baltic to Adriatic, a medieval trade route linking Bohemia (Czech Republic) with Italy also passed directly through the city. Thus, Vienna enjoyed many privileges as a trading post. It came to pass over the centuries that the Viennese middlemen took a larger and larger commission from goods passing through their domain, until the point where anything that came through the city had to be unloaded on the spot and bought and resold by Viennese merchants—at a considerable profit for them, naturally. Even if the goods came by water and were to proceed by the same means past Vienna, this fine little commercial game had to be played. This made for an easy life for the Viennese—that is, in good times when trade flowed. They were entitled to a large share of all goods passing their door without any personal risk or effort. But, conversely, they went hungry in bad times. It has been argued that this double-edged knife of easy security versus helpless insecurity has done more to create the middle-class Viennese temperament than any other one factor. It bred the Viennese love of state monopolies, of guilds, charters, and concessions. It created a pensioner mentality where protectionism and connections (*Protektion*, as the Viennese called it) were all important. To this day one cannot simply open a shop, put out a sign, and be in business. There are concessions to buy, licenses to take out, and a myriad of other bureaucratic inanities that discourage competition.

There is little to see on Fischhof; let's move on to the left (facing the Anker Clock) past the Nuptial Fountain to the enormous apartment and office building at **Hoher Markt 8**. (It actually runs between the streets of Judengasse and Marc Aurel-Strasse.) This is another of those postwar buildings that are scattered about Vienna. Allied bombing of the city began in the spring of 1944, but Vienna was spared the massive destruction that many other cities in the Reich suffered, even though the Hoher Markt was badly damaged in the closing months of the war—so badly damaged, in fact, that it is hard to recognize this as the second-oldest square in Vienna.

This building at Hoher Markt 8 stands on the site of Vienna's oldest post-Roman fortress, the **Berghof**. The exact date of the building that once stood here cannot be determined; but what is known from archaeological finds in the area is that it was built using parts of the old Roman baths that once stood on the corner of Hoher Markt and Marc Aurel-Strasse. The Berghof is mentioned in chronicles as early as the thirteenth century—that is, a century after the advent of the Babenbergs. It was used as the law court, and it was here that the vintners came to pay taxes on their fields. Such a complex as the Berghof is difficult to reconstruct in one's mind—it was a grouping of buildings rather than one massive block as we have today. There were inns, shops, and private houses all included in this complex, as generations of building succeeded each other. It must have been a ragtag affair in

On the Hoher Markt:
a Fiaker *and the Anker Clock*

many ways, something like a medieval castle with cluck-
ing hens, muddy paths, and smoking chimneys on the
peaked roofs. Both an administrative defense center and
an urban neighborhood, there must have been bustle and
constant activity.

The fate of this medieval housing complex was that
of so many of the other houses on the Hoher Markt. By
the late Middle Ages, the Hoher Markt was the center of
Viennese urban life with markets, a small fortress, the
new law courts across the way where we first came into
the square, and fine houses of the aristocracy. But by the
late eighteenth and early nineteenth century, attention was
turning to other quarters of Vienna, and many of the fine
old Gothic houses on this square were razed to make
way for new buildings. Such was the fate of the Berghof.
In 1805 this became the site of the Palais Sina, built for
the powerful Sina family. This *palais*, city palace or mansion, was renovated in the mid–nineteenth century by
the architect Theophil Hansen (whom we will meet in
Walk 4) and was destroyed in the 1945 bombing.

The building now on the site was built between 1955
and 1959 and looks as if it might itself have gone through
two Turkish sieges.

We'll leave the Hoher Markt now for the narrower
and more medieval lanes of the old Jewish ghetto. The
street directly in back of the Nuptial Fountain, between
the Anker building and the site of the old Berghof, is
Judengasse (Jewish Lane). This medieval street was a
connecting route between Vienna's oldest squares: the
Hoher Markt and the Kienmarkt (Kindling Market), which
is the oldest square in Vienna, the present-day Ruprechtsplatz. The medieval houses of the Judengasse are
long gone; the oldest on this street is from the late eighteenth century. But the cobbled, market aspect of the lane
gives us something of the feeling of medieval Vienna.
This street is now known for the bazaarlike clothing and
secondhand shops that line it.

The second house on the right, **Judengasse 4**, has a

baroque statue of St. Barbara set in a niche on its second story. The statue is more than two hundred years old; the house, if you look at the red lettering just to the right of the statue, is from the 1950s. This is an example of Vienna's municipal housing, and not very inspired at that. The interwar years saw some interesting municipal housing solutions with blocks-long complexes built around a commons. These are now the landmarks of "Red Vienna" (such complexes as the Karl Marx-Hof and Engelshof) because they were built by the socialists and encompass rather utopian ideals in their total plan: schools, parks, and shops were built right into the complex to achieve the feeling of neighborhood within the apartment houses themselves.

But this house at Judengasse 4 is not really representative of those older municipal housing blocks; it's remarkable only for the contrast with the baroque statue in its façade.

To the left, **Judengasse 7** is an apartment house from 1837, the Biedermeier age, built in the classicist style with that typical trademark of such buildings, the rounded, arched windows on the first floor. Such signs of age as these arched windows can come in handy—I know one apartment house owner who used the windows as proof of the age and style of his apartment house when applying for a subsidy from the municipal government to refurbish the façade. Since the early 1970s, Vienna has been making a concerted effort to save its old buildings; such subsidies and low-cost loans for repairs are part of this scheme.

Just past this point, on the right, is the western end of the Fleischmarkt (Meat Market), which ends in a tiny attempt at a square. Go to the right, to the steps that lead down to the Fleischmarkt, and look at the building to the immediate left of the stairs. It bears red and white flags and a plaque: one of a couple of hundred designated buildings and memorials in Vienna. This building is the **Kornhäusel Tower**, Vienna's first attempt at a skyscraper, built from 1825 to 1827 by the architect Josef Kornhäusel. (He also built the Theater in der Josefstadt and the Jewish Synagogue just around the corner.) The Austrian writer Adalbert Stifter lived in this same house in the 1840s and described a total eclipse of the sun he witnessed from here in his *Aus dem alten Wien* (*Out of Old Vienna*). Legend has it that Kornhäusel built this tower as a studio (without steps, only a ladder) to get away from his nagging wife. He simply pulled the ladder up after him and shut the trapdoor behind him.

Back on the Judengasse, take a look at the yellow house at the top of the street, **Judengasse 16**. There is now a print gallery in the lower floor of this building, but in the last century this was one of Vienna's better-known beer houses. To the left of this lovely building is a gray monstrosity, **Judengasse 11**, that one would never expect to be baroque. Damaged in World War II and given a renovated façade, this house was built in 1786, a fact that a quick visit to the courtyard could verify: the typical baroque arched hallways are evident inside.

The street going off to the right at this point, past the former beer house, is **Seitenstettengasse**, which holds both the **Orthodox Jewish Synagogue** at **number 4** and also the **Jewish Community Center** at **number 2** (the front of the Kornhäusel building—see the plaque near the Judengasse corner). This street was known in the Middle Ages as the Katzensteig, the Cats' Steps, after a Viennese nickname for this stretch of the old Babenberg town walls. This lane was the oldest connecting street between the old Kienmarkt and what is now—after nineteenth-century regulation of the river—the Danube Canal. Between the buildings at **Seitenstettengasse 5 and 6** was the oldest gate in the city walls, the Katzensteigtor; it was destroyed in 1825.

This area still preserves something of a fortress aspect. Look at the closed-circuit television cameras playing on the synagogue and the community center. They are there to monitor the comings and goings of potential enemies. On any Jewish holy day, members of Cobra, Austria's elite antiterrorist squad, will be found, automatic weapons at the ready, on duty at both ends of the narrow Seitenstettengasse. Neo-Nazi groups and assorted Arab terrorist groups continue the centuries-long persecution of European Jewry.

As early as the thirteenth century there was a Jewish synagogue on the Seitenstettengasse. Jews were among Vienna's earliest medieval inhabitants, though it is not known when the first Jewish immigrants arrived here. One account has Jews arriving in the Vienna region 859 years "after the Deluge"; certainly there were Jewish traders at the time of the Roman encampment, but no accurate records of Jewish population were kept until the eleventh century. As early as 1234 there was one of the first Jewish ordinances—this one to "protect" the Jews from hostilities perpetrated by the Catholic majority. The first segregated Jewish quarter, at Judenplatz (which we shall be visiting soon), began about this same time. More Jewish ordinances "protecting" (actually limiting) the activity of Jews in commercial life occurred in the mid–fourteenth century as a result of a decade of severe persecution following a catastrophic year: floods, locusts, earthquake, and the plague all were blamed on the Jews. Finally, in 1421, the Jews were expelled from Vienna—those lucky enough to get away, that is, for two hundred were burned at the stake. It was not until a century later that Jews were allowed back, and there followed quickly more restrictive laws, excluding Jews from the trades and forbidding them to own land. With the failure of German banking houses in the mid–sixteenth century, Jewish merchants and bankers were again allowed in under a special status to shore up the failing Habsburg finances, but—a cruel foreshadowing of Hitler's decrees—they were forced to wear a yellow circle of cloth on their clothes. More expulsions followed in 1572 and again in 1614.

Later in the seventeenth century a Jewish settlement was established across the canal in the present Leopold-stadt, Vienna's Second District (at that time known as the Judenstadt). There have been ups and downs in the history of Vienna's Jewish population ever since—periods of reform followed by repression. It was basically (not wishing to be too cynical now) the power of Jewish finances more than liberal regimes that was responsible for any freedoms accorded Vienna's (and Europe's) Jews. By 1781 Jews had won the right to attend public schools and to attain official positions—it always helped, however, if they became baptized Catholics. But it was not until 1848 that the Jews were given anything like relative equality before the law. Even such illustrious members of the Jewish community as Salomon von Rothschild were not exempt from medieval laws forbidding Jews from owning property. This Viennese member of the famous banking house circumvented such laws, however, by renting an entire floor of one of Vienna's grand hotels. He was also the first recipient of the Act of Civil Equality in 1848, and, after a donation of 340,000 florins to the city of Vienna (in effect, a very low interest loan), he was accorded municipal citizenship.

It was the second and third generations of Jews in Vienna who were responsible more than any other single group for that amazingly rich flowering of the arts and culture of fin de siècle Vienna, which we will examine in Walk 4. The modern mentality is unimaginable without the achievement of such Jews as Freud, Mahler, Schoenberg, Herzl, Kafka, Wittgenstein, Buber, Stefan Zweig, Schnitzler, and legions of other philosophers, writers, and scientists.

By the advent of Hitler (who was himself a product of fin de siècle Vienna), Vienna's Jewish population was about 200,000. Today it numbers slightly more than 8,000. Of the twenty-two synagogues and houses of prayer in Vienna before 1938, only this one on the Seitenstettengasse remains; most of the others were destroyed on Kristallnacht (Crystal Night; so-named because of the shattered glass on the streets the next morning) of

November 9–10, 1938. This synagogue on the Seiten-stettengasse hardly looks like a house of prayer: You must go into the courtyard before it can be recognized for what it is, for building restrictions forbade Jews from having their temples face the street; they had to be hidden away from the rest of Vienna.

Let's proceed now to the top of Judengasse, the **Rup-rechtsplatz**, to the lovely Romanesque **St. Rupert's Church**. It is thought that this church has connections dating back to Roman times, most likely the site of a Roman shrine. It was at this point also, or hereabouts, that the major gate of the Roman encampment, the *Porta principalis* (which opened directly over the Danube and was unusable), was located. Looking out from Ruprechts-platz over the canal, you have a good view into Vienna's Second District, its bank lined with tall, modern office buildings, and the Salztorbrücke to the left.

This square was the center of the village of Vienna that began to grow after the successive passage of German and Mongolian tribes. As early as the ninth century the bishopric of Salzburg was busy consolidating this area for the Empire (and of course for the Church). The present church is thought to have portions dating from 740, but it is positively known that portions of the nave and lower floors of the tower stem from the eleventh century. Since the thirteenth century St. Rupert's has been considered the oldest church in Vienna. Overgrown with ivy, its square stump of a tower almost cozy in its dimensions, St. Rupert's may be the loveliest church in Vienna. Be-tween services the church remains locked. We can, how-ever, catch a view of the interior from the side door. The middle windows, opposite this door, are the oldest stained-glass windows in Vienna, saved from destruction during the last war by the simple expediency of having them taken out and stored (as those in Paris's Notre Dame were). These windows are the *Enthroned Mary* and the *Crucifixion*. Note the restored wooden-beamed ceiling and the simple vaulting of the nave. It is a pleasant, quiet, homely sort of church, reminiscent in its strong simplicity of an English village church. A statue of St. Rupert is to be found at the base of the tower outside. In his left hand he holds a jug of salt, symbol of the commercial power of that commodity from the days of the Celts. (St. Rupert was the patron saint of Danubian salt merchants.)

Opposite the church, at **Ruprechtsplatz 1**, is a building constructed on the former site of the Salt Ministry. This was a logical spot for such a ministry, since for centuries the salt was unloaded just below this point at the Danube. The architect and set designer Oskar Strnd was born in this house in 1879.

Also on Ruprechtsplatz, in the upper floors of the old beer house we have already seen from the other side, **Ruprechtsplatz 5**, were the **headquarters of O5**, the Austrian resistance movement in the last war. The *O* stood for the first letter of Oesterreich, and the number 5 stood for the second, representing the fifth letter of the alphabet, *E*. The location of these headquarters is ironic since the headquarters of the Gestapo were at the **Hotel Metropole**, which stood on the empty lot at **Salztorgasse 6** (now a section of Morzinplatz) just below St. Rupert's Church. Another irony in this same context is that the present offices of the Bund Jüdischer Verfolgter des Nazi Regimes (the Federation of Jewish Victims of the Nazi Regime), Simon Wiesenthal's operation, is located near here, at **Rudolfsplatz 7**. Wiesenthal, best known for his role in helping the Israelis track down Adolf Eichmann (an Austrian, by the way, as were more than 50 percent of the wardens in the death camps), was himself a victim of the Holocaust, having lost most of his family in the camps. Wiesenthal and his Documentation Center continue to search for war criminals, a search that the Austrian government is less than willing to promote. Austria would very much like to forget that chapter in its history, and the "conquered nation" status accorded it by the Allies has helped to act as a rationale for this covering up of the past. Austria, for example (and unlike Germany), has never given any compensation payments to its displaced Jews.

From Ruprechtsplatz, it is well worth going down the steps to the vacant lot, not only to gain a look back up to the church and to get a feel for what the medieval city must have looked like, but also to take a look at the old Roman wall. A carved stone relief on the house to the left of this little square shows what this section of Vienna looked like, fortification walls and all, in the eighteenth century. The effect must have impressed anyone thinking to attack the city from the north. Also, in the right-hand corner of this empty lot, protected by a metal railing, is an exposed section of the fortification wall. Brick and rubble from the Roman age have been used by successive generations—truly a time line of Vienna.

From here we go back up the steps to the Ruprechtsplatz and back down Judengasse to the first street on the right, Sterngasse, where we turn. In recent years there has been an attempt at revitalizing this ancient section of Vienna, and the shops on this street are a good advertisement for such efforts. Especially interesting for English-language travelers is the **English bookshop** in the second house to the right, with its excellently stocked shelves.

The street takes its name from the building to the left, **Sterngasse 3**, which at one time was known as At the Sign of the Seven Yellow Stars (*Stern* means star). Note first the façade of this building and its curving, elliptical shape. Though this building was constructed in 1734, it still retains the shape of the early medieval houses that were once grouped, elliptically, around a little square just under the shadow of the Berghof in back. This building was originally the court of the Cistercian Abbey in Wiener Neustadt and still bears that name (Weiner Neustädter Hof) even though it is now owned by the abbey at Heiligenkreuz (some twenty miles south of Vienna). The courtyard of this building is cool and quiet and deserves a visit. Be sure and see the cannonball to the left of the entrance on the street façade. This seventy-nine-pound monster was shot into the Inner City from the Leopold-stadt across the canal during the Second Turkish Siege on July 20, 1683. No one bothered to record what damage it did.

Back out on the Sterngasse, we turn left. Directly ahead of us over the rooftops is the filigreed spire of Maria am Gestade, which we will see later. In a few paces we come to steps leading down to the intersection with Marc Aurel-Strasse. This little area in back of the Berghof, including the Ruprechtsplatz, was truly a citadel in itself, all but towering over the river and the ground around it. To the immediate right at the bottom of these stairs is what looks at first sight to be a plinthlike modern abstract sculpture. In reality this is part of the wall of the Roman baths, uncovered during the razing of a house in 1962.

To the right, at **Sterngasse 4**, is the **Marc-Aurel-Hof**, an apartment building from 1891 with a statue of the Roman emperor Marcus Aurelius on the corner of the second-story façade. Look also at the ornate cupola on the roof of this corner "tower" section of the building, as well as that on the building across the Marc Aurel-Strasse—pure ornamentation and fancy without any practical architectural purpose.

Continue along Sterngasse across the intersection. This part of the street is not remarkable. Here we have the beginnings of the textile quarter between the Hoher Markt, Salzgries, and Franz Josefs-Kai (also known as the Fetzenviertel, or rag quarter), an area settled by Jewish textile merchants from Bohemia and Moravia. The building at **Sterngasse 13** has a monumental doorway, usually reserved for palaces and similar buildings, which looks out of place in this nondescript street. Turn around and you can get a good view of the upper Sterngasse, toward the Judengasse. This view really makes one realize what a hill-fort the early medieval core of Vienna was.

To the right once you reach the Fischerstiege you can catch a glimpse of the greenery surrounding Rudolfsplatz and see the hectic stream of cars where once the Danube streamed on the Salzgries (northern limit of the Roman encampment and landing stage for medieval salt boats), one street parallel to Sterngasse.

The **Fischerstiege** (Fishermen's Stairs) has had its name since at least the fourteenth century. It is the ancient path for fishermen from the Danube to bring their wares into the city. Fish from the river, salt from the mines: they were all unloaded and brought up steps like these to the little settlement of Vienna hovering over the banks of the Danube.

Turn left, and as you mount the stairs, you can see the steeple of the tiny Chapel of the Saviour, **Salvatorkapelle**, to the left in the street crossing the top of the steps. This chapel, located at **Salvatorgasse 5**, has its entrance on the Wipplingerstrasse, which we will soon come to. It originated as a small house chapel for the powerful Haymo family in the late thirteenth century. At that time, the chapel was located in the upper story of the Haymo house. But the house and chapel fell into the hands of the city in 1316 after the discovery of Otto Haymo's complicity in a plot to overthrow the new overlords of Vienna, the Habsburgs. Over the next two centuries, the chapel was expanded to its current size. As we shall see later in this tour, the confiscation of the Haymo property also made way for an expansion of the old Rathaus, City Hall. We will be visiting presently both the chapel and Rathaus. For now, we should take a look at the doorway of this end of the chapel, one of the few examples of northern Italian High Renaissance ornament left in Vienna. (Yet even this portal is largely reconstructed; the original decoration is found mostly in the Museum of the History of Vienna.) The columns on either side of the door bear military campaign emblems, reminding us of the militant nature of the Renaissance Church. Be sure to look at the fine sculpture in the niche over the doorway.

Continue to the right along Salvatorgasse, one of the

A detail on the porch of Maria am Gestade

many narrow, cobbled streets of the Inner City with tall buildings lining both sides; this creates a valley effect, which more than one traveler to Vienna has commented upon. Around the first curve in the street you will catch a glimpse of the rear of Maria am Gestade, a Gothic gem in this heavily built-up quarter. Stop for a moment at the corner of the first intersection, **Stoss im Himmel 3**, to see the decorative work around the entrance of what was formerly a Royal-Imperial commercial school. This little side street, whose name means "a push into heaven," takes its name from a sixteenth-century merchant family named Stossanhimls. Notice how massive the doors are here, large enough indeed to allow a coach and horses through the portal.

Continue down the Salvatorgasse toward the church of **Maria am Gestade**. From this vantage point you have a good view of the sixty-yard-high steeple crowned with finely carved stone—probably the loveliest remaining bit of Gothic art in Vienna. Now the Czech national church,

Maria am Gestade was founded in the mid–twelfth century as an adjunct to the Scottish Monastery that the Babenbergs founded in Vienna. Built at first as a Romanesque chapel, it was expanded in the Gothic style in the fourteenth and fifteenth centuries and has long been the "church of the fishermen," for it was in those days a little parish church over an arm of the Danube.

The interior of the church is worth a quick visit, simply because the contrast between the dark, narrow, and high nave and the bright and spacious choir is so sharp. Sitting in the nave, locked out of the choir (except during services), you feel like a penitent awaiting admission to the golden realm. The Redemptorist priest, Clemens Maria Hofbauer, later canonized and made a patron saint of Vienna, was for many years the priest of this church and his relics are buried here, in the right side altar. (Hofbauer, who was once a baker, was responsible for revitalizing religious life after Joseph II's Enlightenment.)

Maria am Gestade is an intimate church, not one to wander around in too much and click off hundreds of photographs. Before going back outside, also look at the windows behind the high altar. These have been patched together from fourteenth- and fifteenth-century originals. Stained-glass art never rose to a high level in Vienna, and much has been destroyed over the centuries, which makes these windows even more special.

Go to the right out of the door and walk around to the west front, near the steps leading down to the Tiefer Graben. This west portal has a mosaic series above the door of scenes in the life of Mary. Most of the rest of the decoration here, and indeed in the entire church, is a nineteenth-century reconstruction. The church was used as an armaments depot by the French army in 1809 and caught fire through carelessness.

In front of the west façade the steps of the Passauer Platz lead down to the Tiefer Graben, which was until the late fifteenth century an arm of the Danube. Stand to the left of the steps and look out to the west. In the distance, on a clear day, you can make out the hills of the Wienerwald, always a refreshing sight from the middle of this busy metropolis. To the left, just past the clump of trees a few blocks to the west, is the corner of the **Börse**, or Stock Exchange Building. Just to the right of this is a tower of the **Arsenal**, a neo-Gothic pastiche, just beyond the Ringstrasse. And just below us, to the right, is the heart of the textile quarter, a good place to shop for cut-rate sheets and towels.

Now go to the left, to **Schwertgasse 3** and the house **"Zu den Sieben Schwerten,"** "At the Sign of the Seven Swords." The street takes its name from this seventeenth-century building, whose façade dates from 1720. The street could just as well be called Puttengasse, for the floating *putti*, or little angels, which people the enormous stone relief over the portal. A fine, simple Pietà stands in the niche over the door and a rough-hewn statue of St. Rochus can be found inside the front door, to the left just before the courtyard. And all this in a private apartment house.

Return to Salvatorgasse and go to the right back down the way we came, until **Salvatorgasse 7**, where we can enter the courtyard of the **Altes Rathaus**. One can translate this as the Old City Hall or the Old Guildhall. Perhaps the latter name better reflects the medieval sense of purpose for this building.

It has never been determined where the oldest Rathaus in Vienna was, but by the beginning of the fourteenth century, there was one located in the Salvatorgasse, approximately where the north aisle of the Chapel of the Saviour is now. When the Haymo family lost their property in the unsuccessful plot to overthrow the Habsburgs, renovations began on the Rathaus to expand it. Over the centuries these expansions continued until the present ornate façade was added in 1699 in the style of Johann Bernhard Fischer von Erlach. (We will see it later, on the Wipplingerstrasse.) When a new Rathaus was built on the Ringstrasse in the late nineteenth century, the main

A detail from the Andromeda *fountain*

city offices were moved. The Altes Rathaus is now used as a district museum as well as boardrooms for several business concerns. The impressive main room of the building, the Grosse Ratsaal, can be visited only once a month, when guided tours are given. (Ask the porter for times if interested.)

To the immediate right of the entrance is the **Museum of Austrian Resistance** (open Monday, Wednesday, and Thursday from 2:00 to 5:00 P.M.). This provides, in effect, a quick history of modern Vienna in pictures and words from the end of World War I through the end of World War II.

Enter the courtyard of the Altes Rathaus and go to the fountain to the right, the *Andromeda* by Georg Raphael Donner. Donner was a baroque sculptor who also did the fountain in the Neuer Markt. This one, in lead, tells in part the story of Perseus and Andromeda: Andromeda, the daughter of Cepheus, was tied to a rock and left as an offering to a sea monster to appease the wrath of the gods. Perseus subsequently killed the beast and took Andromeda for his wife. After her death she was changed into a heavenly constellation. Here we see Andromeda and Perseus in the upper part of the relief battling the monster. This monster, instead of breathing flames, however, blows water into the fountain. Interesting too is the fine wrought-iron work on the balustrade over the fountain.

In the courtyard opposite this fountain, to the far left, we come to the **Salvatorkapelle**. You may want to take a quick peek inside, where, despite its many renovations, the chapel still retains that intimate, magical spell of the Gothic.

We proceed from here out the entrance in front of the chapel to the Wipplingerstrasse, one of the oldest streets of Vienna; it approximates the course of the old Roman *Via principalis*. The present name is a garbling of two names: the Bilpingers, a wealthy burgher family who lived near here in the sixteenth century, and Wildwerker, the name of the district then (after the game butchers who had set up shop here). As you pass out of this portal, directly to the right you will see the sign of one of Vienna's stronger contemporary handicrafts, the wrought-iron trade, or *Schlosser* (which means simply key maker, but is much more). The sign in front, a dangling key in ornate wrought iron, proclaims the business.

Opposite the Altes Rathaus is the former **Bohemian Court Chancellery**, Böhmische Hofkanzlei, now the seat of Austria's Constitutional Court and of the High Court administration. This baroque and marvelous façade and building were built between 1708 and 1714 to plans by Johann Bernhard Fischer von Erlach. Fischer von Erlach first introduced into Austria the style of Palladian classicism, which greatly influenced the Austrian high baroque. The sunbursts and gild work over the portals (representing the coats of arms of the house of Bohemia) are quite a site in this narrow, cobbled street.

At **Wipplingerstrasse 8**, to your right a few paces, are the main portals of the Altes Rathaus, decorated with four columns that represent Justice, Goodness, Piety, and Trust, the basic attributes of good municipal administration. (Somebody forgot to tell that to Tammany Hall.)

Return to the intersection of Wipplingerstrasse and Jordangasse, turn into the latter, and walk for a few steps to the point where Jordangasse and Schultergasse split. The house on this corner, a large, yellow apartment house from the eighteenth century, is where Fischer von Erlach the Elder died in 1723. Note the star over the **Jordangasse 5** entrance—this sign gave the name to the house, Sternhof.

There is a plaque on the **Schultergasse 5** side of the house telling about Fischer von Erlach; it also says that the Austrian playwright Johann Nestroy grew up in this same house in the next century.

The Schultergasse takes its name from the fact that shieldsmiths worked and lived here as early as the thirteenth century. Opposite the Sternhof, at **Schultergasse 6**,

A Schlosser's sign on Wipplingerstrasse

is an antiquarian book and print shop. Here you can find everything from antique guides to Vienna and Austria to prints of the city dating from the Middle Ages on to the present.

Follow the narrow course of the Schultergasse, past small shops and boutiques on either side, to the intersection with the heavily trafficked Tuchlauben. German cloth merchants set up their shops in this locale, just to the southwest of the Berghof. Because of the arcades of their shops, the area began to be known as *In den Lauben*, "In the Foliage." *Tuch* means cloth, so put the two together and you have the origins of the street name. Turn right onto the **Tuchlauben** and go to **number 19**, in the first block, on the right-hand side. This building, enlarged in 1716 around a medieval core, held a treasure for twentieth-century renovators. In 1979, when a floor of flats was getting a face-lift, a series of **Gothic frescoes** were uncovered. Painted around 1400, they tell the four-seasons story of the Neidhart cycle of poems, a well-known medieval cycle. The oldest nonreligious frescoes in Vienna are located on the first floor of this house, which is open daily except Monday, 9:00 A.M. to 12:15 P.M. and 1:00 P.M. to 4:30 P.M. Since the discovery of the frescoes, the house itself has gotten a shiny new paint job on its well-ornamented façade.

Continue along Tuchlauben past the Neidhart frescoes toward the large, yellow building that seems to sit right in the middle of the street and past one end of the tiny horseshoed Kleeblattgasse on your right. To the left, at **Tuchlauben 12**, is a late–nineteenth century house richly ornamented with garlands and such gewgaws. This is the sight of the former "Zum roten Igel," "At the Sign of the Red Hedgehog," the meeting spot of Vienna's brightest literati in the 1840s and later the concert house of the Musikverein, until it moved to its new house on the Dumbastrasse in the late nineteenth century.

Ahead of us, the yellow house that appeared to sit in the middle of the street in fact does, as we can now see.

Around 1100, a triangular "square" was formed at this point with Tuchlauben to the right, Kühfussgasse to the left, and Milchgasse to the rear (by the green dome of St. Peter's Church—the milk market in medieval times). It is not known exactly, but perhaps this triangular area was the earliest seat of Viennese government, with the courts and guildhall on the location of the present house at **Tuchlauben 8**. Here in the little lump of free space won from traffic is the **Tuchmacherbrunnen**, the Clothiers' Fountain.

To the right of the fountain at **Tuchlauben 11** is the **Kleeblatt building**, named after the house sign, a clover in metal relief on the second story. The linen shop, Gunkel, has been here since 1796. Nestroy the playwright parodied its owner in one of his better-known plays, with one of those titles of ten words with twenty letters each, which only a native-speaking German could truly understand. (This goes a long way to explain the almost total neglect of this master satirist outside of the German-speaking world.)

At the second intersection with Kleeblattgasse (the little street which takes its name from the building), there is a pharmacy on the right, **Tuchlauben 9**, called **"Zum weissen Storch,"** "At the Sign of the White Stork," which has borne this same house sign since 1693.

Turn right on Kleeblattgasse and follow the curve to the back of the Kleeblatt building. Notice at this first curve, to the right and left, the curved bumps that project from the sides of the houses at street level. These are, in essence, bumpers, set up originally to protect the houses from carriage wheels in the narrow lanes. They serve equally well today to protect from cars. After another fifty paces the Kleeblattgasse curves abruptly to the right again. At this point, **Kleeblattgasse 9**, you go left through the *Durchhaus* that connects Kleeblattgasse and Kurrentgasse. This *Durchhaus* is full of activity, from the *Tapezierer* (up-

The Tuchmacherbrunnen on Tuchlauben

Von 1385 bis Ende
des 19. Jahrhunderts
stand hier der

„Schöne
Brunnen"

holsterer) on your right to the bakery ahead that you will be able to smell immediately upon entering the passageway. You might want to stop off here for a quick cup of coffee and a roll—the bakery antithetically is called Grimm's.

Out on **Kurrentgasse** our ultimate direction is to the right, toward Judenplatz. But first, take a look at some of the buildings to the left. The street, especially on the even-numbered side, is full to bursting with gorgeously renovated baroque houses. **Numbers 4, 6, 8, 10, and 12** are all from the eighteenth century.

Going to the right then, we quickly come out onto **Judenplatz**, one of the more intimate and truly piazzalike squares in Vienna, despite the cars. This was the site of the original Jewish ghetto, a word which, in its original Italian meaning, was not quite so pejorative as we today know it. (It most likely comes from the Italian *borghetto*, the diminutive of *borgo*, or a settlement outside of the city walls.) The original ghetto was somewhat larger than the dimensions of the present square; it was bounded by Wipplingergasse, Färbergasse, Drahtgasse, Schulhof, Kurrentgasse, and Jordangasse, nestled actually to the back of the Babenberg fortress on Am Hof, and comprised about seventy houses. The doors and windows fronted inward toward the ghetto and blank walls faced outward to the rest of the world. But what had begun as a closed society slowly took on the form of an urban prison, and avenues of access to the ghetto were ultimately blocked off by gates or chains.

The Judenplatz was then the midpoint of the ghetto and was known as Schulhof, a reminder that the first Jewish school in Vienna was at **Judenplatz 2**—it was one of the most important schools in the German-speaking world until the expulsion of the Jews in 1421. After this date the house was razed, and the land fell into the hands of one Jörg Jordan, after whom the present house (mostly

The Durchhaus *to Judenplatz*

MUSIKVERLAG

GEOR. CARL HASLINGER qdm. TOBIAS

I. Stadt
Kleeblatt
Gasse

9
Kleeblatt

BÄCKEREI

from the seventeenth century but still with some bits of the fifteenth century to be seen) takes its name: "Zum Grossen Jordan." We are left with a linguistic problem, however. Was Mr. Jordan, the owner of several properties in this area in the fifteenth century, simply a large man (*gross* meaning large) or a truly great man (*gross* meaning great)? The historical record gives us no answer. On the façade is a relief of the baptism of Christ; under it in bas-relief lettering is a plaque attesting to the gruesome occurrences of the 1421 expulsion of the Jews from Vienna, when more than two hundred women and men were burned. The synagogue, then tucked into the far northwest corner of the square, at about where **Judenplatz 9** is now, was the scene of rabbinical suicides, when the rabbis took kosher butcher knives to their own throats rather than be burned by the Viennese. Next door, **Judenplatz 10**, now the headquarters of the Viennese tailors' union, was formerly the Jewish hospital. On the ground floor, a fine old *Gasthaus* serves one of the better Austrian beers, Puntigamer, from the province of Styria. In the summer months there is a sidewalk terrace sheltered from the street by ivy and sweet peas trailing on lattices (a *Schanigarten* in Viennese).

At **Judenplatz 8** in the far corner, next to the site of the old synagogue, is a house from 1682, which still serves as a Jewish school, house of prayer, and restaurant; it has a police guard in front day and night.

The building on the corner of Kurrentgasse and Judenplatz (**Judenplatz 3–4**) is now the **Haus der Wiener Gastwirte**, Viennese Caterer's House, where young cooks, waitresses, and publicans are trained for their professions. In Vienna being a waiter is still a prestigious job and the apprentice must study several years before donning the white jacket of an underwaiter or busboy. After serving a decade or so, he may finally gain promotion to the black tuxedo of "Herr Ober," something akin to our headwaiters but with infinitely more class. Also of note is that Mozart composed some of the melodies for his opera *Così fan tutte* in 1790 in the house that existed before this one.

The Viennese playwright Franz Grillparzer wrote in the house at **Judenplatz 1**, and there is a statue to the playwright Ephraim Lessing in the middle of the square. This statue has a twisted history. First installed in the square in 1935, it was destroyed by the Nazis (because Lessing was a Jew) in 1939. After the war, the same sculptor created a new Lessing statue, the one we now see, but it was placed near the Danube Canal. Only in 1982 was this statue finally brought back to its original location in the Judenplatz.

We leave the Judenplatz by **Parisergasse**, which runs parallel to Kurrentgasse. At **number 4** you will see some fine *Jugendstil* balcony decoration, if you can crane your neck to see that high in this narrow lane. Parisergasse is a short lane that leads to **Schulhof**, a small court to the back of the church on Am Hof, the **Church of the Nine Choirs of Angels**. The Gothic chancel of this church gives Schulhof a truly medieval flavor, as do the little shops built higgledy-piggledy between the buttresses of the church.

To the immediate left coming into **Schulhof**, built into a niche over **number 6** and now protected by glass, is an extraordinary little wooden fifteenth-century statue of Mary. As you may have guessed by now, the Viennese are nuts about Mary; they have a real Madonna cult. More than one observer has explained their rapid (and imperfect) conversion to Catholicism in the early Middle Ages as simply a prolongation of their earth-goddess devotion (as witnessed in the Stone Age *Venus of Willendorf*).

At **number 4** is a doll and toy museum, and at **Schulhof 2** and the corner of Steindlgasse is the former **Obizzi Palace**, built in 1690 (but on the site of smaller houses that had been situated here from the eleventh century). This old palace now houses the Clock Museum, one of the most extensive of its kind in the world. There is everything here for the time-conscious: from ten-pound gold pocket watches, to astronomical clocks that fill almost an entire room, to delicately carved cuckoo clocks from the Schwarzwald. It is open daily except Monday, 9:00 A.M. to 12:15 P.M. and 1:00 to 4:30 P.M.

The Obizzi Palace is a bit of a showplace in itself, being surely one of the narrowest buildings in all Vienna. To get a proper look at its façade, we should go out of Schulhof between the museum and the church, to the corner of Steindlgasse. Here you can get a perspective of the front, which looks, appropriately enough, like a great grandfather clock.

A quick detour down to **Steindlgasse 4** takes us to **"Zum goldenen Drachen,"** "At the Sign of the Golden Dragon." (Notice the dragon in the niche over the main door.) This building has housed a well-known Viennese restaurant and beer *Stube* for generations. The street takes its name from a Herr Steindl, who was awarded this house for valorous service to the municipality during the Turkish siege of 1683. The exterior, from the eighteenth century, is one of the more charming in Vienna, with its wrought-iron decoration and baskets of geraniums spilling over the window sashes in the summer.

Backtrack then to Schulhof and go the left, along the length of the church and through an archway into **Am Hof**, the seat of the Babenbergs, who were the first German family to use Vienna as a princely seat. It was Duke Heinrich II, "Jasomirgott," of Babenberg who in 1155 first brought the ducal palace from Leopoldsberg (today Kahlenberg), in the Vienna Woods overlooking the little village of Vienna, down to the square of Am Hof. The palace-fortress stood approximately where the offices of the Bank Austria are today, far to the left in the square at **Am Hof 2**. This palace was cut off from other areas of settlement by gates to the east and north.

It is amazing how use and purpose carry through the ages: though the character of this square changed drastically over the centuries after the removal of the city fortress to the Hofburg in the thirteenth century, its military nature remains. In the ornate building tucked into the right corner (as you are standing at the entrance to the square from Schulhof) with the gilded globe atop the façade, the civic arsenal or armory was housed from the sixteenth to the eighteenth centuries. The Bank Austria building was the Ministry of War in the nineteenth century. And the hustle and bustle of a military encampment can still be witnessed today whenever there is a fire in the Inner City, for the buildings to the west and north—**numbers 7, 9, and 10**—are now used for the fire engines of the **Vienna Fire Department**.

The great open area of the square was used for jousts and tournaments in the Middle Ages. With the advent of the Habsburgs in the thirteenth century, the old Babenberg palace complex became a mint; then, in 1386, it was given over to the Carmelites, who had the building razed for the construction of their church. The church, to the immediate left of the point where we entered the square, has undergone enough renovations since its Gothic beginnings to make it almost unrecognizable as a church. Inside it is even worse: the first impression one gets upon entering is little better than that of going into a very airy and uppity train station. Gothic vaulting battles with baroque decoration on the capitals of columns; baroque altars and sunbursts fall plaintively to earth amid the severe lines of the earlier Gothic. As a living example of what restorers should *not* do, this church is worth a visit.

A couple of more noteworthy points in the square before moving on: tucked between the buildings of the Vienna Fire Department at **Am Hof 8** is a narrow red building, built originally in the 1570s and quite overpowered by its weightier neighbors. The house gives an air of the elegance of a bygone world with its façade decoration. Fittingly enough, **Hochriegl**, a fine Austrian *Sekt*, has its headquarters in this house. Around the square toward the Judenplatz, at **Am Hof 12**, is a baroque house, the **Urbanihaus**, diminutive and quite human in dimension, with a fine bay window in its first floor. In the cellars of this house are some of Vienna's more renowned *Weinkellers*, which were originally used simply as storage cellars rather than wine cellars as they are used today.

Next to the Urbanihaus, at **Am Hof 13**, is the **Collalto Palace**, which was built in 1671 on the former gardens of the Jews who had lived in back of Am Hof. Mozart performed for the first time before the Viennese public here as a boy. Note the way the arch from the Collalto Palace attaches to the church, keeping this square integrated to itself.

In the center of the square is the **Mariensäule**, or Lady Column, which was put up to pay off a bribe to God: this time the Swedes were threatening Vienna toward the end of the Thirty Years War and Vienna was saved, so the debts were paid. Mary surmounts the column looking rather bellicose, surrounded by four armed *putti* putting to rest beasts representing the plague, hunger, war, and—equally fearful to the Catholic Viennese—heretics.

We leave the square past the Bank Austria building at **Am Hof 2**. Note the plaque on the façade of this building, to the right of the door, honoring J. H. Dunant. The Swiss Dunant was the founder of the Red Cross and initiator of the Geneva Conventions, and won the first Nobel Peace Prize in 1901. One wonders if the irony was lost on the people responsible for the placement of this plaque—that it should go on the former Ministry of War. About the Nobel Peace Prize: it was an Austrian woman, Bertha von Suttner, who was responsible for talking Alfred Nobel, the Swedish inventor of dynamite, into creating such a prize in the first place. A bit of mea culpa for Nobel, which nuclear scientists would do well to emulate. Suttner, herself an important personage in the pre–World War I peace movement and the author of the important *Lay Down Your Arms*, was greatly disappointed not to be the first recipient of the prize. But her disappointment lasted only four years. She won it in 1905—the first woman to do so.

We are now at the Borgnergasse intersection with Am

The Lady Column in Am Hof

Hof. Our destination is directly across the street to Irisgasse and thence to Naglergasse, but detour for a moment to the left till you are across the street from
Bognergasse 9, a pharmacy **"Zum weissen Engel,"** "At
the Sign of the White Angel." This house sign is one of
the oldest in the Inner City, dating back to the sixteenth
century. The current representation of the angel, in mosaic about the doorway in the *Jugendstil* manner, was
done by the artist Oskar Laske in 1902. (Laske came
into his own in the 1930s and was an important Austrian and international painter.) The house to the right,
at the corner of Irisgasse and Bognergasse, is more cas-
tlelike than the Hofburg, with its turret and neo-Gothic
fancy. Just an apartment house.

We cross Bognergasse and go the few paces of Irisgasse—indisputedly the shortest street in Vienna—to its
intersection with the ancient lane known as Naglergasse,
the fifteenth-century location of nailmakers (*Nagel* means
nail) and, earlier, the southern wall of the Roman and
medieval settlements. Along with Graben, the Naglergasse
proved the stretch of the Roman and medieval wall that
was hardest to defend; for that reason a ditch and moat
were dug just outside it. As we stand at the top of Irisgasse just where it meets Naglergasse, take a look to the
left at Haarhof, the little lane that travels off perpendicularly downhill from Naglergasse. We can still see modern
traces of this great moat by the way the land falls away
from Naglergasse. Likewise affected by the ancient fortifications were the houses. The odd-numbered houses (on
the left side of the street when we turn right into the
lane) are the older, mostly from the sixteenth to eighteenth centuries, as the old walls still existed to the right.
Another of Vienna's rightly famous wine cellars is to be
found down **Haarhof**. (The name comes from the flax
merchants who traded here in the fourteenth century;
Flachshaar means flaxen hair or, punningly, flax fibers.)
This wine cellar is a simpler affair than the one in Am
Hof, with what seem to be miles of underground pas-

sages; it's worth the visit for this catacomb look at Vienna alone. The building in which this cellar is located belonged at one time to the estate of the Esterházys, who have their city palace in the nearby Wallnerstrasse (literally just around the corner). It was a branch of this powerful family who were for many years the employers of Josef Haydn at Eisenstadt and for whom he wrote so many of his pieces as simple evening entertainments.

Naglergasse 13, almost directly in front of you, is a Renaissance house (with baroque façade) called **"At the Sign of the Holy Trinity,"** and the excellent stone relief work over the front portal shows this scene. A bakery, looking very old and permanent, is on the ground floor. It is actually quite a recent inhabitant of the house, replacing a bakery for diabetics which was here for generations and was quite a Viennese institution.

Turn to the right into **Naglergasse**. This is a pleasant Inner City lane full of activity, shops, restaurants, and pedestrians. A couple of small houses to note on your left: **number 19** is from the Renaissance, with a bow window in miniature that should force the awful words "How sweet!" from the most jaded of lips. **Number 21** is a good example of intimate baroque styling, with a stone relief of the Virgin Mary over the portal and a *Beisl* (that curiously Viennese institution, a mix of pub and restaurant) on the ground floor.

Follow Naglergasse as it curves to the right to meet with Heidenschuss. This curve is historically telling, since it follows the course of the old Roman wall. We'll stop at this point; rather than leading you back out into the hurly-burly of traffic on the main streets, I leave you to wander into a wine cellar or *Beisl* off this quiet, medieval lane and clear your heads of all the facts and details of this tour.

Walk·2

Vienna Gloriosa

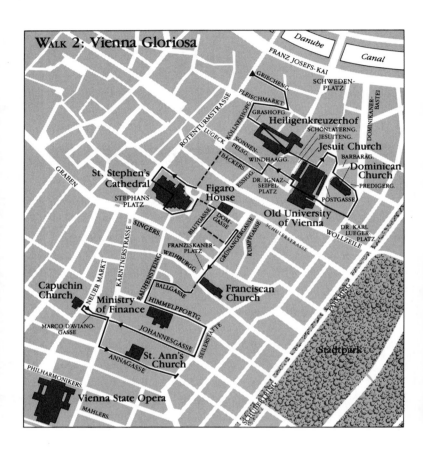

Starting Point: Corner of Griechengasse and Rotenturm-strasse

Public Transport: U1 or U4 subway; #1 tram; or #2a bus—all to Schwedenplatz stop

No right-thinking historian would call the Third Crusade much of a success. It got off to a rollicking start when Emperor Frederick Barbarossa drowned en route. The two other mightiest of the participants, King Philip Augustus of France and Richard I of England—the Lionhearted—fell out early on. And the holy places were not recovered from the Turkish infidels.

The English Richard must have been in a foul mood during this crusade, for he fell out with more than just the French king. Austria's Babenbergs also sent a contingent to this holy war under Duke Leopold V, and Richard managed to run afoul of this duke as well. After one of the Christians' rare victories, Leopold's standard was flown over the battlements of the captured fortress of Acre. (This standard, according to tradition, was a shirt bloodstained in the battle and thus colored red-white-red, still the colors of the Austrian flag.) Richard I was so incensed at this usurpation by a minor German duke that he rashly tore down the standard, replacing his own in its stead.

Leopold V (Jasomirgott's son) was not one to suffer fools gladly. When Richard the Lionhearted was returning from the Third Crusade in 1192 (taking a shortcut across the Babenbergs' duchy in disguise), Leopold managed to capture him at Erdberg in Vienna's present Third District. Leopold clapped Richard in a strong fortress upstream on the Danube at Dürnstein (the source of a thriving tourist industry for that village ever since) and informed the English that they could have their king back for a handsome ransom. In short, kingnapping.

The ransom was paid (and the city of London was in effect pawned to the German emperor to scratch up the enormous sum), but Richard had his back: Leopold was excommunicated for harming a soldier of Christ and died before he could make it up with Rome.

This historical anecdote serves as an introduction to our second walk, for Richard's ransom money enabled the expansion of Vienna into the eastern section, through which we shall be walking. We have seen that the first medieval core of Vienna centered around Hoher Markt, St. Ruprechts, the Judenplatz, and southward to the present-day Graben—basically the perimeters of Roman Vindobona as well. The next growth of the city occurred in the west, where Duke Heinrich II built his court on Am Hof and settled the Irish priests at the Schottenkirche.

But by the twelfth century this early medieval core was tearing at the seams. Most of the population lived in small, peaked, one-story houses crowded along narrow, twisting, cobbled (when lucky) lanes.

With the advent of the Babenbergs things began to percolate in Vienna. Trade picked up as privileges were given to the Viennese to act as middlemen in any transaction crossing their territory; new craftsmen and the luxury trades of silk and tapestry workers were drawn to this ducal center. The old walls were too cramped in their circumference. Already suburbs of merchants and traders had grown up outside of the "city," such as the one we shall be exploring that lay between present-day Fleischmarkt and Wollzeile: weavers, butchers, bakers, candlestick makers—they all were congregating in this new quarter outside the city walls at the Hungarian Gate (so named because it was the eastern portal facing Hungary). Even the new Romanesque church the Babenbergs were creating, St. Stephen's, lay outside the walls of the parish it was intended for.

So, something had to give, and with the advent of Richard's ransom money, it was the walls that gave way to encompass this suburb to the east and newer ones to the south (reaching approximately to the present location of the Hofburg).

This tour begins at Griechengasse, just one street in from the canal off the Rotenturmstrasse. It takes its name from the Greek merchants who heavily settled this whole quarter in the eighteenth century, but as early as the eleventh century it was settled with one type of merchant or another. (Vienna, because of its location on the knife edge of east and west, north and south, has from Roman times been a cultural melting pot, a phenomenon still to be seen in the most recent wave of immigration from the Near East and Eastern Europe).

Griechengasse jumps out of time to us with its gas lamps (however, electric lights replace the cloth filaments), cobblestones, and Gothic tower at the top of the street. A rather dreary lane at first, Griechengasse opens up once we crest its little hill and see the buildings straight in front of us. At the top of this hill, to the left at **Griechengasse 5**, is a Greek Orthodox church built in 1803 with the characteristic plain façade that churches other than Catholic had to bear, even as late as the nineteenth century.

Also from this point, looking straight ahead to the house at **Griechengasse 7** that crowns the lane before its abrupt turning to the right, you can see Vienna's last medieval tower, once a watchtower in the old town wall and now built into the surrounding houses. Look above

this small building, following in a straight line up from the house door, and you will see the red, steeply pitched roof of this late-Gothic (most probably fourteenth-century) tower, which is now divided into apartments. The house itself is from the seventeenth century and has an Our Lady statue in the niche to the left of the house door and a lovely wrought-iron lantern hanging from the façade just below the statue. In front of the house, in the warm months, a restaurant has sidewalk seating bordered with hedges of trellised ivy giving it a cozy, inviting look. Inside the courtyard of number 7 we can get a closer look at this Gothic *Wohnturm*, or residential tower. And in the corridor, just to the right of the door, you can see the pump and marble basin that the inhabitants once used as their main source of water. Such basins (*Bassena* in German, though less ornate than this marble one) are not simply quaint relics of a long bygone past. More than 10 percent of Viennese flats still are the *Bassena Wohnung* type with the water and *Clo* (john or head in Viennese dialect) *in Gang*, in the corridor. The *Bassena* was and is, as can be imagined, the center of gossip in an apartment house. The municipal government is hell-bent to eradicate these substandard units by installing all manner of fold-up, scrunched-up, and all-but-unusable showers in any available niche inside the flat. One rather mourns the eventual passing of an institution such as the *Bassena* that provided such a forum for household discussion. In the *Bassena Wohnungen* there are no anonymous neighbors; no corpses lying moldering for weeks before someone misses them, and the stench finally summons the fire department. The modern trade-off of technology for tradition is still playing itself out in Vienna.

Follow the course of Griechengasse to the right as it narrows down to a tiny alley between two respectably old buildings. To your left as you enter this narrowed length of the street, there is a green door with the date

A view of Griechengasse

"Anno 1500" carved over it. The plaque is a new addition, but the date for the house is true. You come out into a wider street under the buttresslike arch connecting and mutually supporting these two buildings. We are now at the Fleischmarkt, the site of the meat market of Vienna in the early thirteenth century, along with its guildhall.

Coming out onto **Fleischmarkt**, you look straight across the street to **number 18**, the **Tolerance House**. A frieze on the third story reminds us of Joseph II, the Habsburg emperor of the Enlightenment who issued in 1781 a Tolerance Patent, allowing among other things freedom of religion. But as we saw with the Greek church in Griechengasse, this tolerance did not include allowing "offending" religions the right to advertise with a churchlike façade. Today this apartment house is more notable for the excellent bakery housed on the ground floor. This is one of Vienna's better bakeries, and its scent will follow us through most of the course of this walk.

Cross the street to the bakery and look back to the houses on both sides of the Griechengasse intersection with Fleischmarkt. This view provides one of the prettiest, most-photographed little "scenes" in Vienna. To the left at **Fleischmarkt 9** is an apartment house with restaurant and *Stüberl*, or pub, in the ground floor and another restaurant in the upper floor. It is called **Mariahilf**, Mary Help, as are many houses, churches, and even a street and an entire district in this Mary-loving city. Construction on this building began in the fifteenth century. Improvements and enlargements went on through the eighteenth, by which time it was being used as a caravansary for traders and merchants from the Orient. Greek merchants especially seemed to frequent this particular hostelry. Vienna was their turnaround point after coming up the Balkans with their wines, tobacco, spices, and carpets. Over the years these traders made this old gray building their headquarters and stored their goods here.

The narrow, cobbled lanes of the Inner City

The Greeks took to eating their meals at the building adjoining theirs by the arch, **Fleischmarkt 11**. This ivy-hung restaurant has been a tavern for more than five hundred years. On its façade is a wooden carving of one Max Augustin, who is recorded as having died in 1705 in Vienna's Third District and who was immortalized in song as *"Ach du lieber Augustin."* As this carving shows, Herr Augustin was a singer of folk songs and a player of the pipes. He played at many Viennese restaurants, this one among them. The song written about him is one of the great "monuments" to Vienna's seventeenth-century plague (the other being the Plague Column on Graben); it records the misadventures of the singer and piper Augustin, who fell dead drunk in a mass grave for plague victims and lived to tell about it, going on his happy, inebriated way.

This restaurant with the carving was known in medieval times as *"Zum Roten Dachl,"* At the Sign of the Red Roof," but since the eighteenth century it has been known as the **Reichenberger Griechenbeisl**, which is usually shortened simply to the Griechenbeisl. It takes its name from the Greeks who made this their favorite eating spot and from the cloth merchants from the Bohemian town of Reichenberg who also frequented it. Do go inside to see the rooms: they are as tiny and womblike as they must have been half a millennium ago. The guest book here includes such celebrities as Schubert, Beethoven, Johann Strauss, Richard Wagner, and . . . Mark Twain.

To the right of the *Beisl* is another Greek church, which was originally quite a lackluster affair in the late eighteenth century. But Theophil Hansen, a Viennese architect who studied many years in Athens and was the architect of the new (and very Grecian) Parliament, embellished it in 1858. The wealthy banker Baron Sina provided the money for this renovation—his town palace was on the Hoher Markt, as you might recall—and he was also responsible for the building of an apartment house just across from the church at **Fleischmarkt 20–**

22. Sina, himself a Greek, gave an arriviste stamp to this quarter of trading Levantines.

Just to the right of the Greek church (note that rug selling is still a preferred business in this area, with the Oriental carpet shop in one wing of the church itself) is the **Schwindhof**, at **Fleischmarkt 15**. Besides its terrific baroque façade full of window and portal decoration with *putti* filling the air, this house is important because it was the birthplace of Moritz von Schwind. The name probably rings no bells in your head: Schwind was a minor painter of the nineteenth century, particularly of the Biedermeier period, from roughly 1815 to 1848. He did have, however, the good luck to be a close friend of Schubert and to have painted and been included in pictures with the good Franzl, especially in pictures of evenings of art and music that this circle passed together and which have gone down in history as "Schubertiades."

Facing the Griechenbeisl, turn to the left and walk up **Fleischmarkt** in the direction of the Rotenturmtrasse intersection. Go into the courtyard of the first house on the left, **number 16**, for one of those Viennese contrasts that make walking in this city such a joy. From the looks of the shops that have recently settled in this building, the connections of the Fleischmarkt with Asia have expanded and gone even farther east rather than disappeared. In this courtyard are numerous shops and restaurants catering to Eastern religions: a vegetarian restaurant (on the pricey side), a macrobiotic food shop, and a Buddhist bookshop. But there is a strange odor pervading all this, and upon closer inspection you will discover that the bakery on the Fleischmarkt has its kitchens back here as well, wafting sweetly secular dreams among all the spiritually inclined shops.

Back out onto Fleischmarkt, we turn left. The house almost directly across the street, **Fleischmarkt 7**, has rich gilding work to tell some of the history of the supermarket chain of Meinl's. Cross the street here to the odd-numbered side, so as to be able to get a better look at

number 14, now opposite you. This house is our first introduction to what I call heavy-duty *Jugendstil*. Not much subtlety to this one, but all the design tricks of the turn-of-the-century style are there in full force, even down to the gilt laurel wreaths. A director of the Court Opera was born in this house, and yet another director of the State Opera (same institution, different governments) was born at Fleischmarkt 1, making this old butchers' den quite a musical tract.

Continue along Fleischmarkt until Köllnerhofgasse, a most unremarkable street, where we turn left. Follow this latter street for about fifty paces, to the intersection with another short street, Grashofgasse. Two things to take in at this point: The long building to the right, **Köllnerhofgasse 1–3 and 2–4**, is the former **Cologne Court**, where merchants from that part of the Empire had their seat in the Middle Ages. The current house with twenty-two windows in each of the four floors was built from the old buildings in 1792. Such merchant courts were to be found all over medieval Vienna, as the Babenbergs and then the Habsburgs tried to attract needed services and industries and luxury crafts to their capital by the granting of special privileges and titles.

The second thing to notice at this intersection: across Grashofgasse on the corner with Köllnerhofgasse is another of Vienna's wonderful specialty shops. This one sells brass and bronze pulls, keys, and other such accessories. Its display windows on Grashofgasse give you a full sampling of designs and patterns to fit the most elegant drawers and chests.

Turn left on Grashofgasse, a street that takes its strange name (Grasscourt Lane, but not of the tennis variety) from a house shield that once hung here; that house must have had grass in its courtyard—a rarity even in fourteenth-century Vienna. Grashofgasse ends abruptly after fifty paces, and the wall in front of you bears a painted relief of the **Holy Cross Abbey**, Stift Heiligen-kreuz, some twenty miles south of Vienna. This abbey is represented here because, in the thirteenth century, it had one of its city seats just on the other side of this wall. Go through the green doors at **Grashofgasse 3** into the quiet, cobbled elegance of the Heiligenkreuzerhof. Roses trail from the old streetlamps, pigeons swoop in after a bit of food, slow and painful first scales are being learned by some child behind one of the windows on the courtyard. The only thing that spoils some time-traveling here is the presence of cars, for this court is used for public parking during the week.

In Walk 1 we came across another of this abbey's town possessions, on the Sterngasse. In the Middle Ages it was quite common for wealthy abbeys and priories to own large tracts of real estate in the city, although the abbots and priors themselves stayed in the country. Vienna, not yet a bishopric in the early Middle Ages, did not attract the big guns of the Church, only their money. And money the Holy Cross Abbey had, too, for it had one of the original wine properties in Austria and to this day produces some of the finest white wines in the country. Though ownership of such large tracts of tax-free land by the Church must have seemed terribly unfair to the ordinary citizens who bore the brunt of taxation and billeting of soldiers, it is fortunate for the ultimate growth and texture of Vienna. Until the Josephinium reforms of the late eighteenth century, these Church-owned properties retained large tracts of open land right in Vienna, land available to later generations for parks and open squares.

The courtyard we are now standing in is still owned by the abbey, redesigned twice since the original plan of the thirteenth century. We pass out of the large court by a little passageway in the far right-hand corner, past the applied arts department of the University of Vienna set back to the right off the square, and then past the tiny Bernard Chapel, also to the right.

From the large courtyard we come out onto Schön-laterngasse, so named after the wrought-iron lantern at

Schönlaterngasse 6, to your right. (Actually what we see now exposed to the elements is a copy of the original, which is stored for display in the Museum of the History of Vienna.) This house is from the sixteenth century. Just to the left of the lantern, those things that look like smudges on an otherwise well-preserved façade are actually baroque frescoes uncovered during the 1972 restoration of the building.

Actually, 1972 was a landmark year for Vienna's old buildings. At that time the Vienna Provincial Diet adopted the Old Town Conservation Act, an attempt at preserving some of the traditional appearance of Vienna's city center as well as the villagelike atmosphere of what were once the old suburbs just beyond the wall.

In addition to delineating certain houses, streets, blocks, and zones of historical importance that must be preserved, the act also made money available at low cost for the refurbishing of such buildings. Later, in the 1970s, attempts were made to plug loopholes in the law by imposing new building restrictions in zones not covered by it. The laws tried to prevent landlords allowing their buildings to deteriorate to the point where they "had" to be torn down and new, multistoried apartment and office buildings put up in their stead.

Such attempts came just in time, and many parts of Vienna have been redecorated using these *Kultur Schillings*, as the renovation loans are called. The Schönlaterngasse is one of these protected neighborhoods that have reblossomed in the last decade: beautifully painted façades, *Clos* in the apartments; new uses (coffeehouses, galleries) for old houses. To the far right, as you stand at the exit from the Heiligenkreuzerhof, at **Schönlaterngasse 4**, are a series of rounded bay windows on this baroque house that take the curve of the street itself into mind with their own sweeping curve.

To the left, at **number 7**, is a building whose ground floor stems from the early 1200s, at the height of the Babenberg rule of the city. This house is called "**At the Sign of the Basilisk**." The basilisk is a mythological rep-

Schönlaterngasse

tile of the African desert whose breath and look were reputed to be fatal. In a niche of the third floor here you can see what this house's basilisk was reputed to look like: a sandstone reproduction of the beast that looks like nothing but an obscene cross between a straining hen and a pregnant walrus. Below this statue is a mural telling the story of Herr Garheibl, a master baker who one fine June day in 1212 found to his horror a very unfriendly and smelly basilisk in the house well. The tenants cleared out and finally the smell and "animal" went their own way, but the house was ever after known as *"Zum Basilisken."* Scientists and historians now agree that this critter was nothing more than poisonous natural gas that found its way into the well. This whole story is not unlike the terribly anticlimatic reduction of UFOs to the refractory powers of swamp gas. You might take a look in the tiny courtyard of this house to get a feeling for medieval Vienna, with supporting arches between the wings and tiny terraced landings to the apartments.

Continuing left down **Schönlaterngasse**, we come to **number 8** on the right, a courtyard that is ringed around in the terraced landings called *Pawlatschen*, but also "bridged" by connecting terraces in the middle on the second and third floors. These "bridges" actually connect the two tracts of the apartment house like breezeways and connect flats on opposite sides of the buildings that otherwise would have no connecting door.

Renters in Vienna are as clever as the owners. Flats in these old baroque houses are charming but tiny. What fits a newlywed couple becomes a pressure cooker with the addition of children. Instead of moving to new quarters—always an iffy situation in Vienna—many Viennese keep their ears open for possible openings in their own apartment buildings, hoping, not unkindly, that the old bird next door might be carried away peacefully in the night and that they then might be able to buy the lease on her apartment, knock out a wall, and, presto, have a superapartment. The tenants in this house obviously were not so lucky as to find a second flat next door to theirs, but make do with the use of these breezeways to the new additions to their homes.

Back out on **Schönlaterngasse**, across the street at **number 7a**, Robert Schumann passed the winter of 1838–1839, a winter important to all who love music, because it was during this time that he uncovered unknown Schubert symphonies stuck away in the flat of the latter composer's brother. Schubert, appreciated by his own coterie as a genius, never won large public acclaim in his lifetime. He made a miserly $1,000 per year for the dozen years of his creative life. (He died at thirty-one, a victim of typhoid fever.) During his lifetime he had only one public performance, and, because Paganini was in town simultaneously, there was never a review of this concert, only raves for Paganini. When Schumann came to Vienna, only seven years after Schubert's death, Schubert's name, outside his circle of intellectual friends, was all but forgotten. It was Schumann who acted as PR man for the Schubert symphonies, none of which had been published during the composer's lifetime. Still, it would take another generation before the world really accepted Schubert for the genius he was.

Besides connections with Schubert/Schumann, this house has a fine gabled roof and a drain right out of the Middle Ages. Look to the left of the portal, at the junction of numbers 7 and 7a, and follow the drainpipe up to the top to see the excellent design work on the water basin leading into the drain. Elegance in the small things in life.

The next house to the right, still across the street from us, **Schönlaterngasse 9**, is called the **Alte Schmiede**, the Old Smithy, and has a blacksmith workshop fully outfitted as a museum in the cellar. Go in the front door and you can take a look at it through the glass partition. The top story of this building houses the Alte Schmiede—a coffeehouse where readings are given by writers and poets from all over the world.

From here we follow the Schönlaterngasse past the small intersection with the Jesuitengasse and in back of the Jesuitenkirche, Jesuit Church—you can catch a glimpse of the twin steeples from the little alleyway of the Jesuitengasse. Schönlaterngasse curves around to the left and comes out onto Postgasse, which takes its name from the Main Post Office that is located in this quarter. This street is actually one of the oldest sections of Vienna, containing the thirteenth-century Dominikanerkirche, Dominican Church, and the rear portions of the fourteenth-century university and university library.

Just to the right as you join the **Postgasse**, at **number 9**, is the **University Archives**, with the history of this German university presented through the means of original documents. Across the street, the yellow building at **Postgasse 10**, looking more like an apartment house than a place of worship, is **Saint Barbara's**, yet another Greek Orthodox church in this culturally mixed neighborhood. Originally a sixteenth-century Jesuit seminary, it became a Greek Orthodox church after the fall from favor in Vienna of the Jesuits. (Beethoven lived next door, **number 8–10**, the winter of 1815–1816.)

Turn to the right on Postgasse, crossing the street as you do so to the even-numbered, left-hand side. Keep on Postgasse past the intersection with Barbaragasse. Across the street from us, the long gray tract that looks like it could be another ugly postwar building is actually the rear end of the old university. We'll visit a more attractive portion of that institution in a bit. For now, however, turn left on **Predigergasse** (Preacher's Lane), with the baroque **Dominican Church** to your right. The Dominicans were called to Vienna in 1226 by Duke Leopold VI of Babenberg and established their first church on this site a decade later. The present church is from 1630. You may want to take a look inside, for this church (along with the Jesuits', which we shall pass in a short while) is a living, breathing symbol of baroque. From the pomp of the high altar to the sorrowful and murky oils in the side altars, this church is a personification of that architectural style.

The integration of the style is truer here than in other churches—it is not a matter of baroque overlaid on Gothic, for the church, as we have seen, was completely rebuilt in the seventeenth century. No overzealous rococo nonsense about this stolidly Italian baroque edifice.

Continue down Predigergasse and you will soon discover that the Dominican Church is on a different level from the quarter of town you are approaching. The street that Predigergasse meets up ahead is **Dominikanerbastei**, literally, the Dominican Bastion. We are coming to one of the few remaining pieces of the old city walls, in this case one of its projecting triangular bastions.

With the first Turkish siege of 1529, the city's defenses were found wanting. It was more a matter of luck—winter set in early that year, upsetting the sultan's plans—than skill or might on the part of the Viennese that saved the day. The new defense system was begun in 1544 with this very bastion, built on a rather elaborate design. Basically, military architecture in the sixteenth and seventeenth centuries focused on keeping the besieger at a distance for as long as possible, making him spend lives and, even more valuable, his resources. Lives for the Turks, heaven-bound as warriors for Allah, were much more expendable than loaves of bread, of which the attacking Turkish army of 1683—more than 100,000 strong—consumed 60,000 daily. They also tore through 32,000 pounds of meat each day. They surely did not carry such supplies with them from Constantinople, and the land around Vienna soon was raped of all crops and livestock. Thus, such military philosophy was sound enough—keep the enemy at arm's length until they get too hungry to fight any more. So with the defenses of Vienna basically what was constructed was a forty-foot-high and sixty-foot-thick stone main wall around the Inner City. Outside of this was a moat some twenty feet deep and nearly a football field in width. On the outer rim of this moat another "wall" was built up of timber and palisade, with a covered walkway from which soldiers could fire at the enemy. This weaker outer wall was built in zigzags so as to command a greater field of fire. On the far side of these fortifications was a bare no-man's-land of several city blocks wide called the glacis, which denied attackers the benefits of any cover. Bastions such as the one we are now on were built onto the main wall, projecting into the moat at intervals as strong points protecting tracts of the inside wall. In the sixteenth century the architects also developed a series of ravelins, little islands of defense in the moat that covered areas of the wall not protected by the bastions and also shielded the gates into the city.

Approaching the junction with Dominikanerbastei, you can get an idea of the height of these walls and the obstacle they must have presented to any invading army. Security in those days was not a warm blanket, but cold stones surrounding your city.

Turn right on the upper part of the *Bastei*, directly in back of the church, and follow the course of this sidewalk above the traffic past the rear end of the Dominican cloister to the intersection with **Dr. Karl Lueger-Platz**. This square takes its name from one of Vienna's more illustrious and notorious mayors, Karl Lueger, who served from 1897 to his death in 1910. *"Schöne"* Karl, handsome Karl as the Viennese called him, was one of the first modern demagogues to enlist the aid of the newly enfranchised petite bourgeoisie. At first a liberal, Lueger quickly learned his political lessons in the anti-Semitic air of Vienna and was soon using anti-Semitism as his campaign plank. Once in office, however (Emperor Franz Joseph disallowed him office several times because of his rabid policies), handsome Karl played his constituents falsely: *"I' bestimm' wer a Jud' ist,"* "I'll decide who's a Jew," became his new policy, and he took into his municipal cabinet powerful Jews as well as Christians. Lueger's brand of municipal socialism cared for the Viennese from cradle to grave, and he became in his own way one of the best mayors the city has ever had. Among his admirers was a struggling young artist from Linz who trekked all the way from his men's hostel in the northeast corner of Vienna to the Inner City to see Lueger's 1910 mammoth funeral: Adolf Hitler.

Soon we come to steps leading down from the *Bastei*. To our left, at the top of the square, we can see parts of the old wall unearthed and reconstructed during the building of Vienna's subway system.

We take our first right off the *Bastei* on a little street that looks more like a *Durchhaus* than a road, an extension of Dr. Karl Lueger-Platz, and continue past shops and a wine cellar on the right and then back out to Postgasse. To our right are the ivy-covered cloisters of the Dominicans and the church next to them. Across the street is the old university again, and to our immediate left down Postgasse is the street known as Wollzeile. This street formed the southern limit of the eleventh-century merchant quarter, which was then outside the old city walls. In Wollzeile were the wool merchants (*Wolle* means wool), weavers, and dyers.

Our way, however, leads us across Postgasse to the old university. The street going at right angles to Postgasse is Bäckerstrasse, a street that took its name, logically, from the plenitude of bakers, who had their market here from early medieval times until the advent of the university in the fifteenth century and the subsequent upgrading of the entire neighborhood. We follow its course, but via the *Durchhaus* just to the right of the street through the old university.

It is high time we get to the Habsburgs, for the university and the high southern tower of St. Stephen's were their first real achievements in making Vienna *their* city.

The Babenbergs, especially under Duke Leopold VI, as we have seen, brought a new sort of glory to Vienna, creating monasteries and some elegant court life. Vienna became the most important city of the Holy Roman Empire after Cologne, and Austria was one of the richest duchies. The trade from the Orient to Venice and thence through Vienna to Central Europe turned the city into a major trading center, a contender for a bishopric and a city destined to last. But the last of the Babenbergs, Frederick II, was a restless sort, ever trying to take more than he could reach. He was turned out of his city at one point because of his fight with Emperor Frederick II of Hohenstaufen. He died in 1246 in a battle with the Magyars. Since he left no heirs, his death left a power vacuum in Vienna and the duchy of Austria. Vienna was given as a protectorate for a time to a lesser margrave or prince of the Eastern Marches of the Holy Roman Empire. Then when Emperor Frederick II died, King Ottokar II of Bohemia seized the chance to take Vienna for his own. During his quarter-century rule he once again extended the walls as well as the building of the Hofburg, which had already been moved by the Babenbergs closer to its current location. All in all, he ingratiated himself to the Viennese, especially with new municipal privileges for the growing class of burghers.

Enter the Habsburgs. Although small beer in the Empire, Rudolf of Habsburg was elected Holy Roman Emperor in 1273 just so that he could be controlled and manipulated by the Electors. Or so the Electors in Frankfurt thought. But Rudolf proved them wrong with one of his first actions. When King Ottokar refused to recognize him as emperor and to quit Vienna, Rudolf marched on the city. The Viennese patricians sided with Ottokar—it was not the last time they would choose against a Habsburg. Rudolf threatened perhaps the worst thing any public-spirited Viennese could imagine: the destruction of the vineyards surrounding the city unless Ottokar went. Ottokar went. After all, the vines had been in cultivation for millennia by this time, and kings last only a matter of decades. It was a wise choice.

Two years later, in 1278, at the Battle of the Marchfeld just to the east of Vienna, Ottokar lost his life trying to retake the city, and the Habsburgs were to be indelibly linked with Vienna for the next six centuries. The first two hundred years they spent consolidating their lands; the next two hundred were an era of expansion; then came a century each of concentrating their power within Austria and of terribly belated modernization within their realm.

The Habsburgs did not always live in Vienna, and neither was Vienna always an imperial nor even royal city. Though the Habsburgs were for the most part emperors of the Holy Roman Empire until its dissolution in 1806, they often chose other seats for their royal residences: Maximilian I, the marriage broker par excellence, preferred Innsbruck; Charles V, who ruled over an empire upon which the sun never set, did so from Madrid, and his brother Ferdinand from Wiener Neustadt; the enigmatic Rudolf II formed a Renaissance court at Prague with the astronomers Kepler and Tycho Brahe in attendance.

Rudolf I's son, Albert I, was the first of the Habsburgs to live in Vienna. The family came from Alsace and Swabia and their name comes from one of their castles, Habichtsburg, or Hawk's Castle, in present-day Switzerland. The Viennese promptly repaid Albecht's courtesy of living in their city by revolting against him.

The Habsburgs did not play much of a role in the life and growth of Vienna until the advent of Duke Rudolf IV, called The Founder. Notice that the Habsburgs, like the Babenbergs before them, were merely dukes of the Empire if not elected to the emperor's crown. In the fifteenth century they were raised to archdukes; only in the nineteenth century with the collapse of the paper Holy Roman Empire of the German Nation and their subsequent taking of the position of rulers of Austria and Hungary did they assume the title of kings.

The sobriquet of The Founder was given to Duke Rudolf IV because he raised the position of St. Stephen's to that of a diocesan foundation. But, like the Babenbergs before him, he was unsuccessful in his bid to win the vital bishopric for the city—that would come a century later. This Rudolf also laid the foundation stone for the south tower of St. Stephen's and for a new Gothic nave in 1359. Six years later he founded the University of Vienna, near which we are walking. Rudolf IV expanded the small school started in the thirteenth century, increasing the number of Latin and philosophy classes and creating new courses in medicine and law. This was the second university, after Prague, in the German-speaking world. (Austrian historians like to sidestep the fact of Prague by calling theirs the first *German* university.)

We turn right in the university square from the passage parallel to Bäckerstrasse. To our immediate right is the oldest tract of the university, formally inaugurated in 1425, but with buildings from the seventeenth century incorporated into it as well.

Schubert was a student here in the days when the school had become a *"K und K"* (Imperial-Royal) seminary, from 1808 to 1813, and also served in the choir of the court chapel as a soprano until he was sixteen and his voice finally broke. At the seminary he was already composing prolifically. Dressed in his three-cornered hat, cutaway dark-colored coat, and short breeches, he was also taking on the roly-poly dimensions that would later earn him the nickname of *Schwammerl* (Tubby) among his closest friends. Never an imposing figure at only 5 feet 1½ inches, Schubert was yet a giant of music.

Straight ahead of us is the **Jesuit Church**, built from 1623 to 1627 and renovated with the twin towers and the new façade in the early eighteenth century. The Jesuits were called to Vienna in the mid–sixteenth century to put a stop to the Reformation. Emperor Ferdinand summoned them. He had his seat at Wiener Neustadt to the south because of all the "heretics" in Vienna. His was a small court but easily protected from the Protestants. Ferdinand, grandson of Maximilian I, was born and bred in Spain. Very Catholic indeed. And during the Reformation, the Viennese had become very Protestant indeed. It was reported that in the heydey of the Reformation, there were only four Catholic priests in all of Vienna and that more than 70 percent of the population had converted to Protestantism. Thus Ferdinand, staunch Catholic and stickler for the Spanish court protocol, called in the Jesuits to combat these backsliders. The Jesuits set up shop at first on Am Hof and then moved to this church some seventy years later, also taking over control of the university next door (always a hotbed of liberal thinking, as far as they were concerned) and strictly limiting the number of Protestant students allowed to enroll. Within a century of the Jesuits' arrival, the "evil" bud of Protestantism had been all but eradicated from Vienna (and is still today, when approximately 95 percent of the Viennese are Catholics).

The interior of the Jesuitenkirche, with its spiraling marble columns, is well worth a visit. The Viennese dubbed such Jesuitical architectural flourishes as these twisted columns and the swirls and curlicues that you see on the façade "Jesuit snails." Lovely carved pew decorations inside, as well.

To the left of this square is the former **Aula**, or Great Hall, of the university, Vienna's premier rococo attraction. In the days before the advent of the concert halls, composers had to play in private homes or in such multipurpose halls. Thus, in the eighteenth century, the so-called *Liebhaberkonzerte* (connoisseur's concerts) were held here. Haydn's *Creation* premiered here, and Beethoven conducted his Seventh Symphony here.

The square in which we have been standing is now known as the **Dr. Ignaz Seipel-Platz**; formerly it was Universitätsplatz. Dr. Seipel was a priest, a theology professor, and twice chancellor of Austria after World War I.

We leave the square by the far left-hand corner, turning into Sonnenfelsgasse. This lane was known until the nineteenth century as Johann Sebastian Bach-Gasse, after the German composer. With the renaming of the street

129

after a well-known *Hofrat* (advisor) to Empress Maria Theresa, Josef von Sonnenfels, Bach has never had another street named for him in this city of musicians. There is a Bachgasse in the Sixteenth District, but it is named after the brook (*Bach* means brook) that once flowed there. But this name change was not such a bad thing, for Sonnenfels deserved some such honor after his long and arduous career of public service. A product of a long line of rabbis from Brandenburg, Sonnenfels seemed the least likely candidate as an advisor to her Apostolic Majesty Maria Theresa. She so detested Jews (not racially but because they were heretics; dogmatists insisted they had been responsible for the death of Jesus) that during audiences with Jewish bankers in order to borrow their money to finance the building of Schönbrunn, her summer palace, she had to sit behind a screen.

That Sonnenfels was considered a Jew is yet another index to the conservatism of Vienna: his father had migrated to Austria, converted to Christianity, changed his name to Wiener (meaning Viennese), and written a treatise on the Holy Communion that had earned him a chair at the university. Ennobled, he changed his name again. His son, after seeing the world and learning a dozen languages as a common foot soldier in her majesty's army, studied law at this same university and won a name for himself as a reformer of the Enlightenment, striving to bring Austria into the main current of European thought. German with a passion, Sonnenfels was still considered a Jew by the powers that were, as if fresh from the shtetl. But Maria Theresa listened to Sonnenfels; he staked his career bucking her on issues such as the use of torture in prisons and of breaking on the wheel as a form of capital punishment. As late as the 1780s, instructional manuals were still being printed for the staff of prisons with vivid illustrations on the use of torture. Sonnenfels was instrumental in putting a stop to these medieval

Interior of the Jesuit Church

practices and was largely responsible for what little light entered Vienna with the Enlightenment. He was honored by more than a street name: Beethoven also dedicated his D Major Piano Sonata to this strong-willed and rather pedantic man.

At any rate, Sonnenfelsgasse is one of the older Viennese streets with houses from the Renaissance and Baroque creating a particularly pleasing atmosphere.

The first building on the right, **Sonnenfelsgasse 19**, is the former **proctors' house** of the university, built in 1628 after the Jesuits had taken over administration of that school. Next door at **number 17**, there is a lovely bay window in a seventeenth-century house, and at **number 15** there is an exceptionally good example of a Renaissance portal from the sixteenth century.

Sonnenfelsgasse was also part of the handworkers' and merchants' quarter that settled here in the eleventh century. With the advent of the university, however, and especially with the coming of the Jesuits, this quarter became fashionable and patricians moved in, building fine city palaces and mansions. Even simple apartment houses took on rich baroque ornamentation, as you can see much farther up the street at **Sonnenfelsgasse 3**. But we are not going that far: you can catch a glimpse of the façade of number 3 from the corner of Windhaaggasse and Sonnenfelsgasse. This is the sixth building on the right-hand side from the intersection and is called the Hildebrandt House because its decoration is in the style of that famous baroque architect. We'll be seeing some examples of that architect's work soon; he was also responsible for the design of the Kinsky Palace to be seen in Walk 3. One of Vienna's more touristy wine cellars is to be found in the cellar of the Hildebrandt House.

Turn left on Windhaaggasse and follow its short length to Bäckerstrasse again. Directly facing you at **Bäckerstrasse 12** is a Renaissance house with an amazing bit of fresco remaining to the right of the portal. The façade of this house was updated in the eighteenth century, but still the old house shield was left: **"At the Sign of the Cow and Wolf."** If you look closely, you'll see the two animals, representing the Protestants and Catholics during the Reformation, playing backgammon. The Viennese have one fine attribute among others: though they outwardly are obedient to authority, they still make fun of it. Not much is taken seriously in this city where the "situation may be desperate but not serious." I grossly overgeneralize, of course, but one does get the impression in Vienna that the only things that really matter are the quality of the new wine and the ever-decreasing size of Wiener schnitzels in an ever-increasingly inflationary period. Even as disturbing and violent an era as the Reformation and Counter-Reformation was dealt with by a bit of levity: this mural in front of us is contemporaneous with those hard times.

By 1551, when the Spanish Habsburg Ferdinand called the Jesuits to Vienna to restore Catholic order, Vienna was, as has been noted, a Protestant city. To establish a new balance of power, a major revolution had to take place. In 1578 all Lutheran preachers and teachers were banned from the city and Jesuits took over the education of the young. Soon no one of the Lutheran faith was allowed to own property or to obtain academic degrees. Yet there were no Inquisitions in Vienna: the zeal of the Jesuits was tempered by the Viennese temperament. What executions there were took place only infrequently and for the grossest of offenses, such as during the peasant uprisings when churches and manor houses in the countryside were sacked and their occupants slaughtered. This is not to condone the Habsburg retaliation of such incidents, but as compared to the rest of Europe, such retribution was mild.

The Counter-Reformation was not a smooth operation, nor was it accomplished overnight. It had its ups and downs and successes and failures and lasted well over a century. More than one commentator would still agree that Austria and Vienna were never fully re-

Portal decoration in the baroque streets

Catholicized. One plus for the Catholic Church: it had more feast days than the Protestant, and the Viennese were and still are always ready for a day away from their jobs, a nice walk in the woods (with perhaps a quick visit to a church thrown in for good measure), and a hearty meal. Interesting to note in this lack of zealousness vis-à-vis work to be found in the Viennese: up until the late nineteenth century the institution of Blue Monday, a semiofficial holiday, still held sway with Viennese workers. Blue Monday was an antidote to the Sunday afternoon blues of knowing one had to go to work the next day. To make Sundays more pleasant, Mondays were simply taken off now and again.

One interesting side effect of the Counter-Reformation was caused by the fact that a good proportion of the moneyed nobility and patricians were Protestants. At one point in the early seventeenth century, many of these wealthy families refused to swear loyalty to the newly elected Emperor Ferdinand II of Habsburg, preferring his Protestant counterpart, Frederick V of the Palatinate. Things were complicated with the political maneuverings around the incident, for these were the years of the Thirty Years War. The long and short of it was, however, that the Catholic Ferdinand won out. Thus began a most unhealthy exodus from Vienna of wealthy Protestant families, who were allowed to take 90 percent of their wealth with them. At the peak of this exodus, one thousand families left in one year. The confiscated property resulting from this exodus (along with the destruction and explosive spirits following the Turkish siege of 1683) in part made the Baroque age possible: building sites were won. But the loss to Vienna, not only in money but in talent, was incalculable. As one historian puts it: "Austria has probably never quite repaired this loss, it has left deep and permanent marks on her character."

The Jesuits themselves very directly gained by this mass exodus: their church was built on the site of about a dozen homes of Protestants who had built around the university.

There are a couple of houses of interest to the left while standing at this intersection. **Bäckerstrasse 14** is another Renaissance building with an interesting **Madonna statue** in the niche over the doorway—yet one more example of Vienna's Mary Cult. Next to it, at **Bäckerstrasse 16**, is a baroque town mansion, a fine example of such structures in Vienna. A house like this would be inhabited by the new burgher class, wealthy merchants and manufacturers. At one time in its history, this house had an inn called Schmauswaberl, one of those frustrating German diminutives that all but defy translation. Loosely translated, this inn was called The Little Feast Hive. This diminutive referred not so much to the tiny size of the many eating rooms, but to the food that was served: untasted dishes procured from the court kitchens, which were sold on the cheap to the students from the nearby university. The building now houses the offices of the Austrian Tourist Club, of great service to hikers in Austria, selling walking maps and backpacking itineraries.

We turn right into **Bäckerstrasse**. Immediately, at **numbers 8 and 10** to the left, we come upon two of those patrician/lesser nobility palaces that were built in this quarter in the seventeenth century, when it became one of Vienna's smart addresses. From both of these buildings you can get an idea how Vienna's Baroque architects used the limited space of these narrow streets to the best of advantage. Magnificence is shown off in detail, not in grandiose façade effects. After all, no one could ever catch a glimpse of the entire façade in these tiny streets: there simply was not room for such a vantage point. It is often difficult even to be able to see to the top of the building next door, a fact that more than one eighteenth-century traveler duly noted in his diary. To the right in the courtyard of number 10 you can see the old stables, for such palaces also had their own equipages and teams of horses, while the burgher classes relied on the public fiacres (there were also sedan chairs for hire at the main gates to navigate the narrowest of lanes), and the lower classes stayed to their feet.

By the time these palaces were built, the population of Vienna was nearing 70,000. When the university was first built, the population was 40,000. Even with this relatively slow growth rate from the Middle Ages to the Baroque epoch, one can imagine that crowding was an endemic problem in Vienna, for the habitable space within the city walls had not increased. Yet most lived well. Visitors to Vienna in the early fifteenth century—as the following account of a German traveler shows—liken it to one grand palace: "Entering the city you might fancy yourself walking amongst buildings of a royal castle . . . everything delights the eye of the observer; each house seems to stand more proudly than its neighbor." The same diarist records that the insides of the houses were well-appointed: "The dining rooms are often splendidly panelled with pine and heated with great stoves. The windows are all glazed; some of them are beautifully painted and protected with an iron trellis. The houses have bathrooms and kitchens, offices and bedrooms which can be rented. All of them are provided with cellars to store wine and provisions." These cellars are a constant feature of early diarists' reminiscences about Vienna: more the result of the wine trade, when most property-owning families also had their own vineyard, than of any Roman building scheme, they proved of use more than once to the Viennese during sieges.

From these two baroque palaces at numbers 8 and 10, we pass the Essiggasse (Vinegar Lane) to the left and go into the courtyard of **Bäckerstrasse 7**, the most beautiful courtyard in all of Vienna. It's arcaded, an actual Renaissance masterpiece in this overly baroque city. The parts of the building with the arcades are from 1587; those without are from 1748. Notice the arcade over the portal. On the first floor there is a collection of wrought iron from the collection of the painter Amerling. In the far right-hand corner of the courtyard is an old stable that is preserved as it was—sans horse—four centuries ago. And best of all, this house is still a private apartment house. It looks the way it does because the inhabitants care about it, not because it is maintained by the park bureau.

Turn to the right once back on **Bäckerstrasse** and go to **number 5** on your right, where you can see an example of the old house number from the first official house-numbering of 1770. At that time still, there were few enough houses—some fifteen hundred in the Inner City—to make street names unnecessary, and so the houses were simply given a serial number.

Next door, at **Bäckerstrasse 3**, there is a lovely baroque portal. The balcony above it is overhung with ivy and sparkling red geraniums in the warm months. Cross the street and notice to the left of number 4 the *Durchhaus* in a building from the late nineteenth century. Note all the glassed lower floors, which were formerly stables for the well-to-do inhabitants. **Bäckerstrasse 2**, also to the left, has a courtyard with smart design studios—patterned materials in this case—and a tower from the seventeenth century. (Look back over the entryway once you have entered the *Hof* to catch a look at this.)

Come back out onto **Bäckerstrasse**. The corner

137

building across the street at **number 1** is a gaudy nineteenth-century tribute to what was formerly on this site: the **Regensburgerhof**, one of those medieval seats of the foreign merchants who gained privileges by coming to this (at the time) Danube outpost. This medieval Regensburgerhof was quite the noble in spot for sixteenth-century Vienna, used for special city ceremonies by the burgomaster. Going to the left, we see in the square called Lugeck, straight ahead, a statue of Johann Gutenberg, the inventor of movable type.

We turn left off Bäckerstrasse (Lugeck now) into the *Durchhaus* through **Lugeck 5**, which exits onto Wollzeile at number 5. This courtyard-passageway and house have received the name of "Zum schmeckenden Wurm," "At the Sign of the Stinking Dragon." There are conflicting stories about this name, as there are for the translation of *schmecken*, which means to taste, but in dialect can mean to smell (i.e., both to stink or to sniff something). And the intrigue grows: Tradition has it that one Salome Schmiedhuber, the lovely daughter of the proprietor of Schmiedhuber's leather goods shop, had her bedroom window directly above the crocodile that acted as the trade symbol for her father's shop. The locals called the crocodile the dragon, *Lindwurm*, and one night a student who admired this pretty girl put a bouquet of flowers for his beloved in the claws of this crocodile—a gift to the girl, except it looked as if the "dragon" were actually sniffing the flowers. This story is all a bit too pat, like something out of a Waldmüller painting. The truth is that there was as powerful a stink in the cellar of this building a couple of hundred years ago; the locals thought it was some terrible dragon there and that's how the house got its name. Most probably the stink was of the same origin as the smell the baker encountered back on Schönlaterngasse, "At the Sign of the Basilisk"—more natural gas seeping into the structures. You choose the story you like best. There was, until recently, a sniffing dragon adorning the portal on the Lugeck side, now replaced by a drinker advertising the wine house inside.

Inside this *Durchhaus*, which is really a proper shopping passage, you'll find one of Vienna's favorite eating institutions, **Figlmüller's**, which is an old-time wine house and restaurant. A bit touristy now, but the *Schnitzel* still drapes over the plate. The wine served here is *Eigenbau*—the Figlmüllers have their own vineyards and produce their own wine.

We pass out onto Wollzeile, the old wool merchants' and weavers' district of the Middle Ages and now a busy shopping street, and cross the street to another *Durchhaus* at **Wollzeile 4**. To your right, you will pass another Viennese institution: Schönbichler's Tea Specialties, which specializes in more than teas, as you will see inside.

From the single-headed eagle on the door (no more double-headed eagles—the symbol of the dual monarchy—since 1918 and the creation of the Austrian Republic) to the row upon row of English marmalade, Ceylon teas, and specialty schnapps, this shop is symbolic of aristocratic shopping in the "good old days." In a shop like this, you'll get the full treatment: no phony *"Grüss Gott, Herr Doktor,"* but a gracious and simple greeting, heavy use of the subjunctive ("What is it the sir or dear lady would care for?"), and at least a one-to-one assistant to customer ratio. And if all this seems rather grandiose and a bit too much, then listen to how the musicologist Charles Burney described how the middle classes shopped in 1772 in Vienna: "They [Viennese] do not go to the shops to make purchases; but the shops are brought to them; there was literally a fair at the inn where I lodged, every day. The tradespeople seem to sell nothing at home, but like hawkers and peddlers carry their goods from house to house. The stranger is teased to death by these chapmen."

But in the midst of this somewhat anachronistically noble shop, the Viennese scale of things has made inroads: every day you can find neighborhood kids buzzing in and out between the heavily laden bags of blue-haired matrons, snatching one of the sample cookies and a quick cup of free tea from the day's sample in the samovar.

We continue through this *Durchhaus*, which exits at
Stephansplatz 6, part of the **Zwettlhof**, formerly an abbey founded by the Cistercian monks from the Abbey of
Zwettl in Lower Austria. In the fourteenth century Rudolf
IV of Habsburg purchased it for the cathedral, which he
was then enlarging, using it as the priory. The building
now houses the **Dom and Diocese Museum** (open Tuesday to Saturday, 10:00 A.M. to 4:00 P.M.; and Sunday,
10:00 A.M. to 1:00 P.M.). Some good Gothic sculptures as
well as oils are to be seen here, especially a portrait of
this first Habsburg to truly attempt to enhance Vienna's
international repute. Granted, such an attempt was not
all a matter of impartiality: since the time of the first
Habsburg emperor, Rudolf I, and his son, Albert, who
was also Holy Roman Emperor, the Habsburgs had con-
solidated their *Hausmacht* (power of their own house) by
the acquisitions of Styria, Carinthia, and Tyrol. But for a
full century no Habsburg had been elected emperor. In
1356 insult was added to injury by Emperor Charles IV,
of the house of Luxembourg, with the publication of the
Golden Bull, an attempt at making the office of emperor
a more permanent, hereditary affair. Falling short of his
intention, Charles IV did succeed in limiting the election
of the emperor to a select seven princes of the Empire,
whose lands would be inherited intact. The Habsburgs
were not among these seven. Duke Rudolf IV of Habsburg did not take kindly to this slight, nor did he appre-
ciate the elevation of Prague to the role of imperial city.
And worst of all, Charles IV's daughter, Catherine of Bohemia, was married to Rudolph IV, thus adding to the
tension.

By heavily taxing the property of the nobility in Vienna and by boosting the alcohol tax, Rudolf IV was
able to gather enough funds to build the university we
just visited, thus rivaling Prague's. And with the laying
of the cornerstone for the immense south tower in
1359 (and a planned north tower that never was completed), Rudolf continued the competition with Prague,

Memento mori on St. Stephen's north wall

for Stephansdom was, with these two planned towers, to be a replica of the most important church in Prague, Veitsdom. Rudolf, wanting to establish a diocese, had to make do with his Viennese church elevated to a collegiate church under the administration of the Passau bishopric.

It was this same Duke Rudolf IV who was also responsible for one of the poorer forgeries in history. Not content to battle Charles IV with architecture and grandeur alone, he also attempted to raise the position of the Habsburgs in the Empire by producing a set of documents "recently uncovered" in his chancellery that supposedly exalted the Habsburgs above all other princely families. The Habsburgs were, he declared, now archduchesses and archdukes. The articles were clearly a forgery, but the Habsburgs bulled ahead with their new titles in spite of the furor—even the poet Petrarch riled vehemently against this usurpation. But the Habsburgs were so undaunted in the face of this criticism that the newly "won" titles were not taken away from them, and when Frederick III of Habsburg became emperor, he confirmed the title and, indeed, from 1440 to 1806 (save for a few years in the 1740s) the Habsburgs were all but hereditary emperors of the Holy Roman Empire.

Once out of this *Durchhaus* you will find yourself back at **Stephansplatz**, near where Walk 1 began. **St. Stephen's** began life as a little wooden church outside the old Roman walls in 1130, and from the earliest times it (like Vienna itself) has had rich associations with the grape. The Bishop of Passau obtained jurisdiction over St. Stephen's by a simple barter of a vineyard to the south of the city to the ruling Babenberg duke. The new church begun here in 1137 was named after the patron saint of Passau, St. Stephen, and was from this early date on intended as a sort of administrative center over other Viennese churches.

But soon the Babenbergs regretted their decision in allowing the Bishop of Passau jurisdiction in what they were coming to see as the capital of their duchy. It became first their, and later the Habsburgs', mission to make St. Stephen's an independent bishopric, which came about only in 1469 under Emperor Frederick III (who is buried inside, in one of the more lavish Renaissance tombs).

More grapes: This same Frederick III also, according to legend, summoned the Viennese vintners to the building site of the north tower in 1450. It had been a bad harvest and the wine was much too sour. He had the vintners mix their sour wine with the lime to pour the mortar of the foundation, so that "we'll build it right," as the emperor put it. It is said that the wine in the quicklime is responsible for the strength and durability of this north tower, which we will be looking at now from our perspective at Stephanplatz 6.

The church was totally rebuilt twice in the thirteenth century, and what we have today is basically a Gothic

Detail of St. Stephen's Romanesque west portal

church enhanced by Romanesque leavings from the time of King Ottokar's interregnum in Vienna, with Renaissance statuary and baroque altars. Building on this church continued for four centuries.

If you have not already done so, now might be the appropriate time for a visit inside. A tour of St. Stephen's is a book in itself (and indeed several have been written). Some quick points of interest: From our same position looking at the north side of the church, you can see the outside pulpit straight in front of you, adorned now with baroque sunbursts and the usual panoply of baroque design. Originally the main interior pulpit, it was moved outside with the advent of the Pilgram pulpit we shall see soon. This exterior pulpit is named after the Franciscan monk Johannes von Capestrano, who came to Vienna in the mid–fifteenth century and preached against the Turks.

If you are going inside, follow the north wall to the right, around to the main entrance, the west Romanesque portal called the *Riesentor*, which is usually mistranslated as Giant Gate or Portal. (*Riesen* means giant.) But actually this name is a bastardization of the old German, *Ristor*, for draw gate. As much fortress as place of worship, St.

Stephen's had a defensive portcullis in those days. Of the amazing statuary over this front portal I will point out one: that of Christ directly over the main door. He is seated on a rainbow with his left knee bared—something all but unknown in iconography. Many art historians argue that this is a symbol of Freemasonry, an Enlightenment movement that was said to have its origins with the church masons and cathedral builders. Their initiation ceremony included the entrance of blindfolded journeymen into the workshop with their left knees bared.

The two matching towers on this west façade are called the Pagan Towers, because of their minaretlike shape. Anything looking like a minaret reminded the Viennese of those fearful pagans, the Turks. Inside you *must* see at least two of the thousands of pieces of statuary in the cathedral: the Pilgram pulpit and organ loft by the same master stonemason from Moravia. The pulpit is just inside the iron gates to the main nave, to the left. This tour de force is a late-Gothic masterpiece carved from seven blocks of sandstone—it was the only stone that could be worked with such woodlike precision. Four church patriarchs gaze out at us from the filigree stonework of the balustrade: St. Augustine, St. Gregory the Great, St. Jerome, and St. Ambrose. Along with this celebrated assemblage is the stone carver himself, Anton Pilgram, a magician of his craft, staring out of a window at the foot of the pulpit. Such foppery was enough to antagonize the mason's guild, for in the 1500s stonemasons and architects definitely did not go about signing their work—intended for the glorification of God—so ostentatiously. But if this antagonized the masons, the capturing of a second commission in St. Stephen's sent his fellow guild members flying to Emperor Maximilian I demanding that he "remove this artist from St. Stephen's." Maximilian did not comply, happily, and thus we are all the richer with a second Pilgram sculpture, to the left of the pulpit, just past the entrance to the elevator in the north tower—the organ pedestal, which bears another of these distinctive signatures just at its base.

Maximilian I also showed common sense in things besides hiring and firing practices. It was he who married Mary of Burgundy and thus won, without a bullet being fired, all of Burgundy and the Low Countries for the Habsburg domains.

Let's move on through the Stephansdom and get back, figuratively and historically, to the streets of Vienna. Cross the church to leave by the side entrance, to the right of the high altar, at the foot of the huge south tower. One other sight of interest before going out, however: in the right side altar, in what is known as the Apostle's Choir, is the tomb of Emperor Maximilian's father, Emperor Frederick III. It has been compared to the pyramids of Egypt, and with its 240 statues and the almost half-century it took to complete this monumental work, such a comparison is not all hyperbole. Frederick, unlike earlier and some later Habsburg emperors, set up his imperial court in Vienna. But the Viennese were not easy on him, this first of the Habsburgs to go in for marriage brokerage in a large way. Twice the Viennese besieged him and his family in the Hofburg, in the intermittent strife of the late fifteenth century between city and nobility. This was because Vienna, unlike most other cities of the Empire, had no city charter. There had been charters before the Habsburgs, but with the advent of that family the city was reduced to a mere appendage of the Empire. Independent self-government came only after centuries of bickering between town and crown. This complicated position as city and imperial seat still affects Vienna today, most especially in its relationships with the rest of Austria. There is still great rivalry between the other cities of Austria and Vienna (which many Austrians look on as a foreign place, a den of court intrigue, a syphon for tax money better spent elsewhere in the republic).

Poor Frederick was even turned out of his city by the Hungarian king Matthias Corvinus in 1485 and had to set up court in Linz. But through all these setbacks Frederick proved that he possessed the one true Habsburg gift: staying power. It was he who used the forgery of Duke Rudolf IV to raise the house of Habsburg to archducal status, above all other princely houses in the realm. It was he who devised the voweled device that we will see on so many Habsburg relics: A E I O U. This signified *Austriae Est Imperare Orbi Universo* ("The house of Austria is destined to rule the world"). Of course, when Frederick was driven from Vienna by the Hungarians, the joke-hungry Viennese said it meant *Aller Erst, Ist Oesterreich Verloren* ("In the first place, Austria is lost").

(Ironically enough, it was the Hungarian usurper Matthias Corvinus who coined the saucy *mot* describing the Habsburg conquer-by-marriage policy: *Bella gerant fortes; tu, felix Austria, nube: Nam quae Mars aliis, dat tibi regna Venus.* "Let the strong fight wars; thou, happy Austria, marry: What Mars bestows on others, Venus gives to thee.")

Frederick intended this tomb to be an imperial symbol—today it is difficult to visit this monument to a dead age. Usually this marble slab is roped off, so that one can visit it only if going on one of the regularly organized tours of St. Stephen's.

Passing out of the south side door, we come out onto the Stephansplatz just opposite the *Churhaus*, the curate's house, built on the site of the former Burgher's School, the most important educational institution in Vienna before the founding of the university. The former *Bauhütte*, or headquarters for the masons constructing the cathedral, was also located on this spot.

Go to the left once out the side entrance and continue around to the back of the church, with the massive cloisters and old administration buildings (to the right) of the **House of the Teutonic Order**, whose church is on the Singerstrasse in this same complex. The Order of Teutonic Knights, one of those chivalric orders formed during the times of the Crusades, has had a building on this site since the thirteenth century. This present complex, which forms the southeastern corner of Stephansplatz, is from the mid–seventeenth century.

A couple of things to look for around the back of St. Stephen's: Just as you come around to the back of where the high altar is situated inside, there is a series of six Gothic frescoes of the Passion to the left. It is striking to see these frescoes, if only to realize that they have endured all kinds of weather for more than half a millennium, and only fairly recently have they been properly protected from the elements by an overhanging roof. Next to these frescoes is the *Zahnweh-Herrgott* (Our Lord of the Toothache), another instance of the Viennese at their nickname-happy best. The story goes that drunken students, returning home from an evening on the town, stood in front of this statue and joked that it looked as if Jesus was suffering from toothache, rather than the agonies of crucifixion. In the morning, all of these students awoke with their own toothaches (hangovers?) and could be relieved of their pain only by begging forgiveness in front of this figure.

We leave **Stephansplatz** at **number 5a**, a *Durchhaus* that leads through to **Domgasse**. Notice the shop to the immediate right on Domgasse once you have come out of the *Durchhaus*. It is a specialty shop that supplies party favors and fireworks for Viennese carnival, or *Fasching*, one of those periods of permitted craziness in Vienna. Though it is no longer the extremely frivolous and libidinous season it was in the eighteenth and nineteenth centuries, the Viennese *Fasching* is an occasion for frolic in the midst of the dreary winter, when children dress in all sorts of costumes and adults attend masked balls. In its heyday, Viennese *Fasching* would see more than one thousand balls scheduled in one night across the city! The Opera Ball is still the premier *hochnasig* (literally, high-nosed; hoity-toity) ball of the season, but every profession, union, and club seems to hold its own ball. The Washerwomen's Ball, to which scamps from the aristocracy would go "slumming" on the lookout for a *süsses Mädel* (sweet young thing), is no more, but there are still holdovers from the days of old Vienna: the Zuckerbäcker Ball (Confectioner's Ball) and even a Fiacre-Driver's Ball, where the rough and rugged characters who drive the city's horse-drawn carriages gather with their wives and sweethearts for a night of merrymaking.

At **Domgasse 5**, down the street to the left, is the **Figaro House**, built in the early eighteenth century and famous because it was among the eleven residences that the Mozarts inhabited in their ten years in Vienna from 1781 to 1791. Wolfgang and wife Constanze (sister to the girl who earlier threw him over for a brighter prospect) had four rooms in this house, from 1784 to 1787. Among other things, Mozart wrote *The Marriage of Figaro* here, as well as seven piano concerti and the *Haydn Quartets*. It was here Mozart first met Papa Haydn, already something of a historical figure in Vienna. When he heard the quartets dedicated to him, Haydn was compelled to exclaim: "Before God and as an honest man, I tell you [he] is the greatest composer known to me, either in person or by name."

Mozart had been recognized as a child prodigy (he spent fourteen of his short thirty-five years on tour) and had won raves from audiences for such tricks as playing from sight, playing the piano with the keyboard covered with a cloth, demonstrating his absolute pitch, and so on. After his meeting with da Ponte, he turned out three great operas in succession: *The Marriage of Figaro*, *Don Giovanni*, and *Così fan tutte*, all of which were successes in their day. He even won the supreme honor of being appointed chamber composer to the emperor, Joseph II. But such honors rarely filled the larder: his court appointment, for example, brought in only 800 gulden annually, about $1,000. Mozart composed with a fervor—not only in quality but in quantity. But in those days before the recording of music, indeed even before public concerts, the musician/composer was more a lackey to a noble household than an independent artist (as was partly the case with Haydn, himself employed for decades by the powerful Esterházy clan and living in splendid isolation in Eisenstadt to the southeast of Vienna). Compositions were rarely even printed, so that the composer made little from them above the immediate salary allotted by his patron.

In Mozart's case things were different. He was one of the first composers to become independent of patrons; his finances suffered accordingly. And that he fell out of favor with the court—though not the public—because of *Figaro* did not help: It is surprising the opera was ever staged, for in that age of censorship and the beginnings of class strife the subject matter—the undoing of an aristocrat by a pair of quick-witted plebians—was an explosive one.

The rooms at Domgasse can be visited daily except Monday, 9:00 A.M. to 12:15 P.M. and 1:00 P.M. to 4:30 P.M. To the left, on entering the street door, you will notice a door with a round window. This formerly led to the *Portier's* lodging on the ground floor. Some say that the concierge or building superintendent of Viennese parody is a dying breed, but I have witnessed no signs of their giving up the ghost. Tiny empresses (for they are usually women) in their own right, they live rent-free in a ground-floor flat and maintain the building and order. They close the house doors at nine or ten each night and you need a house key to get back in. If you've forgotten yours or are unfortunate enough simply to rent a room in somebody's flat and are thereby unworthy of a house key, you have to ring for this frighteningly imposing figurehead, take all the abuse and wrath she feels it her right to pour onto you for having awakened her in the middle of the night—though it is only ten past ten—and tip her besides. This *Sperrscherl* (*sperren* means close) is just one of the perks these women take for granted. But they are a hearty and crusty lot for all that and long may they live, for there is ultimately something comforting about knowing that a dragon is between you and the world as you sleep at night.

But back to Mozart. Upstairs, except for the lack of furniture, the apartment is much the same as when the

Mozarts lived here and will be one of your few opportunities to get behind the façade to see what the skeleton
of a Viennese apartment looks like. It is an eerie feeling
to know that Mozart—that short, pockmarked genius
with the pudgy hands (great pianists seldom have the
long, tapered fingers one imagines they possess)—walked
these very floors, composed here, had domestic squab-
bles here. Most definitely worth your time for a short
visit.

Our tour proceeds right after you exit the Figaro
House on the Blutgasse, but first there are some sights to
the left. At **Domgasse 6** is the **Former Lesser Bishop's
Court**, where that prelate once resided. It is from the
mid–eighteenth century and was built by a well-known
architect, Gerl. For generations, legend has stated that it
was at the former house on this site that Vienna's first
coffeehouse, "**At the Sign of the Blue Bottle**," was established. (See Walk 4.) Not to daunt you coffeehouse pilgrims, but the reason for this legend is that the proprietor
of said café, George Kolschitzky, died in the house next
door, **number 8**, "**At the Sign of the Red Cross**." You'll
see a plaque on the house put up in 1983 by Polish
pastry cooks (!) to commemorate that fact.

Kolschitzky is one of those fascinating footnotes to
history who become symbolic for an entire epoch. He
was simply one of many messengers who, for a high
price, braved the Turkish lines during the 1683 siege of
Vienna to tell the relieving army to advance, that the
situation inside the walls of the town had greatly deteri-
orated (in other words: Help!). Kolschitzky and his servant had made this treacherous round trip through enemy
lines by wearing Turkish garb (Kolschitzky was a Pole
who had worked for a time as an interpreter in Constantinople), and each was paid two hundred ducats upon
their return. But Kolschitzky refused a second offer, which
his servant took up and successfully completed. There
were other messengers as well, each bringing back reas-
suring words that the relief force would soon attack. Such

a situation continued for another month before the relieving army struck.

At any rate, Kolschitzky must have been a master of
public relations, for it is his exploits that chroniclers of
the siege chose to report over other messengers. Indeed,
Kolschitzky's deeds take on a magnitude in league with
the commander of the Viennese fortifications, Starhemberg, and the burgomaster, Liebenberg, who died
defending the city. After the Turks were routed on September 12, 1683, by a relieving force of 120,000 Germans and Poles, the spoils were handed out all around.
The Turks had taken most of their treasury with them,
but among other things left behind were sacks and sacks
of coffee beans. Kolschitzky, in reward for his services,
was given these "useless" beans (the Viennese did not
yet drink coffee) and he proceeded to establish Vienna's
first coffeehouse, "At the Sign of the Blue Bottle," where-
abouts now unknown.

So, back at the Figaro House, we dogleg to the
right onto Blutgasse, a most sanguinary description for
this narrow, cobbled lane. The name (*Blut* means
blood) of the street may come from a massacre of Templars that occurred in 1312. The Knights Templars was
one of the triumvirate of military religious orders that
were formed during the Crusades. Others were the
Knights Hospitalers (later the Knights of Malta) and the
Teutonic Order, alongside whose building the Blutgasse
runs. The Templars were suppressed when, quite simply, they became too powerful and rivaled the power of
sovereigns. It is unclear if one such massacre occurred
on this spot or not, and if so, whether the nearby Teutonic Order, rivals of the Templars, played an instrumental role in it.

We turn left out of Blutgasse at the *Durchhaus* through
Blutgasse 3. (The next house after this is the old Fähn-
richhof, one of the oldest building complexes in the city:
a smattering of smaller houses from the Gothic age,
which, in the Baroque age, were knocked together into

the large and forbidding building you now see at Blutgasse 5–9.)

But we follow a path through the much smaller and
cozier series of baroque buildings at **number 3**, with their
wrought-iron *Pawlatschen* and tiny nooks and crannies.
This is another example of the recent city renewal of old
buildings and entire neighborhoods. Go straight through
this *Durchhaus*, down the stairs, past the little bit of green
on the left and the intersecting passageway to the right,
out onto the **Grünangergasse**, which takes its name from
the green meadow (*Anger* means meadow) that was still
to be found in this locale before the second great city
expansion in the late twelfth century. The name was
changed through the course of time, when the fact that a
green or commons could have stood here was all but
unthinkable and a *Gasthaus* took the name of *"Zum grünen Anker,"* "At the Sign of the Green Anchor." Its successor is still to be found on the street, directly to your
right as you come out onto Grünangergasse. Our first
destination is directly across the street, up the walkway
to the right of **number 7**, and out onto an open "park"
built on top of a parking garage. Filled with potted plants
and abstract sculptures, this little open area is one of
those surprising oases in the midst of the metropolis that
make life so livable in Vienna. A fine view of the *Steffl*
can be had from here, turning around and looking back
over the buildings of Grünangergasse and Blutgasse. At
the far end of this park platform, you are overlooking
Kumpfgasse, a crooked little street that lies in the oldest
and farthest line of the Babenberg city expansion of the
late twelfth century, which the unfortunate Richard the
Lionhearted helped to finance. This tiny street is full of
baroque and classicist buildings. The composer Hugo
Wolf lived at **number 9**. Johann Strauss the elder lived
at the house that formerly stood on the site of **number 11** and wrote his reactionary (politically, not musically)

View of the Steffl *from Grünangergasse*

Radetzky March, celebrating the deeds of the general who helped to put down the 1848 revolution and "commune" in Vienna, at the same time that his son (the one most of the world thinks of as *the* Johann Strauss) had taken to the barricades with the students and workers.

Go back to **Grünangergasse** and turn right for a short detour to **number 4**, the old **Fürstenberg Palace** with some lovely hunting dogs as statuary over the portal. One guess what the ruling passion of this noble family was. The hunt was as important to Austrian nobility as it was to the British. And it was not always the stag that was victim: Maximilian I lost his wife, Mary of Burgundy, to a fall from her horse during a hunt. The nobility retained huge hunting preserves all around Vienna and farther out in the country. Joseph II opened one of the largest of these, the Prater, to the public in the late eighteenth century. He also turned the huge preserve of the Lainzer Tiergarten west of Vienna into a walled enclosure, with a fifteen-mile-long wall built of mortar by one Herr Schlucker. To this day, the Viennese expression *arme Schlucker* ("poor bastard") recalls the impossible task given his harried court architect. But whatever one thinks of the sport of hunting, it did have the positive result here that huge tracts of land surrounding Vienna were saved from development. The Vienna Woods exists in part because of this noble passion for the hunt.

Things of course got out of control in the nineteenth century with the decline of the house of Habsburg. The heir apparent, Franz Ferdinand (who was assassinated at Sarajevo), was an avid hunter, and his grotesque hunts beleaguer the imagination with their statistics: many thousands of birds shot in the matter of a few hours; countless deer and chamois slaughtered for royal whimsy. As ironic symbol of such slaughter, the double suicide (murder?) of Crown Prince Rudolf and his mistress in 1889 occurred at the royal hunting preserve of Mayerling to the south of Vienna.

The hunt still does go on, but now it is big business.

All through the Vienna Woods you can see, in every available meadow and open field, high, wooden shooting stands for deer season. Rich Europeans pay thousands of dollars for the privilege of hunting on large tracts of government- and privately owned land in the Alps. Trophies of horns can cost the hunter up to five thousand dollars, and the meat goes to the local warden. Even fishing rights to streams in Austria come high: up to twenty dollars per day to cast a fly, and all the fish must be set free.

Housed in the old Fürstenberg Palace now are the headquarters of the Association of Austrian Booksellers; across the way at **Grünangergasse 1** is a building in which the offices of Vienna's earliest book printers were found in the sixteenth century. Bookshops line the streets of Grünangergasse to this day. Tradition, as we have seen, dies hard in Vienna. Also in number 1 is the Galerie Nächste St. Stephens on the second floor, one of the most important exhibiting rooms for Austria's postwar artists. The Fantastic Realists, that school of fantasy painters so important in Vienna in the past couple of decades, got their start with exhibitions held here.

Backtrack down **Grünangergasse** past where you entered the street from the *Durchhaus*. Look over the door of **number 8**, to the right, for a remembrance that fifteenth-century bakers plied their trade in the house that formerly stood on this site: stone reliefs of buns, crescent rolls, and other baked goods are represented there.

Continue past the Restaurant zum Grünen Anker, a Viennese institution with its *Stammgäste*, or regulars, who come back again and again to the same table and are on a first-name basis, or *per Du*, with the waiters and proprietor. *Stammgäste* at this restaurant and at the *Gasthaus* of the same name that preceded it have included such notables as Schubert, Brahms, and the painters Klimt and Schiele. The playwright Grillparzer also spent part of his youth in the apartments above.

Grünangergasse ends with its intersection with Sin-

Beer delivery at an Inner City Gasthaus

gerstrasse. We won't turn into the latter street, but rather examine a few sights from the vantage point of this corner. The name of this street has, however, nothing at all to do with singers, but comes from a family of weavers and dyers who settled here from their home of Sünching (later corrupted to "singer") near Regensburg in the twelfth century. But the street has musical connections for all that: both Brahms and Mozart lived for a time in the House of the Teutonic Order, to your right at **number 7**. It was here in fact that Mozart, still in the retinue of the archbishop of Salzburg, who was visiting Vienna in 1781, was literally kicked out of that personage's service for the rank effrontery of asking that he be allowed to perform in public a piece that the archbishop had commissioned. A swift kick on the rump by the archbishop's secretary sent Mozart on his way, and thereafter Mozart settled in Vienna and began that decade of writing in which his mature genius came to the fore. It was a kick for which the world should be grateful. And when Brahms was living here in the 1860s, Johann Strauss the younger, living in the nearby Weihburggasse, is said to have paid a visit to the German master, humbly (for Brahms was by this time world-famous) requesting an autograph. Brahms obliged him with a further act of humbleness: after the first few notes of the *Blue Danube*, Brahms inscribed "Unfortunately not by Johannes Brahms!" Brahms, the intellectuals' musician, and Strauss, the king of the waltz, became fast friends, played that fascinating Austrian card game called Tarock together, and were generally each other's best audience.

Other famous musical inhabitants of the street include Richard Wagner, who passed part of 1861 at Singerstrasse 32 at the home of Dr. Standhartner. Wagner shed no tears over the thought of departing from Vienna, yet he returned to the Austrian capital time after time; his trail leads us all over Vienna, since he changed lodgings numerous times, one step ahead of his creditors. Interestingly enough, one of his champions in Vienna was Strauss, who first played Wagner overtures in his Sunday morning concerts in the Augarten in the Second District, the home of that famous porcelain and of the Vienna Choir Boys, that five-hundred-year-old institution started by Emperor Maximilian I.

Any examination of music in Vienna has to take into consideration the role the Habsburgs played in the encouraging of musical growth. It was no accident that Vienna was the home of Gluck, Haydn, Mozart, Schubert, Beethoven, Brahms, Bruckner, Wolf, Mahler, Schoenberg, Webern, and Berg. This fostering of musical Vienna is perhaps the finest Habsburg legacy.

Beginning with Emperor Maximilian I, when he established the *Hofmusikkapelle* in 1498 to provide song at his court (whether it was Vienna or Innsbruck) until well into the nineteenth century, the Habsburg princes, empresses, and emperors were a musical lot.

Maximilian, something of a Renaissance man beyond the Alps, did not limit his love of art to music. It was he who befriended Dürer and ennobled him, after a German noble refused to hold the ladder of this "commoner" when Dürer was painting the ceiling of a banquet hall for the meeting of German princes. "I can make a noble of a peasant," Emperor Maximilian barked at this prince, "but I can never turn a noble into an artist such as he." Granted, Maximilian's taste for the arts was not without its self-gratification: had he been a ruler in the electronic age, he would have won the world, for he had a natural gift for controlling the media and for self-advertisement. He had a sort of comic-book version of his life and deeds (largely imaginary) created from 137 woodcuts and 109 miniature paintings, *Triumphzug*, which remains one of the treasures of the northern Renaissance. Along with his schemes for marrying off the Spanish branch of the house of Habsburg to win Bohemia and Hungary, he found time to write scores of books, not only about fishing and hunting (he was an avid chamois hunter), but also autobiographies and philosophical works on leading the right life.

Despite the fact that Maximilian's court was at Innsbruck and that his successor's, Charles V, was in Madrid, a sixteenth-century Viennese poet who taught at the Scottish monastery could report of the "profusion of singers and instrumentalists who may be heard here, come from all parts of the kingdom and often indeed from abroad. Nowhere, assuredly, are so many musicians gathered together."

When Ferdinand I succeeded his brother, Charles V, as ruler of the Austrian Habsburg lands, he brought to Vienna not only the ornate court manners of Madrid and the haute école of riding (which still lingers in the Riding School), but also his love for music. It was no accident that in his official portrait a piano stands next to his writing desk. It was this Ferdinand who brought the love of Italian opera to Counter-Reformation Vienna, as well as the baroque and the Jesuits. A later Ferdinand, the third, along with Leopold I (the emperor during the Turkish siege of 1683), Joseph I, and Joseph II, continued the Habsburgs' musical tradition. Ferdinand III himself composed oratorios and operas, some of which show real originality. Leopold I did his bit by increasing the court orchestra to one hundred singers and two hundred instrumentalists, a size it has never since surpassed. Joseph I was a truly gifted flautist and composer. His compositions show the influence of Alessandro Scarlatti, but that is no mean comparison. The Vienna of Maria Theresa and of her son Joseph II was no less hospitable to musicians. The empress herself could sing a soprano part on sight; her husband, Francis, played the violin. Her father, Charles VI, who had commissioned the Karlskirche and turned Vienna into a "Roman" capital with Fischer von Erlach's help, was said to have never missed a concert given at the Hofburg, and he often conducted these concerts as well. One only has to recall the welcome that the six-year-old Mozart received at Schönbrunn to realize the paramount position of the musician at court: that stern Empress Maria Theresa was not averse to having the most highly exploited child prodigy in history jump up into her ample lap after his performance and give her a big hug.

Even Maria Theresa's rather dour offspring, Joseph II, who refused to wear pompous court clothing and cavorted about Vienna in his old hat and frock coat patched at the elbows, still sponsored the musical arts.

This feeling for music spread into lesser layers of the aristocracy as well, and thus musicians flocked to this capital where patronage was plenty: the Kinsky, Lichnowsky, Liechtenstein, Waldstein, and Razumovsky families have all been written into history as sponsors of Mozart symphonies and Beethoven concerti. The great palaces were the scene of premiers of more than one immortal piece of work from the greats of the Vienna musical heritage.

There are some additional sights of interest you can take in from the vantage point at the intersection of Grünangergasse and Singerstrasse before moving on. Directly in front of you, across the **Singerstrasse** at **number 22**, is a lovely courtyard of the former court of the cathedral provost. One last musical association: The *Domkapellmeister* (cathedral musical director) Albrechtsberger died here in 1809—he was a friend to both Mozart and Haydn and a teacher of Beethoven.

Farther to the right and on the same side of the street, **number 18** is where the Fröhlich sisters lived. One of them, Katharina, was the "eternal bride" of the playwright Grillparzer. The two were engaged for decades but never married, and they finally settled down in old age to a platonic ménage with another of the sisters.

At **number 16** you can just make out part of the grandiose façade of the **Neupaurer Palace**, with its Fischer von Erlach look-alike doorway (pure copying of that architect's Bohemian Chancellery, which we saw on the Wipplingerstrasse in Walk 1). The palace itself is nothing terribly important to see, but the idea of it is. This was built in 1715, amid that huge surge of baroque building that came with the threefold victory of Catholicism over Protestantism (when many aristocratic families left town, leaving building sites for the newly powerful), of Christianity over the Turks, and of life over the plague of 1679. Neupaurer, small potatoes in history (he was a town councillor and militia captain), bought up three small buildings, knocked them down, and had this palace built in the grand style with groaning Atlantean figures holding up the portal. We'll see many such examples of these baroque palaces during the course of these walks.

Farther up the street to the right, on the right-hand side, you can see the green spire of the **Church of the Teutonic Order**, a Gothic gem undisturbed through the ages of thoughtless baroque renovation that most Viennese churches suffered. Coats of arms of the Knights of the Teutonic Order can be seen on the walls. Gregorian chants are to be heard here Sundays at 7:00 P.M.

Just up from the church is the **Hotel Royal** at **Singerstrasse 3**, site of the apartment house where Salieri, Mozart's great competitor and a court favorite, lived. He opened the first voice school for the Society of the Friends of Music in 1817. Mozart and Salieri were such unfriendly rivals that the latter was proclaiming even on his deathbed that he had not poisoned Mozart, as rumor had it at the time of Mozart's death.

Closer to where we are standing, to our immediate right in fact, is one of those old pharmacies for which Vienna (though not necessarily medicine) should be proud. All over Vienna the pharmacies, in particular, have made it a point to retain the old-world look—even new pharmacies are built with wainscoting and paneled ceilings to lend the weight of authority and age to their sales. To the left, on the left-hand side of **Singerstrasse** at **number 17**, is the former **Rottal Palace**, built in the style of that other baroque master, Johann Lukas von Hildebrandt. As with so many Inner City palaces, this is now used for government offices, housing the Austrian Ministry of Law.

Just across the street from here, in the cloister of the Franciscan Church, is a wonderful wine shop, almost a city block long, that stores its wine in the cellars of the cloister. Do not be put off by wine sold in the *Doppelliter*, "double liter." It is generally of better quality than U.S. bulk wine sold in jugs and can be quite refined. Here you can sample wines not only from wine areas close to Vienna, but also from the Wachau region of the Danube, where the Grüner Vetliner, a tart, fruity wine, is king.

Gumpoldskirchen, the wine village and vineyard area just to the south of Vienna, has for centuries been considered the finest wine region of Austria, especially in the export market. So strong was this tradition that the newer

161

Wachau wines were for decades used only to make vinegar. Try some of these tart wines, especially those from the Krems region, and discover a new viticultural experience.

And way down the **Singerstrasse** to the left, at **number 28**, is the well-known Viennese *Beisl* "Zu den drei Hacken," "At the Sign of the Three Axes," an inn since the Biedermeier days, where the playwright Nestroy and Schubert, among others, gathered for lunch.

So, finally back at the intersection of Grünangergasse, let's cross Singerstrasse and, jogging a little to the left, enter the street that is an extension of Franziskanerplatz. Just before entering the square, at the top of this street on the right-hand side is another little specialty shop typical of Vienna: a sign shop where you can get everything from door plaques to street signs made to order.

The **Franziskanerplatz** is one of the lovelier tiny squares of Vienna, dominated by the Franciscan Church to the left along with its cloisters. The Franciscans were one of the many orders who settled in Vienna during the Catholic resurgence of the Counter-Reformation. Inside the church are some paintings by the famous Austrian baroque painter Martin Johann Schmidt, otherwise known as Kremser Schmidt. Like the Jesuitenkirche, the **Franciscan Church** has no Gothic underlying structure, as it was built in style and is *very* baroque. There is a stunning high altar with floating *putti* and sunburst galore. From in front of the church we can survey the square. In the middle of the square is the Moses Fountain, from 1798, with that old Jewish leader looking very European. To the right, just next to the sign shop, is one of Vienna's smaller cafés, aptly named the Kleine Café (Small Café). All over the First District and out into the old *Vorstädte*, or districts outside the Ring, such small, intimate spots have been opening for the past decade. Somewhat Pepsi Generation–ish, these *Lokalen*, or in spots, provide something of a haven from the usual *Kraut* and *Knödel* fare of *Gasthäuser* and inns.

They are symbols of Austria's greatly delayed postwar affluence.

Note the chimney on the house at **number 2**: newer apartment houses encircled this tiny building, and it was forced to send its chimney towering up like a small skyscraper just to get the smoke over the newcomers. At **number 1**, directly opposite the church, is the apartment house in which Egon Caesar Conte Corti lived and wrote from 1933 to 1953. Something of a Viennese Barbara Cartland, Corti wrote historical novels about the Habsburgs.

Take a look at the entrance hall to this building: with its low, arched ceiling, it is like entering a grotto. In the courtyard is the back entrance to one of the few old-time wine houses in the Inner City.

To the left of number 1, Weihburggasse leads back to Kärntnerstrasse. This entire area is known as the Weihburgviertel, after the numerous churches and cloisters that settled here from the fourteenth century on. (*Weih* means holy or consecrated.) From the church you can get a glimpse of the house at **Weihburggasse 10–12** just to the left, where that street leaves the square: a typical and lovely *Jugendstil* building among the classicist and baroque buildings of the area.

To the left in the square itself, at number 6, is a house with a most checkered past. It was recently renovated in the style of Vienna's Fantastic Realism tradition. The street number over the portal, the wrought-iron work and mosaics in the court, and even the flooring of the corridor are all kept in style. This house now encloses a chic passage with smart shops on either side. But this building was not always so elegant: at one time the Franciscans made a habit of saving women of the night and housing them in this house until "rehabilitated." Rehabilitation in this case meant marriage, since **Franziskanerplatz 6** became something of a marriage brokerage firm for the nouveau riche looking for a wife with beauty rather than breeding.

As you stand in front of the church, to your far left at **Weihburggasse 14** is a handsome apartment house built in 1722 in the style of Hildebrandt with excellent wrought-iron balconies.

We leave the Franziskanerplatz by the narrow alleyway between this building and Franziskanerplatz 5. Actually, this alley, which looks more like a doorway than a street, has a name, **Ballgasse**. The street curves up to the right, and it is at this curve that the old game house was located. It later was rented to the city of Vienna and became an Italian theater; since 1772 this "new" house located here has been the guild house of the Viennese cabinetmakers. As you'll notice by the sign and wood smells at **Ballgasse 8**, they are still making tables and cabinets here—a tradition that is older than the U.S. Constitution.

Ballgasse is narrow and winding. Medieval streets were meant to be so for two reasons: as a defense measure and to cut the wind. In recent years this street has been upgraded with a couple of cafés and restaurants.

Before the eighteenth century, Ballgasse led only into Blumenstockgasse to the right (down which you'll find an excellent English bookshop). We follow Ballgasse now to the left, however, past **Ballgasse 4**, where Beethoven lived during the French bombardment of 1809 and in which Grillparzer had an apartment from 1823 to 1826. Turn left into Rauhensteingasse. A few quick things before proceeding: Across the street and two houses to the right is an excellent old-time bakery. Just across the street from the Ballgasse-Rauhensteingasse intersection, at **Rauhensteingasse 8**, next to the rear end of one of Vienna's first department stores, is the site of the Mozart "Death House." The house that stood here until the late nineteenth century was Mozart's unlucky thirteenth Viennese address. Here he wrote *Die Zauberflöte* (*The Magic Flute*), *La Clemenza di Tito*, his last piano concerto, and the *Requiem*. Mozart died on December 5, 1791, at the tender age of thirty-five, from a kidney disease and overwork.

Legend has it that he died with his cheeks puffing out to whistle the manner in which the trombones should play their part in the *Requiem*. *Die Zauberflöte*, Mozart's mystical, Masonic opera, was a smash hit in Vienna, but it came too late. Mozart died a poor man, leaving the world 626 compositions richer. He received the simplest funeral possible at St. Stephen's and was buried in an unmarked common grave in the cemetery of St. Marx in Vienna's Third District. Revisionist historians would have us believe that such a no-fuss funeral and burial were symptomatic of the times rather than of Viennese indifference to the passing of a genius from their midst. In fact, Vienna was still rocking from the reforms of Joseph II, going through a period of austerity and court simplicity that even extended to the attempted suppression of funereal pomp. Joseph II did put a stop to burials in the overcrowded and diseased catacombs under St. Stephen's. It was he who was responsible for the so-called nose pinchers: coffins of simple construction without all the funereal pomp and carving of expensive sarcophagi. Mozart, like Joseph II, was a Mason in those days when that organization had not declined to its current nonstatus. In the eighteenth century, the Masons fed the Enlightenment in Austria and were most definitely persona non grata with the royalty (though some royalty did belong, like Joseph II), for they were seen as a revolutionary element. The Masons did not have any dictum per se about simple funerals, but such could have been the case with this liberal, enlightened society.

At any rate, the argument goes that Mozart chose the simple funeral he had rather than having it imposed upon him from lack of care by his Viennese public. Poppycock, I say. It was simply the case that before Beethoven's time composers were grouped in that netherworld of entertainer, along with traveling players, jugglers, and other such freaks of nature. All very good to hire once in a while to compose a charming ditty, but most definitely not of the level to be buried with the pomp of a general or minister. It took Beethoven's perpetually grumpy ways and world-weary frown (actually more the result of his hearing loss rather than a real antisocial or troubled personality) to convince the good burghers that the composer was an artist rather than artiste and deserving of— if not respect—at least elbow room.

So we proceed to the left on Rauhensteingasse until the intersection with Himmelpfortgasse. Across the street is the Café Frauenhuber, at **Himmelpfortgasse 6**, one of Vienna's finer Inner City cafés. It's a good spot to catch up on correspondence or the newspapers while sipping a cup of coffee. In the late eighteenth and early nineteenth centuries this was the location of a noble restaurant, Jahns Traiteurie, established by the former pastry cook of Maria Theresa, Franz Jahn. Mozart as well as Beethoven conducted their works in the concert hall here.

We turn left on **Himmelpfortgasse**. The buildings to the left stand on the spot of the old cloisters of Himmelpfort (Heaven's gate), which give the street its name. To the right, at **number 8**, is the **former city palace of Prince Eugene of Savoy**, now used as the Ministry of Finance. Eugene was an international soldier-statesmen whose very name demonstrates his trilingual roots: Eugenio von Savoy. Born to a branch of the House of Savoy, Eugene was connected on his father's side to the Spanish Habsburgs and through his Italian mother to Cardinal Mazarin. He was brought up at the court of the Sun King, Louis XIV, at Versailles, and was earmarked for holy orders. Louis derisively called this puny youth the *petit abbé*, but more than one witness noticed that he ran with a very fast crowd—indeed a crowd that "engaged in immoral pleasures" with the young Eugene wearing female clothes. Eugene was not cut out for life in a monastery, and he ran away from the French court to become a soldier in the Imperial (Holy Roman Empire) army at the time of the 1683 siege of Vienna. He distinguished himself at the subsequent battle near Kahlenberg, in which the Turks were routed, and subsequently threw himself into the new profession of military man with a passion he had earlier reserved for his "immoral pleasures." He was a major general at twenty-two; by the age of thirty the emperor had placed him in supreme command of the operations against the Turks. Prince Eugene was responsible for ridding the Turkish menace from Europe and for holding the French, traditional Habsburg foes, at arm's length.

For his services to the Empire, Eugene was richly rewarded, not only in titles (as head of the Privy Council and president of the Imperial War Council, his power was second only to the emperor's), but also in hard cash and domains. But Eugene had class; he did not squander his wealth on fast horses and faster women. He was a great collector: of books, of engravings, and of intellectuals. (He was friend and confidant to Leibniz, among others.) In 1694 he bought several houses in the Himmelpfortgasse, had them razed, and commissioned the court architect, Fischer von Erlach, to build the palace in front of which we are now standing.

We have already seen other work by Fischer von Erlach. This architect was largely responsible for the Austrian baroque. Before his time, Viennese architecture was an Italian hand-me-down. But Erlach, himself a student in Rome for more than a decade (and influenced by the school of Bernini), created a specifically Viennese style, blending Italian baroque and Palladian with English manor house style. His Atlantean figures holding aloft portals and lintels, his pilastered façades and Leibnizian "perfectionism" all played their part in forming a distinctive imperial baroque style for Vienna.

But Erlach suffers on narrow streets like Himmelpfortgasse. Confined as the building site was, his monumentalism had to be worked out in a more refined and subdued style with tall windows and a pilastered façade. The narrowness of the street itself made division and articulation of the façade by projecting parts impossible. Erlach borrowed heavily also from French architecture, creating a triumphal gate typical of French classical architecture. This solution was, moreover, a statement about Prince Eugene, who had left the French court—that he had "arrived" in Vienna.

But before the final extensions were completed (Eugene had to wait some time to acquire all the necessary property), Eugene changed architects. He picked Johann Lukas von Hildebrandt, a pupil of Borromini, to complete this building and to design his summer palace, the Belvedere. Hildebrandt had a somewhat lighter touch than Erlach; his architecture was not of the monumental proportions of Erlach's, and there is a particularly Viennese kind of playfulness at work in his façades.

Go in the central doorway of this palace, and look at the statuary of the main staircase with its sculpted Atlantean and Herculean figures, representing Prince Eugene's own Herculean struggles.

Continuing down the **Himmelpfortgasse**, we pass another palace, on the left at **number 13**, the **Erdödy-Fürstenberg Palace** from 1724, which leans more to the monumental style with its Atlantean figures on the portal. Next door to this, **number 15** is a refreshing change from imperial baroque; it's a gabled house from the seventeenth century on a more human scale. Other nearby houses are from the Baroque and Classicist age. The Austrian playwright and librettist Hugo von Hofmannsthal lived for a time at **number 17**. Hofmannsthal, who is best known outside Austria as the librettist of numerous Richard Strauss operas, was something of a wunderkind, penning poems as a student, under the name of Loris, that won him recognition from the best writers of the day. It must have been an embarrassing surprise for the literati who invited this unknown Loris to coffee to have a pimply *Gymnasium* student turn up instead of the sad and timeworn poet they had imagined the author to be.

Across the street to your right at **number 14** is the site of the Hungarian Crown Gasthaus, where the Schubertians met in the early 1800s and where Carl Maria von Weber lived in 1823. (It is a curiosity, not specifically

Antique row on Himmelpfortgasse

Viennese, that men of genius are often completely ignored during their lifetimes and then posthumously every niche and corner connected with them is searched out and plaques are mounted to their honor.)

We turn right at the intersection of Seilerstätte, the old work area of the rope makers of Vienna. Across the street at **Seilerstätte 9** is the **Ronacher**, a building that has served for more than a hundred years as theater, dance hall, vaudeville stage, the radio and TV studios of the Austrian Broadcasting Corporation and has been restored recently to accommodate live theater.

To the right, notice the double-headed eagle in relief over the door at **Seilerstätte 22**. This is the old Habsburg symbol, rulers of Spain and Austria and then Austro-Hungary: dualism in the most literal sense. But since the fall of the monarchy in 1918, the double-headed eagle has lost one head and the single-headed eagle is now the symbol of the city of Vienna.

The next intersection is that of **Johannesgasse**; that's the **Ursuline Convent** on the far right corner. Turn right up Johannesgasse past the Ursuline Church to the left—the street is so narrow that until recently I was not even aware of the existence of this church, not having had a full view of the façade.

Across from this baroque church is one of the loveliest of all baroque buildings in Vienna, the **Savoysches Damenstift**, the Savoy Institute for Gentlewomen. Besides some sculptures on the façade by one of the finest Austrian baroque masters, Messerschmidt, there is also a lyric, serene, utterly unexpected courtyard to experience. Originally a palace of the Savoy-Carignan family, the house for gentlewomen was created when two other houses were joined to the original palace. In the courtyard there is a lovely wall fountain, The Widow of Sarepta, also by Messerschmidt.

Out on the street again we look across to the other side to **number 8**, a former part of the Ursuline Cloister and since 1960 a part of the **Hochschule für Musik und darstellende Kunst**, one of Austria's major voice and instrumental academies. For those with enough ingenuity and talent, a fine education can be had here for less than one hundred dollars per semester.

The far end (toward Kärntnerstrasse) of these old cloisters also houses a collection of religious folk art in what was once the old cloister apothecary (open Wednesday, 9:00 A.M. to 4:00 P.M., and Sunday, 9:00 A.M.

to 1:00 P.M.). More interesting than the oil paintings inside are the nichelike rooms and display cases of the old pharmacy.

Across the street at this point, at **Johannesgasse 9–13**, is another of those 1950s Viennese housing complexes that are a feeble copy of the interwar "Red Vienna" projects such as the George Washington-Hof and Karl Marx-Hof. This one is named after Franz Karl Ginzkey, a founder of the Salzburger Festspiele, one of the biggest summer music festivals of Europe. The garish painting over the entrance is a reminder that this was built on the sight of a hostelry for impoverished students in happier times.

About midway up **Johannesgasse** we come to the **K und K Hofkammerarchiv** at **number 6** on the left-hand side. This former cloister was turned to state use during Joseph II's "cloister offensive," in which he closed a couple of hundred convents and cloisters in Austria that he found were basically useless—they did no nursing or teaching. This one became a part of the Imperial-Royal Archives; its director at one point was the dramatist Franz Grillparzer. Grillparzer is acknowledged by the Austrians as a German Shakespeare for his fifteen dramas and small body of lyric poetry. He was the successor to Nestroy, but a much different sort of dramatist. He wrote in the grand tradition and was compared in his lifetime to Goethe. But he did not have the staying power of a Goethe or a Schiller and preferred to play an observer's role in life as well as drama. (Witness his decades-long engagement to Katharina Fröhlich.) From 1838 to his death in 1872 he refused to submit his plays for production because of unfavorable comments about them. He was appointed director of the archives in 1832 and held the position until his retirement in 1856. The workroom that Grillparzer had here can be visited (Monday to Friday, 9:00 A.M. to 2:30 P.M.) by going through the first corridor and ringing the bell on the first door to the right in the courtyard. A voice will come across the intercom, and you should ask for the "**Grillparzer Zimmer**." If all goes well another buzzer will sound and you can open the door and take the elevator up to the second floor, where a custodian will be waiting for you. To get to the Grillparzer room, you have to pass along row after dusty row of Habsburg records, from the fifteenth century to modern times, covering all sorts of Imperial-royal business in the financial and economic spheres. (The political and war archives are elsewhere.) This archive will give you just a small example of the tons and tons of paper that went into the running of the Habsburg Empire. Actually, the journey through the archives is more impressive than Grillparzer's workroom, which is set rather too formally.

Back out onto **Johannesgasse**, directly across the street we see what looks to be another baroque palace at **number 7**. Actually this is a piece of kitsch from the 1890s, built to exactly resemble a baroque palace (down to the painted sandstone steps that look like marble). It now houses an American Junior Year Abroad program, which might explain the amount of English you've been hearing in the street.

Continue up the **Johannesgasse** toward Kärntnerstrasse. The next building to the left, **number 4a**, is the **Music Conservatory of the City of Vienna**, which turns out musicians and singers. The conservatory is municipally run, while the Hochscule für Musik und darstellende Kunst, which we saw at Johannesgasse 8, is federally operated.

Across the street at **number 5–5a** is the **Kaunitz Palace**, built after a plan by Hildebrandt. It now connects with Prince Eugene's palace on Himmelpfortgasse and houses, along with that one, the Ministry of Finance.

From here, Johannesgasse narrows into a pedestrian zone and you pass several restaurants (including— shudder—the golden arches of an American chain) and come out onto the "Broadway" of Vienna, Kärntnerstrasse.

Since ancient times, Kärntnerstrasse has been one of

the main traffic arteries of Vienna. In the early Middle Ages it was the road that led to Carinthia (Kärnten) and over the Brenner Pass into Italy. Despite the street's age, the houses of Kärntnerstrasse are not very old. In the late nineteenth century many old houses were destroyed in order to widen the street for increased traffic. More destruction followed in World War II, so that the street now consists almost entirely of new buildings and is so covered with neon and other advertisements that it is all but impossible to make out the façades. Kärntnerstrasse has been a pedestrian zone since 1971, with traffic allowed only in the morning hours for delivery of goods to the businesses that are located in the street. During the warm months the Kärntnerstrasse is one of the best people-watching streets of Vienna, and even in the winter the Viennese do the Sunday after-church stroll here in their finery. Some of the best music in Vienna (by street musicians from around the world) can be heard in this street during the summer months.

At this point we are going to partake of a short detour to Neuer Markt and visit a couple of sights, and then turn around and come back to this same point on Kärntnerstrasse. To do so, cross over Kärntnerstrasse and continue up the short Marco d'Aviano-Gasse, named after a Capuchin monk famous for his good deeds during the Turkish siege of 1683. This short street leads us directly into **Neuer Markt**, almost opposite the Kapuzinerkirche, **Capuchin Church**. You're right to think this church looks pretty new: the façade was restored between 1933 and 1936, albeit in an ersatz old style. The church is more than three centuries old and the most famous thing about it is that the crypt of the Habsburgs, the *Kapuzinergruft*, lies below it. (It may be visited daily, from 9:30 A.M. to 4:00 P.M.) You may recall from Walk 1 that this is one of the three great "storehouses" for bits and pieces of the Habsburgs. Most of their bodies lie in fancy and less than fancy coffins-cum-sarcophagi here; the hearts are in St. Augustine's Church and the entrails in the crypt of St.

Stephen's. Habsburgs have been buried here since 1633, and a visit to the crypt is all but obligatory for the ghoulish. Underground it is cold and musty, and row after row of Habsburgs provide a very dead history to the city and times. Maria Theresa's casket is the centerpiece here, and the empress is depicted with her consort, Francis of Lorraine, in a less than ethereal pose. Her son, Joseph II, is also down here, buried in one of the simple "nose-pincher" coffins that he recommended for the overly showy Viennese. Joseph was, as expected, unsuccessful in his attempts at reducing pomp at court and at burials. He rescinded his edict requiring simple burials finally, but not without a broadside at the Viennese:

> Since a great many subjects do not wish to understand the reason for the regulation concerning burial sacks, which were instigated out of regard for the health of the people with a view to accelerating putrefaction; since, moreover, they evince so deep an interest in their bodies, even after death, without appearing to understand that they are nothing but stinking corpses, His Majesty no longer cares how they bury themselves.

The only non-Habsburg interred here is one Countess Fuchs, governess to Maria Theresa and her daughters. To counter critics of such a breach of court manners, Maria Theresa said, quite logically, "She was always with us during her lifetime—why shouldn't she be so during her death as well?"

Back up in the daylight, with your back to the church, you can get a good view of this square, formerly known as the Melhmarkt, or Flour Market. It was here that grain dealers found guilty of fraud were pilloried; the square was also a popular eighteenth-century sleighing ground. Vienna was always a bustling city in its center. If we rue the fact that cars now litter Neuer Markt, we should consider the similarly noisy and odiferous activity to be found here in the early nineteenth century, when seventy-five coaches departed from the old White Swann Inn in the square every day and an equal number arrived. The Neuer Markt has been terminus for transport ever since 1200, when the foreign trade to and from the south was based here. The beginnings of Vienna's excellent public transport system lie here as well, with the first coaches that plied their trade between the suburbs and the center of the city: every hour on the hour from Neuer Markt to Hietzing, or Dornbach, or Hütteldorf by the 1820s.

In the center of the square, to your left, is the **Providence Fountain**, perhaps better known as the Donner Fountain (1737–1739) after its creator. What we see now is a copy of the original (which is to be seen in the Lower Belvedere). Four near nudes represent four rivers: water as a providential gift of the gods.

Maria Theresa, libidinous enough in her own marital relations—her sixteen children testify to that—was a public prude. She disliked public displays of nudity, so she had Donner's fountain dismantled and sent well along the bureaucratic way to being melted down for a cannon. It was saved by an art lover in the arsenal and hidden away, to be reconstructed in 1801.

Such a social prude was Maria Theresa—some say it was out of self-defense to curb her husband's wandering eye—that she instituted the Chastity Commission in 1747. This commission's function was to decree morality as another might fair prices on firewood. Commissioners were empowered to search houses on suspicion of hanky-panky, to arrest men for entertaining an opera singer, a dancer, or any other woman of suspected loose morals. Offending ladies could be imprisoned or banished from the Empire. Ironically, Casanova was in Vienna during this "sexual terror" and was forced to take lodgings separate from those of his current mistress. He noted that there was plenty of money and luxury in Vienna, but that "the bigotry of the empress makes Cytherean pleasure extremely difficult."

175

As usual, the Viennese managed to find a way around the new regulations—a favorite ruse was for the aristocrats to find a sympathetic elderly marquise who might employ the current mistress as a "chambermaid." Worst of all, the commission was notoriously unsuccessful in containing the passions of the empress's husband. All in all, the Chastity Commission made the empress the laughingstock of Europe and had to be disbanded only six months after its institution.

So, let's retrace our steps down Marco d'Aviano-Gasse and turn right into Kärntnerstrasse. One of the first buildings we pass, at **Kärntnerstrasse 37**, is the **Maltese Church**, founded by the Knights of Malta who were called by the Babenberg Duke Leopold VI to found a pilgrim's house on this location. The subsequent knights' hostelry was later turned into a Gothic church of the Order of St. John the Baptist. It gave the name to Johannesgasse on which we walked earlier. The façade had a retouching in the classicist style in the early 1800s; otherwise, inside the church maintains its Gothic appearance. Three houses from the church, at **Kärntnerstrasse 41**, is another of the few older buildings in the street, a one-time Esterházy palace, the core of which stems from the seventeenth century. This graceful Schönbrunn yellow palace now houses a gambling casino.

We turn left off the gawdy bright lights of Kärntnerstrasse at the next street, **Annagasse**. This is one of the prettiest of the little streets off of Kärntnerstrasse that have received much renovation in the past decade. Full of little boutiques, antiquarian bookshops, and galleries, it is strolling in Vienna at its best (also very little traffic!). The street takes its name from the lovely and delicate **St. Ann's Church** at **number 3b** (Church of the Followers of St. Francis of Sales), which was built on the sight of an earlier pilgrims' hostel and cloister dedicated to St. Ann. Inside, the incomparable Daniel Gran (we'll see more of his work at the Hofbibliothek at the Hofburg in Walk 3) did the ceiling frescoes as well as the altarpiece on the high altar.

Some other interesting and good-looking buildings on this quiet street: **number 4** across from the church is the **Kremsmünster Court**, owned by the Kremsmünster Monastery in Upper Austria, home of the famous Austrian school of statecraft since 1675. Next door at **Annagasse 6** is the **Herzogenburger Court**, another of the monastery-owned tracts in the middle of Vienna—this one dates from 1365, but has a baroque face-lift from 1720.

And next to this, at **Annagasse 8**, is the **Täubelhof**, built after a plan by Hildebrandt, which was used for a time (1768–1789) as the School of Drawing and Engraving, a forerunner of the current Academy of Fine Arts. (See Walk 4.)

At **number 14** you will see the relief of a fish over the main portal. This is the former *"Zum blauen Karpfen,"* "At the Sign of the Blue Carp," built in the seventeenth century; it housed a famous beer house in the eighteenth century. The owner of this inn, one Herr Göschl, was known as one of the most popular *Wirts*, or publicans, of all Vienna and bore the nickname of Knödelwirt (dumpling publican) because of the prodigious size of dumplings served here.

On the right-hand side, at the bottom of **Annagasse** at **number 18**, is the gallery of Christian Nebehay, one of the early promoters of the work of that fine Viennese artist Egon Schiele. The end of the Annagasse also brings us to the end of this walk.

Walk · 3

Noble Vienna

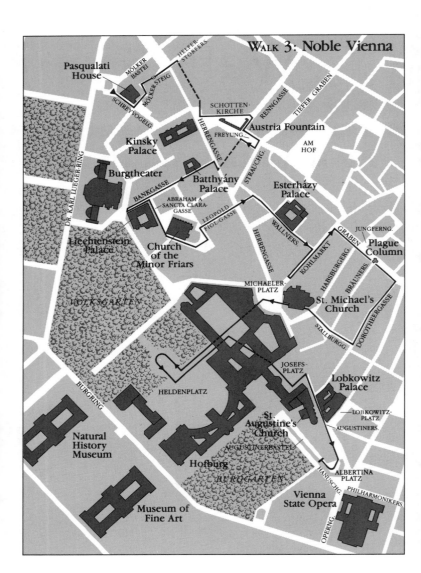

WALK 3: Noble Vienna

Pasqualati House

MOLKER BASTEI

HELFER STORFERS

MOLKER STEIG

SCHREYVOGELG

SCHOTTEN-KIRCHE

RENNGASSE

TIEFER GRABEN

FREYUNG

Austria Fountain

HERRENGASSE

AM HOF

Kinsky Palace

Burgtheater

Batthyány Palace

STRAUCHG.

Esterházy Palace

DR. KARL LUEGER-RING

BANKGASSE

ABRAHAM A SANCTA CLARA-GASSE

LEOPOLD FIGL-GASSE

WALLNERS.

JUNGFERNG.

Plague Column

Liechtenstein Palace

Church of the Minor Friars

HERRENGASSE

KOHLMARKT

HABSBURGG.

GRABEN

BRAUNERS.

St. Michael's Church

VOLKSGARTEN

MICHAELER-PLATZ

STALLBURGG.

DOROTHEERGASSE

BURGRING

HELDENPLATZ

JOSEFS-PLATZ

Lobkowitz Palace

LOBKOWITZ-PLATZ

AUGUSTINERS.

Natural History Museum

St. Augustine's Church

AUGUSTINERBASTEI

Hofburg

BURGGARTEN

HANUSCHG.

ALBERTINA PLATZ

PHILHARMONIKERS.

Museum of Fine Art

Vienna State Opera

OPERNG.

Vienna was never the capital of the Holy Roman Empire, for such an empire existed only on paper and in the imaginations of the Electors in Frankfurt. But when a Habsburg was chosen emperor (as was most often the case from the fifteenth century until the demise of the Empire in 1806), then likely as not Vienna would be— for the time of his tenure—*the* imperial city.

It was only after the defeat of the Turks in 1683, as we saw in the last walk, that this frontier town began to take on the aspect of an imperial city. In the eighteenth century Vienna took on an imperial façade quite consciously. The great Catholic noble families from all corners of the Empire began sending their sons to court to serve as diplomats, soldiers, courtiers. And other noble families settled near the seat of power, the Hofburg, just as power brokers now gather in Washington, D.C., for the political handouts to be won. Artisans and craftsmen followed; the population skyrocketed, doubling in the course of the eighteenth century to more than 200,000. Vienna the melting pot was created. A glance at the great noble names of Vienna is enough to convince of that: Lobkowitz, Pallavacini, Kinsky, Harrach, Czernin, Esterházy, Schwarzenberg. They came from Poland, Bohemia, Hungary, Saxony—even Ireland.

This walk will take us through the section of Vienna that these aristocratic families built and will end with the largest town palace of all, the Hofburg.

The Mölker Bastei is one of the few remaining portions of the old walls still standing in Vienna. We saw one other such bastion in Walk 2: the Dominikanerbastei. We actually begin this walk atop the Bastei and not at the level of the Ring. Where Schreyvogelgasse and Mölker Bastei come together at the Ring, a small square is formed with a statue of a man, Liebenberg, in the middle of it. (More about him in a moment.) In back of the statue there are stairs that lead to the top of the old wall.

From this vantage point, standing just to the left of **Mölker Bastei 8** (with our back to it), we are looking out over the Ringstrasse to the university, part of that great urban renewal project that replaced the old walls in the mid–nineteenth century. To the far right and beyond the university, stand the Pepsodent-white towers of the Votivkirche. You might think these look quite old and Gothic, and you would be partly right. The church is a nineteenth-century reproduction of a Gothic church, a votive offering actually for Kaiser Franz Joseph after he survived an assassination attempt. In an age of wackos and conspiracies, when presidents, popes, and even candidates are considered fair game for the assassin's bullet, it is hard to imagine the accessibility that the Hapsburgs (and indeed most pre–twentieth-century monarchs) offered all throughout their reigns. Though some were more formal than others, honoring the stiff and distant Spanish court protocol above all else, still they all made themselves available to the little people of the Empire and of Austria, if only to give those people the illusion of benign autocracy. They walked freely among their subjects without Herculean secret service agents encircling them. Joseph II went the farthest in this quasi-egalitarian mixing with the public. Not only did he roam about the streets alone and incognito, but he also demanded that his subjects should in no way demonstrate that they recognized him.

So it was that Franz Joseph, the next-to-last Habsburg emperor, whose reign would last a record sixty-eight years, was found one day in the early years of his reign unprotected on this *Bastei*, strolling along for a bit of fresh air like the commonest of the bourgeoisie. An Italian tailor stabbed the emperor in the neck—he must have been a poor tailor, because he did not allow for the high stiff collar Franz Joseph wore at all times, which deflected the blow. The Votivkirche, erected on the glacis toward which Franz Joseph was looking at the time, recalls this attempted assassination. There would be other more successful attempts on these last Habsburgs: the empress Elisabeth would lose her life to an assassin's knife; the emperor's brother, Maximilian, would be "officially" assassinated—that is, executed—in Mexico, attempting to reestablish Habsburg domains in the New World; Franz Joseph's son was to die mysteriously (suicide or assassination?) at Mayerling with his lover; and the emperor's nephew and heir apparent, Franz Ferdinand, and his morganatic wife would die by assassins' bullets in Sarajevo. It was almost as if this first crude, almost laughable attempt on Franz Joseph's life, ending not in death but in the erection of a church, ushered in the modern age. The age of kings and absolute law—absolutes of any kind, for that matter—had passed.

But the Vienna we will be discovering during this walk was still under the sway of the world of order and caste: a world that was most likely no less violent and chaotic than our own, but one that, nonetheless, demanded a brave face to be borne to the world—an outfit of the utmost finery to be donned for the battle of life.

Just below us, in the midst of the little square, is a statue to the mayor of Vienna during the last Turkish siege, Liebenberg. This burgomaster died just before the end of the siege, and it was one of those timely historic deaths. Liebenberg had been guilty of, as the historians tactfully put it, "administrative irregularities." But with his death all was forgotten. No matter that he had been sick during most of the weeks of the siege; no matter that it was not a Turkish ball that had brought him down, but dysentery. No matter that it was largely his misrule of the city beforehand that caused such great difficulties for the defending garrison during the siege. A mediocre mayor, a man of questionable character, Liebenberg, in death, was exonerated. He became to posterity one of the heroes of the siege. Just as, in Viennese tradition, it was the entire city that rose in arms against the Turks when in reality it was the imperial garrison of less than 10,000 men that saved the city. Food and billeting concessions had to be squeezed out of the Viennese. At the worst point of the siege, the garrison, reduced to 4,000 men (facing an army of 150,000 to 200,000 Turks), had to make a house-to-house search to conscript men to defend their own city. And the court was worse: they scurried to Wiener Neustadt and Linz, jewels in tow, at the first sign of the scimitar.

Turning to more pleasant thoughts, literally, we now face the building at **Mölker Bastei 8**, known as the **Pasqualati House**. This building was constructed in the late eighteenth century as an apartment house by the court physician of Maria Theresa, Josef Benedikt Pasqualati. His son was a friend and admirer of Beethoven, and the composer lived and worked here on and off from 1804 to 1815. This is one of the thirty-odd addresses that Beethoven blessed with his presence in his Vienna years. This ceaseless wandering from apartment to apartment, from the city to the suburbs and country, marks not only the life of Beethoven but also of Schubert, Mozart, Brahms, and to a lesser extent even the staid old near-friar, Bruck-

The view of the university from the Mölker Bastei

ner. One wonders if it was simply their restless spirits that forced these composers to be ever changing their addresses, or if it was purely a matter of money, as in Wagner's case, staying one step ahead of the landlord. In an age of patronage of the arts, where there were no public concert halls and in which compositions were largely commissioned for aristocratic ears, such shuffling around can be perhaps better understood—the "musician" (not yet composer and hardly called a true "artist") was at the whim of his patron. He went where the money was and where neighbors' ears would not be offended by the pounding of piano keys at odd hours of the day and night.

But Beethoven's case was the most extreme of all Viennese composers. Not for him the servant's table frequented by Haydn and (for a time) Mozart. He was the first of the great composers to demand, and be granted, special status as an artist.

"It is easy to get on with the nobility," Beethoven said, "if you have something to impress them with." And impress them he did. Arriving in Vienna at the age of twenty-two in 1792, he was quickly recognized as a new musical force. Not for him the smooth, fluent style of Mozart. The Viennese had never heard such pyrotechnics at the piano as Beethoven confronted them with. Piano makers had to create a tougher, better instrument than the light-actioned Viennese models, which this greatest piano player of his time destroyed like kindling. Beethoven did not woo audiences with insipid harmonies; neither did he kowtow to nobility because of their social position. Like many composers, Beethoven was short (five feet four inches) and anything but socially presentable. He had the nasty habit of spitting whenever he felt like it, and, in the city of the waltz, he was so uncoordinated that he never learned how to dance—shaving was such a taxing physical operation for him that he rarely avoided cutting himself. Yet, despite this unimposing appearance and gnomelike physiognomy, he seems to have had his fair share of romances, with ladies both highborn and low. The perpetual bachelor, Beethoven was most definitely not the misogynist some made him out to be. His deafness, which began when he was in his early thirties and progressed to the point where he could hear none of the exquisite works that he created, made a misanthrope of the man. His Heiligenstadt Testimony, a long complaining letter confessing this affliction that was intended to be read after his death, confirms the character change wrought by it. Beethoven raged against life and death. He did not go gently into that good night; Viennese legend has it that on his deathbed, lightning and thunder broke the stillness. He raised himself and shook a defiant fist at nature. Shortly after this he died. He was fifty-seven, one of the longer-lived composers when one takes into consideration men like Mozart and Schubert. And not for him the third-class funeral of Mozart, all but unaccompanied to the grave: Beethoven's funeral marshaled an enormous crowd (for those days) of twenty thousand: 10 percent of the population of Vienna then.

In this Pasqualati house, Beethoven composed and worked on *Fidelio*, the Seventh Symphony, quartets, the *Leonore Overture*, and the Piano Concerto no. 4. The city of Vienna runs a Beethoven Museum here, open Tuesday to Sunday, 9:00 A.M. to 12:15 P.M. and 1:00 P.M. to 4:30 P.M. You should visit the rooms, if not for love of Beethoven, then just to satisfy your curiosity about what the insides of such buildings look like. This presents one of those few opportunities, as did the Figaro House, to get inside these flats. This one is on the fourth floor.

In the museum are lots of Beethoven facsimile material and little original stuff, which is guarded religiously by Beethoven societies that worship the man as a messiah. Directly upon entering the apartments proper, above the cabinet against the left wall, are two prints of what the view from the Mölker Bastei looked like in the 1820s—this is the same view that Beethoven had out the windows of this room. The house where he died was visible directly across the glacis from this house. In the second room are some oil paintings of friends and patrons—most important the Russian ambassador, Prince Rasumovsky, who was a great Beethoven patron. Beethoven was never desperate for patrons: in 1808 the princes Lobkowitz and Kinsky and Archduke Rudolf gathered together and settled four thousand gulden on him when he was considering leaving Vienna for an offer at the Westphalian court. He took the money gladly: he was not afraid of its compromising his artistry. On the contrary, he felt it was due him just because he *was* an artist (and he even went to court at one point to force the Kinsky estate to keep up with payments after the death of the prince).

There is also a piano in this room, typical of the heartier type that was made for the explosive playing style of Beethoven.

These rooms are all antiseptic and tidy now. One wonders what they looked like when Beethoven lived here. There is a hint from this report by one shocked visitor in 1809:

> Picture to your self the darkest, most disorderly place imaginable—blotches of moisture covered the ceiling; an oldish grand piano, on which the dust disputed the place with various pieces of engraved and manuscript music; under the piano (I do not exaggerate) an unemptied chamber pot; beside it a small walnut table accustomed to the frequent overturning of the secretary placed on it; a quantity of pens encrusted with ink. . . . The chairs, mostly cane seated, were covered with plates bearing the remains of last night's supper, and with wearing apparel, etc.

Also in this same museum are rooms dedicated to the Austrian writer Adalbert Stifter. Part poet, part naturalistic novelist, part essayist, and ever in love with painting, Stifter was one of the bright lights of an otherwise dull Austrian firmament in the mid–nineteenth century. The paintings in the Stifter rooms may convince one that he was better off with writing, however. A symbol of the Viennese and Austrian schizoid nature (Vienna still has one of the highest suicides rates in the Western world), Stifter ended his renowned life by slashing his throat after learning he had cancer of the liver. The Stifter rooms are well worth the visit because all the doors are in place and the layout of the rooms really gives you a good idea of living conditions—on the interior at any rate—of the Viennese in the nineteenth century.

The house directly next to the Beethoven house, **Mölker Bastei 10**, is from the same time (late eighteenth century) as are most of the buildings on this bastion. That parts of the walls themselves were used and heavily built upon should give you an idea of how difficult it was to find building sites. This house was host to a couple of well-known guests. Goethe's granddaughter Alma died here in 1844. She was supposedly the model for the figure of Austria on the Austria Fountain that we shall later see on Freyung. Before this, at the same time that Beethoven was living next door, there resided here Prince Charles de Ligne, who was the commentator par excellence on the Congress of Vienna of 1815, which redrew the borders of a Europe disrupted by a generation of fighting Napoleon.

De Ligne was a Belgian émigré who made Vienna his home. His life was led in a sort of faded elegance, sleeping in the library of his modest flat, riding about this city which was playing court to all the crowned heads of Europe (and half its courtesans as well) in his sprung and battered old gray coach with swaybacked grays pulling it. But despite impoverished straits, de Ligne was invited to the best houses because he was a charming old gaffer, full of wicked stories and bon mots. He had been everywhere and, it seemed, done everything as a youth. Raised at the court of Versailles, he fled during the Revolution and fought in most of the great battles against

Napoleon. His friends and acquaintances numbered all the greats of eighteenth-century Europe: Catherine of Russia, Frederick the Great of Prussia, Voltaire, Rousseau, Goethe. He was in his eighties when the Congress opened, and in its first months he never failed to miss a ball or masquerade, which were all the rage in the eighteenth century. It was he who coined the quotation most often used about the Congress of Vienna: *"Le congrès ne marche pas; il danse."* He thus described in one cutting epigram the frivolous spirit of this Congress, which was captivated by the waltz and beautiful women to the exclusion, almost, of work. De Ligne caught a chill one night waiting out in front of his house here on the *Bastei* for a "lady friend" who failed to arrive. Stood up, in short, and laid low with a cold that eventually killed him. His last act of hauteur was to add to the Congress ceremonies the funeral of a field marshal in the Austrian army (the rank he held).

From de Ligne's house, we go past the Beethoven house and left around the corner, still up on the old bastion, but following now the course of **Schreyvogelgasse**, named after a writer and early administrator of the Burgtheater. To the left, at **number 10**, we come to the so-called **Dreimädlerhaus**, named after the operetta largely written by Schubert. Tradition has it that Schubert lived here while writing that composition, but there is no proof. Most probably the name was given the house because it so exemplifies the sort of cozy, to-scale family dwelling that ushered in what is known as the Biedermeier age.

Much nonsense has been written about this age, which basically encompasses the time between the close of the Congress in 1815 and the outbreak of the 1848 Revolution. (Revolt would be more apposite.) Some historians shrink the end date back farther to the 1830s and the coming of the dim-witted Kaiser Ferdinand and the powerful machinations of Prince Metternich pulling his strings. It's enough, however, to know that the Biedermeier age spanned roughly the first half of the nineteenth century. Contemporaries did not refer to it as the Biedermeier age; that was a later invention. The term itself is not an Austrian coinage, but comes from a fictitious small-town German schoolmaster (Swabian at that), who was the supposed author of a series of poems published in a satirical journal in the 1850s. The terms *Biedermann* and *Biedermeier* came to symbolize all that is solid, respectable, and reliable. (*Bieder* means upright.) There is more than a faint whiff of bourgeois inherent in the term—the Biedermeier age was one of the first true middle-class epochs in history. The homely virtues were accentuated; the family became paramount after the grandiose excesses of the Congress. It was an age of censorship and the iron hand of Metternich intriguing to stem the liberal tide: Austria had found a new mission. Having outlived and undone enemies from the Turks to Magyars to Protestants to the French, the Habsburg Empire turned to a new task: upholding absolutism in an age of increasing liberal, democratic reform. Denied entry into the political world, middle-class and intellectual Vienna turned inward. This partly explains the popularity of the musical evenings, *Schubertiades*, during these times. A proliferation of card games, children's games, cutouts, and so on served to entertain families in the coziness of their own snug homes. Reproductions of such games can still be found in the toyshops and fancy paper shops of Vienna. All of this turning inward was to bear fruit at the end of the nineteenth century, as we shall later see. But the decades before March 1848, the *Vormärz*, were quiet enough, and visitors to Vienna wrote glowing reports of the "most happy and enjoyable people." For the Viennese of today, this Biedermeier age represents the "good old days" of Alt Wien popularized in myth and history.

Biedermeier, though it is a term used in all German-speaking countries, has its real home in Vienna and in other parts of Austria. It has even lent its name to furniture and architectural styles. The chic outer districts of

Vienna—especially Hietzing—and Baden bei Wien are full of this architectural style. In the center of Vienna, fewer examples are to be found, since until the razing of the walls there was no new space for building in the Inner City—the baroque building spree had seen to that. But Biedermeier permeated the walls of all ages, and thus salons and entire suites of rooms were laid out in this cozy style. It is not unusual to enter a drawing room today and be ushered into this 150-year-old style, for of all the Viennese traditions this one has held on the strongest into the ambiguous age of MTV culture.

Notice the humorous doorbell at number 10: a bronze hand holds the pull for the bell. Nice façade decoration as well on this house; nothing too ostentatious but enough to tell of its importance.

Passing on, we come to **Schreyvogelgasse 8**, with its street front rather jogged back from the line of the rest of the street. (It actually leads into the Mölker Steig.) This baroque house from the late eighteenth century is called "Zum Auge Gottes," and if you look closely at the gilded decoration on the second-story façade, you will see this eye of God staring down at you, a holdover from the pagan evil eye that keeps the plague and other such bad luck from the door.

Turn left into the little lane, **Mölker Steig**, that leads between Schreyvogelgasse 8 and 10. Follow Mölker Steig up into the heart of this old fortification *Bastei*, first to the left and then to the right. The monumental buildings we will be passing to the right form the rear of the Melker Hof, the front of which we shall be seeing shortly. This was one more of those immense courts that the wealthy country abbeys developed in the midst of fledgling Vienna. This one was founded by that magnificent Monastery of Melk up the Danube from Vienna (that absolute baroque marvel hanging over the river built by the architect Prandtauer in the eighteenth century). Founded in 1453,

The Mölker Steig

this Melker Hof was greatly enlarged and renovated in the 1770s. The Viennese dialect has broadened the *e* in Melk, and thus this bastion and the lane traversing it have taken the name Mölker.

We go down the picturesque flight of steps to the base of the bastion now, still on Mölker Steig. To your immediate right at the bottom of the stairs is a shop specializing in traditional Austrian apparel, *Trachten*, and folkloric art and housewares.

Continue along Mölker Steig to the crossing of Schottengasse. To the left you can catch a glimpse of the Vienna Woods far out over the houses. Cross the street and look back down to the right in the **Schottengasse** at **numbers 3** and **3a**, the front of the **Melker Hof**, with its simple yet forceful façade decoration. One of the little-known chapels of Vienna can be found in here (sixth stairway, first floor) with an excellent high altar of the Ascencion by Kremser Schmidt. The chapel can be visited, however, only during the Sunday mass.

On the corner of Schottengasse where you are now standing is one of the more elegant cafés of Vienna, the Café Haag, which is famous locally for its pastries and baked goods (sold just two doors down Helferstorferstrasse from this point).

Walk along **Helferstorferstrasse** about twenty paces to the **Durchhaus** at **number 2**, where we turn right and go through the passage into the courtyard of the **Schottenhof**, where the Scottish monastery is located. In this case, the "Scots" were actually Irish monks from Regensburg—medieval man had little patience for the subtleties of geography. Duke Heinrich II, the first of the dukes of Babenberg to settle in Vienna, summoned these monks from his own hometown, a symbolic gesture implying that the Babenbergs intended to stay and settle in Vienna and to bring the light of Christianity, and its cultural offsprings, to the Eastern Marches. Building on the Schottenkirche, Church of the Scots (to be visited presently) began in 1155; this courtyard and monastery were products of the early 1800s, built to plans by the architect Kornhäusl, whom we have already encountered in Walk 1. Kornhäusl seemed to be very catholic in his building styles and commissions, for the other building of his we have seen was a synagogue. In the warmer months there is outdoor seating for the café and a restaurant in this pleasant and unexpected courtyard. To the left, across the greenery from where we are walking, is the entrance to the monastery. This is the main portal, situated between enormous pillars. Visits to the cloister gallery are, unfortunately, held only on Saturday at 2:00 P.M. (entrance here at the main portal). The picture gallery houses some fifteenth-century paintings of Vienna that you may want to see if you want a more accurate idea of what medieval Vienna looked like—for example, *The Flight into Egypt*, which seems miraculously to have detoured via the Kahlenberg to the north of Vienna.

Also in this monastery is the **Schottengymnasium**, the equivalent of England's Eton and the United States's Groton, where the bright young men of Vienna's upper crust have been schooled for the past two centuries. At about the time when these boys are not more than a twinkle in daddy's eye, they are signed up for enrollment *x* number of years hence. Graduation, a *Matura*, from the Schottengymnasium is one of the entry cards to the power elite in Austria.

We come out of this courtyard onto the street-cum-square called **Freyung**. To your immediate left is the entrance to the **Schottenkirche**, an edifice continually built, destroyed, and rebuilt from 1155 through the nineteenth century. Every style from Romanesque through Gothic, baroque, and classicist, can be seen here. The final renovation took place in 1893, carried out by that Ringstrasse architect Ferstel. Though the main hall remains baroque in spirit, the "neo" elements give the insides something of a cartoon appearance.

For those of you braving this walk in the colder winter months, there is a special treat, for the best *Maroni* and *Kartoffel* (roasted chestnuts and potatoes) stand in Vienna can be found directly in front of the church entrance.

To your right, across the street at **Freyung 4**, is the **Kinsky Palace**, built originally for Count Daun, whose son was an important general under Empress Maria Theresa. The palace later came into the possession of the wealthy and powerful Kinsky clan. Hildebrandt, that rival architect to Fischer von Erlach, drew the plans for this palace, built from 1713 to 1716, in the heyday of palace building in Vienna after the siege. You may want to sneak across and steal a glance into the courtyard of this palace and see how all the old outbuildings (stables and servants quarters, even the enormous *Keller*, or cellar) have been put to use: a café, hair boutique, antique shop, and other such posh sorts of establishments. Also, upon entrance, the stairway to the left is the monumental one that is justly famous in art history circles: notice the depth of each step and the horrendous number of steps it takes to cover such a climb when each step is so shallow. Such stairs were made for elegant strolling upward and dramatic, sweeping-frocked departures. Often it is the case, as in this palace, that the stairs on upper floors are much narrower and steeper. The grand staircases were for show and led—as these stairs do—to the ballrooms or main sitting rooms of the palaces.

From in front of the Schottenkirche we can also take a look at the palace directly to the left of the Kinsky Palace, at **Herrengasse 23**; this is the **former Porcia Palace**, one of the few buildings and only palace in Vienna from the Renaissance, about the mid–sixteenth century. Though the interior has undergone many renovations, the façade remains much the same as it was and is a typical example of Italian Renaissance architecture, with its portal winged by columns and the coat of arms of the Porcia family on the second-floor façade. This little diamond of a palace, all understatement and subtlety, makes its neighbors seem abrasive and ostentatious by comparison. It is truly a palace built on a human scale.

The portal of the Kinsky Palace

We go the left around the corner of the church. Just around the corner we have a better view of how this street called the Freyung actually could have been used as a square at one time. The Christkindl Markt was held here in the eighteenth and nineteenth centuries and has recently resumed. Peddlers and hawkers were to be found here always, and even popular theater was represented, when the originator of Viennese popular drama, Stranitzky, set up his show here during the annual market. Stranitzky's major creation was Hanswurst, a simple peasant employed in the service of the great who expressed the plebeian point of view in rather choruslike running commentaries on the thought and actions of the great. Stranitzky began the tradition of the playwright-actor-director in his early–eighteenth century dramas, in which the major complaint of Hanswurst (whom Stranitzky himself always played—foreshadowing Nestroy) was that *"so wird man ja noch reden derffen"* ("surely we can still talk!").

The name of the Freyung comes from the right of asylum granted the Scottish monks in 1181 (Freyung from *Frei* or *Freiheit*, meaning freedom), which remained a tradition until it was revoked during the reign of Maria Theresa.

Across the way at **Freyung 3**, at the **Y** of the intersection of Freyung and Herrengasse, is the **Harrach Palace** from the early eighteenth century, with a reconstruction of a pavilion built onto it by Hildebrandt. Some major bomb damage was done to the building during World War II, but at least the old baroque façade was restored as a result. To the left of it is the Ferstel Palace, which we shall be visiting soon.

Follow the side of the Schottenkirche for about twenty more paces and you will come to a life-size statue of Duke Heinrich II of Babenberg stuck into a niche in the wall. This is a small honor for the man who was responsible for Vienna's being taken seriously as a metropolitan center, for he initiated the first court life in the city in the twelfth century.

Farther along the side wall of the church is the bell tower, which looks more like an Italian campanile than spire. The bells of the Schotten Church are noted in Vienna for their sonority. Plan to be nearby at the sounding of the hours—they really do have a golden, round tone.

Directly to the right on our side of the Freyung is the **Austria Fountain**, erected in 1845 in the heyday of Austrian chauvinism, before the 1848 Revolution, which made the Empire begin to question its efficacy. The base is constructed of four symbolic figures pouring out the four waters of the monarchy: the Danube, Po, Elbe, and Vistula. The fountain is surmounted by a female figure representing Mother Austria. Goethe's granddaughter Alma, who died in the house next to the Beethoven house, modeled for this, as noted earlier. The fountain stands on the sight of a chapel that stood here for three and a half centuries.

To our left, at **Freyung 7**, is the **Chest of Drawers House**, so-called by the Viennese because of its distinctively linteled windows and narrow façade. Built in 1774 as the priory to the Scottish monastery on the grounds of what was once the church cemetery, this building now houses a pharmacy and an herb shop on the ground floor: a hand-in-glove business practice, if I've ever seen one.

Continue to the left to Renngasse, a side street off the Freyung that takes its name from its medieval function as the showplace for horses which were sold nearby (*rennen* means to run): the fourteenth-century equivalent of a car lot. The first large building to the left, **Renngasse 1**, is actually older than it looks. Only the ground floor has been renovated on this century-and-a-half-old building, formerly the hotel "Zum römischen Kaiser." Beethoven lived here from 1815 to 1817; Schubert also made his debut here in 1818 as a composer, as the plaque on the side of the building tells us.

Across the street at **Renngasse 4** is the **Batthyány-Schönborn Palace**, named after the powerful Hungarian count who commissioned Fischer von Erlach to build it in 1699 and after the German Schönborn family who purchased it in the mid–eighteenth century. This palace, now housing the Mexican embassy, is one of Erlach's more noble creations, very much in the imperial style that he adopted in midcareer. In the tight confines of the

Renngasse, Erlach has managed to give weight and importance to this essentially diminutive palace by the restrained elegance of the portal flanked by vases in façade niches, the relief work on the second story, and the pilasters running the height of two stories. As with his palace for Prince Eugene on the Himmelpfortgasse, Erlach's Batthyány-Schönborn Palace reflects the position and deeds of its owner, the governor of Croatia and a military man who took part in the campaign against the Turks. Notice particularly the battle frieze above the central window. The palace of a mere governor of Croatia had, of course, to be less magnificent than Prince Eugene's, the supreme commander of the imperial forces, but still this palace shows Erlach's essential architectural program at work: the tension and symmetry of the buildings were displayed in the façade itself. The narrowness of Vienna's lanes did not allow for magnificent projecting bays or statuary. Instead, Erlach depended on the surface articulation given by his long, tapering pilasters and the splendid and quite sophisticated portal and central window groupings with their complicated curves and angles.

From this point, you should look up to the far right to compare Erlach's work with the **Kinsky Palace**, one of Hildebrandt's major works. Less integrated and more showy in their own fusty, Viennese manner, Hildebrandt's palaces did not really take the "imperial" function into account as did Fischer von Erlach's. When the Schönborns bought the Batthyány Palace, they had intended to renovate it to plans by Hildebrandt, but this never came to pass.

We go back to the **Freyung** and turn left past the **Kunst Forum** gallery with its *faux Jugendstil* sidewalk ornamentation, and on to the Tiefer Graben intersection. This cross street once was the Alser Brook (called before that the Ottakringer Brook) and formed a natural northwestern defense to the medieval and Roman towns. Cross the Freyung at this point, keeping Tiefer Graben on the left. Tiefer Graben now becomes Strauchgasse, which was the medieval site of Vienna's garbage dump. Freyung at the time was referred to as *auf dem Mist*, "on the trash heap." At **Strauchgasse 1** is the old **Montenuovo Palace**, built for Kaiser Franz Joseph's court chamberlain, Prince Montenuovo. This prince's career is itself a metaphor for the increasing hypocrisy inherent in the Habsburg monarchy. Montenuovo was one of those terrific pedants about *Hoffähigkeit*, or who, by the facts of breeding, was acceptable to be presented at court. His name pops up all throughout nineteenth-century Habsburg history: in the fracas over Archduke Ferdinand's romance with the commoner Sophie; in controversy over the converted Jewish composer and director of the *Hofoper*, Gustav Mahler. But Montenuovo himself was of questionable pedigree: his line was spawned by Archduchess Marie Louise and a minor Austrian count who was "commissioned" to cheer the good woman up after her husband, Napoleon Bonaparte, had been exiled.

Notice on the corner of this building the stone relief of a Turk on his horse. This recalls the legend that, during the 1529 Turkish siege, Turkish sappers digging a tunnel under the city walls were discovered by a baker in the cellars of the house that once stood here, thus saving the city.

We turn back up Freyung again, in the direction of the Schottenkirche. The second building on the left, **Freyung 2**, is the **Ferstel Palace**, built in a blend of Romanesque and early Renaissance style by the Ringstrasse architect Heinrich Ferstel between 1856 and 1860 for the Austro-Hungarian Bank. We turn into the shopping passage that now lines this building, one of the smartest arcades in Vienna. At the far end of the arcade is the Danube Mermaid Fountain from 1861. To the left before the Herrengasse exit is the renovated Café Central. In its day—that is, the fin de siècle—this was *the* intellectual and literary coffeehouse of Vienna. The literary all-stars of their day, such as Schnitzler and von Hofmannsthal, gathered here, as did Alfred Adler's breakaway psychoanalytic group. (Freud preferred the more *bürgerlich* Café Landtmann on the Ring.) The Austro-Socialists also met here, and one Lev Bronstein, a Russian émigré, better known as Leon Trotsky, was fond of playing chess in the back recesses of this venerable coffeehouse. Closed for many years, the café reopened only recently after the general renovation of the entire Ferstel Palace.

We exit the arcade onto Herrengasse (Lord's Lane), which in the seventeenth century was "palace row." It was here, and on nearby side streets, that the noble families of the Empire settled near the court and built their magnificent palaces. They hustled after empty building sites or knocked two or three older buildings together to create an effect suitably imposing for their station.

Turn right out of the arcade and then left into the first side street, Bankgasse. The first building to the right, **Bankgasse 2**, is indicative of the entire area. This is another **Batthyány Palace**, built by the widow of the count whose palace we saw on Renngasse. This countess, Lory, was something of a legend in Vienna in the eighteenth century. The daughter of the court chancellor, Count Strattmann, she bought three small houses in Bankgasse and then the Orsini-Rosenberg Palace that stood on the corner of Bankgasse and Herrengasse, and had them knocked together in the style of Fischer von Erlach. (This was in 1718 and Erlach himself was busy with other projects, such as the Karlskirche.) Prince Eugene and Countess Lory were the best of friends, and the two would play piquet every night. It seemed that the prince employed a coachman and a lackey who were both as ancient and frail as he was and that on their nightly trip to the countess's palace from the Himmelpfortgasse, all three would fall asleep. The horses knew the route so well that they would stop in front of the Batthyány Palace automatically, and the countess would wait patiently in her upper salon until the three aged gentlemen awoke.

Across from this palace, at **Bankgasse 3**, are the former administrative offices of the Austro-Hungarian Bank.

Austria and Hungary have had a tenuous relationship throughout their histories. Posing yet another "barbarian" threat to the Empire in the Middle Ages, the Magyars were co-opted into the Habsburg domains in the sixteenth century by marriage. But the Hungarian magnates were always unwilling partners at best to the Habsburg monarchy (though they *were* gentlemen enough to come to the rescue of the young Maria Theresa when set upon by the Prussians and French). In 1867, after the Habsburg defeat by the German states, the Hungarians managed to force the *Ausgleich*, or equalization treaty, with Vienna, which gave Hungary a large degree of autonomy in the monarchy. Then, in 1918, with the dissolution of Austro-Hungary, that nation went its own way . . . for a time.

Farther down **Bankgasse**, at **number 4–6**, is the former **Strattmann-Windischgraetz Palace**. It was designed in 1692 by Fischer von Erlach, who was given the commission (his first for a palace) by Countess Lory's father, the court chancellor. This palace was later purchased by Count Windischgraetz and, by joining with the neighboring house, the present elongated façade was achieved. Since the middle of the eighteenth century the building was used as the Hungarian Chancellery. Today it houses the Hungarian embassy.

From this point on Bankgasse you can catch a glimpse of the roof of the Parliament building on the Ringstrasse, aswarm with chariots and winged charioteers: all neo-classical and Hellenic in inspiration.

Proceed to the end of **Bankgasse** where we come to the **Liechtenstein Palace**, still owned by that rather exotic princely family, virtual owners of their own country. This was but one of two rather sumptuous palaces this family occupied in Vienna; the other, in the Ninth District, was their summer palace and is now the Museum of Modern Art. This particular palace may perhaps be the most oppressively monumental of all palaces in Vienna. "An edifice needs length to be splendid," wrote one of the princes of Liechtenstein, father of the one who had this palace built. "The longer the better, because it makes for renown and magnificence to see a great number of windows and columns." And as the Liechtensteins felt that the Italians held "the secret of majesty," it was an Italian architect, Martinelli, who built both of their Viennese palaces. But such monumentality on a narrow street defeats its own purpose, and this palace looks heavy and in rather poor taste next to smaller neighbors. As with many of the old palaces, this one now houses an Austrian ministry. The Liechtensteins still own it, however, and rooms are maintained in one wing for visits by the family. As the palace is owned by a foreign country, it also has the right of extraterritoriality.

Backtrack a few paces from the palace to the intersection of Abraham a Sancta Clara-Gasse, which we take toward the **Minoritenplatz**. The Viennese could not have chosen a more ironic person to name a street after in this noble quarter, for the fiery Augustinian friar and poet, Abraham a Sancta Clara, was no lover of Viennese hypocrisy or flamboyance. Having failed in his attempts at instilling a bit of the Catholic sense of sin and a touch of Protestant austerity into his unwilling flock, Abraham a Sancta Clara nevertheless gives us in his sermons and poems a thrilling record of late–seventeenth century Vienna and its twin passions (against which he unfailingly preached): pagan enjoyment of sensual pleasures and a sly distrust of all authority and heroics.

At **Minoritenplatz 4**, we come to the side entrance of the **Liechtenstein Palace**, with its gilded coat of arms over the portal held aloft by a pair of groaning Atlantean figures. Next to this, at **Minoritenplatz 3**, is the **Dietrichstein Palace**, which was renovated in the mid–eighteenth century by one very busy architect, Hillebrand (a student of Hildebrandt), who was responsible for many other renovations in this same area. There is a high, gabled tym-

An Atlantean figure on the Liechtenstein Palace

panum on this building, filled with sculptures, and the building, all in all, retains some of the quiet elegance of older Viennese palaces.

In the center of the square is the **Minoritenkirche**, Church of the Minor Friars, a mendicant order. The first church to stand on this spot was built in 1250, and the existing church dates from 1339. Through the course of the centuries this church received numerous renovations, but after its baroque alteration it was returned to the Gothic style in 1784. Inside there are clean and uncluttered Gothic lines. You may want to see the mosaic reproduction of da Vinci's *Last Supper* on the wall to the left of the high altar.

Standing with your back to the main entrance of the church, you can see the former **Starhemberg Palace** across the street at **Minoritenplatz 5**. The Starhembergs were one of the original twelve noble families of the Holy Roman Empire, and one of its members was the commander of the troops inside the Vienna garrison during the 1683 siege. A later member of the family led the proto-fascist *Heimwehr* troops during the turbulent interwar years in Vienna and can be said to have played a significant role in weakening the political life of Austria enough so that Hitler's invasion was welcomed simply because he promised to restore "order."

We go to the left (with our backs to the entrance) along the little arcade on the side of the Church of the Minor Friars, and past the **Austrian State Archives** (on our right) to **number 1**. Here, at the rear of the church, are the recently uncovered foundations of an earlier chapel. Directly opposite the church at this point is the new Federal Chancellery with a subway station at its door—an interesting contrast of old and new in the center of the city.

We continue around the church to leave Minoritenplatz by **Leopold Figl-Gasse** to our right, between two government houses of the province of Lower Austria. As we have seen, Vienna has played a schizoid role in Austrian politics: an Imperial city, it was also the major town of the surrounding duchies (much later to become *Länder*, or provinces, of the Republic of Austria).

Historically, Vienna the city (versus Vienna the seat of the Habsburgs and sometimes administrative center-cum-capital of an empire) has always had to wage a battle for city rights and privileges from the counts and princes who lorded over her in the feudal fashion. This schizoid nature has been held over into modern times with the formation of the republic: Vienna is not only the capital of Austria, it is also a self-contained province in its own right as well as the capital of Lower Austria. This three-fold administrative function employs tens of thousands of bureaucrats, one of the major occupations in Vienna. But it also makes for rivalries with the other provinces, which distrust such concentration of power (and of tax monies) in one place.

Leopold Figl-Gasse leads out to Herrengasse. We cross the street again and continue on to the **Wallnerstrasse**. Facing us at **number 8** is the former **Caprara-Geymüller Palace**, scene of many an elegant soirée in the eighteenth and nineteenth centuries. It was here that the playwright Grillparzer first met his lifelong fiancée. The Geymüller brothers, famous local bankers, held court to luminaries of nineteenth-century artistic Vienna. In the cobbled courtyard of this palace is a linden as old as the palace.

Turn right into **Wallnerstrasse**. At **number 6–6a** is the **Palais Palffy**, which must be the most restrained palace of Vienna, built in 1809 in the prevailing French style. Among other famous visitors to this palace was Bismarck, who lived here in the summer of 1892.

To the right is the intersection with **Fahnengasse**, a fairly recent street in the Inner City, created when an old palace belonging to the Liechtensteins was torn down in 1913. The hulking building on the left-hand side of Fahnengasse, which occupies almost an entire city block and houses offices of the post office on the ground floor, was built in place of the palace almost a generation later, in 1933. If you look to the top of it you will see a glassed-in penthouse. This building is known as the **Hochhaus**, "high house" or "skyscraper," and was the first of its kind in Vienna. Inside the old palace was the famous Bösendorfer Concert Hall, named after the piano firm of the same name and renowned for its acoustics. This hall witnessed the works of such composers as Bartok, Brahms, Grieg, Liszt, Mahler, and even Schoenberg. At the premier of an early Schoenberg work Mahler all but got in a fistfight with one of the ruder members of the audience, who had yelled out after the Schoenberg piece, "Air out the hall before Beethoven is played!"

From this intersection you can also catch sight of another palace back up on the Herrengasse: the **Mollard-Clary Palace** at **Herrengasse 9**, which dates from 1696 and is now the Museum of the Province of Lower Austria. (Like much of the Herrengasse, this old palace has also been converted into serving the purposes of the Lower Austrian capital.) In 1760 this palace was taken over by Count Clary-Aldington, master of the hunt and a man none too little impressed with his own prominence. So impressed was he that he had his monogram— C/A—worked into the window gratings of the first story.

One other thing about Fahnengasse before we proceed along Wallnerstrasse: it takes its name from the celebrated flag-raising incident (*Fahne* means flag) of 1798, which occurred in the nearby Caprara-Geymüller Palace. A French general was renting the palace and decided to hoist the French tricolor from the roof. He started a small riot with such an unpopular action, for Austria and Napoleon's France were then at daggers drawn.

Continue on **Wallnerstrasse** until the **Esterházy Palace**, on the left-hand side at **number 4**. It was built in 1695 for that wealthy and powerful Hungarian noble. The Esterházys, who had larger palaces in the country to the southeast, in present-day Burgenland, sometimes wintered here and brought their court musician, Josef Haydn, with them. Haydn, father of the symphony, string quartet, and sonata, was for most of his creative life a paid servant of the Esterházy family, in charge of their twenty-three-man-strong orchestra and responsible for composing original pieces for the prince's pleasure. His name, however, was known all over Europe as a famous composer while he was still "in service."

More than any other composer, Haydn symbolizes the refinements of the golden age of the aristocracy, which wrought the palatial transformation of Vienna that we are exploring in this walk. It was a time that prided itself on civilization and *Kultur*, when philosophers assured one that reason could direct the workings of this most perfect world. The Leibnizian universe held sway during the eighteenth century. The age of revolution had yet to dawn, and Haydn was firmly in a world of measured proportions, far removed from that of Beethoven's. When Haydn died in 1809 during a French occupation of Vienna, Napoleon himself ordered an honor guard at the composer's door and a twenty-one-gun salute to be fired at his funeral. Born to borderline peasants in 1732, Haydn showed early on a proclivity for music that earned him first a place at a church school and then, at age eight, a place at the choir of St. Stephen's, which he kept for the next nine years, until his voice broke. There followed many years of penury in Vienna, of giving music lessons and composing late into the night. In 1761 he went into service for the Esterházy family, first at the two-hundred-room palace at Eisenstadt and later at the new palace (in present-day Hungary) of Esterháza, a palace so immense (its opera auditorium alone had a four-hundred-seat capacity) that it put every other palace in Europe but Versailles to shame. Maria Theresa acted like a blushing commoner when invited to musical evenings there and became quite dissatisfied with her own meager palace of Schönbrunn. During the four decades of service to one Esterházy or another, Haydn supplied music for two weekly concerts; one authority has estimated that in the ten-year period from 1780 to 1790 alone he conducted more than one thousand performances of Italian operas. In the isolation of the country Haydn was forced to be original; his levelheaded and fair handling of the orchestra under him earned him the nickname of "Papa" from these grateful players, accustomed in those times to dictatorial conductors. Haydn was also one of the most mellifluous and prolific of composers: he wrote 104 symphonies, 83 string quartets, 52 piano sonatas, concertos, chamber music, choral works, songs, oratorios, masses, and even 23 operas. There was no musical form to which he did not turn his hand.

The Esterházy Palace now houses galleries and municipal offices. In the cellars in the rear there is a well-known Viennese wine cellar, serving wine from the old Esterházy estates. Ironically enough, this particular wine cellar, named after one of the noblest families of the Habsburg monarchy, is strictly a *bürgerlich* haunt and makes no pretentions to status.

Across the street at **Wallnerstrasse 3** is the **Lamberg Palace**, from the mid–eighteenth century. In the courtyard there is a wall fountain to be seen, as well as some newly added penthouses. This palace also bears the name Kaiserhaus, after the Emperor Franz I of Lothringen, Maria Theresa's consort, who held audiences here.

Continue along the Wallnerstrasse toward the intersection with **Kohlmarkt**. At **number 2**, to the left, we come to the Viennese furniture-making firm of **Thonet**, which popularized the bentwood coffeehouse chair and rocking chair around the world. They are still in business, still creating the styles that made them famous almost a century ago.

Past this point we come out onto Kohlmarkt, a coal market in the early Middle Ages—but at that time they were selling charcoal, not black coal. With the transfer of the Burg from Am Hof to this area, Kohlmarkt became one of the more important shopping and market areas, first for foreign trade and then later for smart shopping of all sorts. This tradition has remained until today, when we can still see shops from Cartier's to Country Living scattered along the sides of this street (and the odd fast-food fish restaurant as well, or else it wouldn't be truly Viennese—that mixture of snootiness tempered by a sort of middle-class leveling).

We will ultimately follow the Kohlmarkt to the left toward Graben, but first let's stroll to the right to look at a few things of interest. Almost directly across the street from us at **Kohlmarkt 7** is a quietly elegant eighteenth-century apartment house whose courtyard is worth a quick visit.

Next door to this building, at **Kohlmarkt 9**, is a plaque commemorating the fact that Chopin spent the winter of 1830–1831 in the house that once stood on this spot. But the house standing here now is something special itself. A product of *Jugendstil* (see Walk 4), it was built in 1901–1902 to plans by Max Fabiani. This is one of the finer *Jugendstil* houses in Vienna and portrays that Viennese variant of the art nouveau very well. Much less flowing and self-conscious than its French and Belgian counterparts, Austrian *Jugendstil* tended more to be a geometric and lovingly rendered "simplistic" style. See especially the overhanging roof, so typical of that style. The firm of Artaria, music publishers and art dealers, has been in this same spot for more than two hundred years. They published the works of Haydn when he was first becoming known in the world.

Continue to **Kohlmarkt 14**, to the *Zuckerbäckerei* (pastry shop) *extraordinaire*, **Demel's**. Like the Spanish Riding School and the Boys' Choir, Demel's is one of those things Viennese that every tourist already knows about before arriving. The bakery has had a long history of service to the Viennese upper crust, but in the twentieth century it, as most other things, has become more egalitarian. Their hot chocolate alone is worth the visit, and their marzipan-peopled windows are always a treat to see. Service is still done here in the third person ("The good lady wishes . . . ?").

Across the street at **number 11** there is an interesting

Graben: strollers' paradise

shop sign. The current gift shop was not always here: over the door we can still see the old sign letting us know that a watchmaker once had his business here. Interesting is the bit about *Seine Majestät, des Kaisers und Königs*, which means the shop was once licensed by the *K und K* authority (*kaiserlich-königlich*, or Imperial-Royal). This is similar to the British custom, "By appointment to His/ Her Majesty." Compare this to the one-headed eagle, the modern insignia of Austria, adorning shops such as Thonet's down the street. Same principle at work: Such shops now have the good graces of the republic rather than His Majesty.

Now turn around and head back on Kohlmarkt toward the Graben. Kohlmarkt has had many distinguished visitors and inhabitants, but perhaps none quite so bizarre as Herr Mälzel, a conjuror of the most extreme sort: he conjured life out of inanimate objects. Mälzel was a builder of automata, those strange nineteenth-century mechanical contraptions that linked Madame Tussaud with mechanics to create robots. Mälzel had an entire orchestra of these automata, which played at the Theater an der Wien in the early nineteenth century. In his own home, Mälzel set up a septet of these robots to perform almost any known musical piece. The Viennese thought he was a magician—some even suspected him of black magic. When Napoleon married the daughter of Emperor Francis II (the old Habsburg marriage policy all over again), Mälzel had the "couple" greet cheering crowds on the Kohlmarkt from his own window—this when the real couple was receiving guests at the Hofburg just down the street.

There is a tiny building—if it were a book of poetry we would call it a slim volume—wedged between two more massive neighboring houses at **Kohlmarkt 4**, which you should not miss. The façade is done in marble and the top floor bears marble statuary of two fun-loving women, as well as some exquisite relief and inlay work.

This brings us out to the top of **Graben**, which has widened some since its days as the moat to the Roman encampment and the early medieval town. With the city expansion of 1200 under the Babenbergs, the Graben was filled in to gain more building space. By 1300 it was known as a market area. Graben became one of the better addresses of the late Middle Ages and has remained a center of Viennese urban life ever since. By the time that Maria Theresa became co-ruler with her son, Joseph II, Graben had become the center for secular and church festivities: hardly a procession would be organized that did not pass down this street. As with Kärntnerstrasse, in the nineteenth and early twentieth centuries Graben was widened, and many of the old houses were pulled down to make way for new buildings. There is therefore not much left on the Graben of any real age, except for the Plague Column and one baroque palace, which we shall be seeing. But the general effect of the street is a pleasing one, wide and spacious in this city of tortured, winding lanes.

From the Kohlmarkt end of **Graben**, we can see across the street at **number 21** the **Sparcasse** building, a bank from the classicist period. One of the only buildings on the Graben from the early nineteenth century, this particularly fine example of that style sports a gabled pediment and simple, almost austere façade. Note the façade decoration of a gilded bee in the gable, symbolizing the arrival of the industrious, worker-bee middle classes.

To the left, at the top of **Graben numbers 19 and 20**, are two particularly lush examples of nineteenth-century building, complete with sexy caryatids holding aloft projecting bays.

At the top of the building at the corner of Kohlmarkt and **Graben**, to your immediate right, **number 18**, is a bronze statue of a riding Hussar—not the savior Sobieski riding down from Poland to rid Vienna of the Turks as is popularly thought, but simply advertising of a classier type: there was once an exclusive shop on this location called "Zum Hussaren."

We now turn right into Graben—it is best to walk down the middle of the street actually, through the parking area, so that you can get a view of both sides of the street. Take a look at **Graben 16** to the right, a Schönbrunn yellow building from 1909–1911, typical *Jugendstil*. There are some lovely mosaics on the fifth-floor façade and elegant projecting glass windows on the second floor, a favorite motif of late *Jugendstil* architecture.

The fountain that you come to in the middle of the street is one of the two that have been here since the fifteenth century. More than mere decoration, fountains were the main water supply in the medieval world. That a street or area had fountains on it indicated that it had most definitely arrived: People were living here permanently and building was going on.

This is the **Joseph Fountain**, surmounted by a statue of that saint and decorated on the pedestal with reliefs of the *Flight into Egypt* and of *Joseph's Dream*. This lead statuary is from 1804, though there have been decorative displays here for centuries.

Just past the fountain, notice the *Jugendstil* grill work laid out in a rectangle in the middle of Graben. This once surrounded a subterranean men's rest room; now it is just one more piece of decoration.

To the right is the intersection of Habsburgergasse and to the left the crossing is Jungferngasse (Maiden Lane). The latter street takes its name from a most titillating traditional story about the fatal results to a nobleman of his assignation with a young virgin here. The records remain very quiet about how the poor gentleman met his demise: an angry father or a broken heart?

Jungferngasse leads to **St. Peter's Church**, a much built-upon holy spot in Vienna: there may well have been a church of sorts standing on this site since the fourth century. The present church was built from 1702 to 1733, with Hildebrandt lending a hand. Other Baroque artists lent a hand with interior decoration, the most important being Johann Michael Rottmayr, who did the fresco in the cupola. During the Christmas season there is an exhibition of mangers in the crypt of this church—mangers big and small, homely and fine.

Past the intersection of Jungferngasse to the right, at **Graben 14–15a**, is the **Grabenhof**, a monumental building from 1874, when all of Vienna was in the grips of such monumental historical building on the Ringstrasse. This one even has its intermediate stories spanned in a sort of loggia effect, with giant columns meaning lord knows what in the arcane symbolism of such architectural "programs." This was built by Otto Wagner during his conservative phase. We shall be seeing other buildings by this same architect in Walk 4; they make this one look silly and overblown by comparison, for Wagner in old age made a break with traditionalism and joined forces with the revolutionary artists of *Jugendstil*.

To the left, take a look at one of the shop façades of **number 26**. This belongs to a jewelry shop in the far right of the ground floor. It is a fine example of 1970s Viennese innovation, with the use of materials (in this case marble and bronze) that represent what the interior of the shop deals in. Also, this rather biologically organic façade is actually articulated and given meaning by very functional heating and air-conditioning pipes in bronze.

Continue down the middle of Graben to the **Plague Column**, a triangular cloud of floating angels and dead bodies. The plague, or Black Death, hit Vienna in 1679, killing almost 15 percent of the population in a matter of weeks.

During the plague, Emperor Leopold I, from the safety of his court in Wiener Neustadt, vowed to erect a memorial when and if his people were delivered from its ravages. It says something for the importance of this street that such a monument was erected here. And Leopold made good on his promise, commissioning Ludovico Ottavio Burnacini to build the Plague, or Trinity, Column to commemorate the end of the Black Death. Fischer von Erlach was one of the young artists to join in the work on the column. The pedestal is covered in panels of reliefs with everything from the *Creation* to *Plague* depicted, with stops along the way for the *Last Supper* and the *Raising of the Dead*. A Jesuit priest was responsible for determining the complex symbolic program of the reliefs, but one needs only look at the thing, rising as it does in a mist of white stone accentuated by gilding and bronzes, to experience the great sigh of relief Vienna was expressing here, one of the true high points of Viennese baroque. It served as the model for similar columns erected all over Austria.

Back to the right-hand side of **Graben**, at **number 13**, there is another shop front and interior worth a look. Just to the left of the main entrance of this building is the clothing firm of **Knize**, whose quietly elegant façade and interior were done by the Viennese architect Adolf Loos. We'll be seeing more of his work later in this tour.

And to the left of this shop, just on the other side of one of Vienna's classier pastry and sweet shops, at **number 12** is a baroque portal which was left when the building was rebuilt in 1897. The next building, **number 11**, is the only baroque palace on the entire street, the **Bartollotti-Partenfeld Palace** from 1720. One more thing on the right-hand side of the street: Across the Dorotheergasse intersection is the **Anker building**, an office building in that Schönbrunn yellow built by Otto Wagner in the late nineteenth century. On the top is a glassed-in atelier, which the architect himself used for a time and which is now the workshop of the artist Friedensreich Hundertwasser, perhaps the most innovative and creative of contemporary Austrian painters, with his mosaiclike canvases and vibrant colors.

(See the "Other Sights of Interest" section in the introduction for the Hundertwasser museum and architectural gems to be seen in the Third District.)

Across **Graben** at **number 29–29a** is the **Trattner-hof**, built in 1900 on the site of a late–eighteenth century building of the same name. Trattner was a publisher—actually a pirate of Goethe and Shakespeare, to name only two of the many foreign authors he introduced to Vienna. But instead of being punished for pirating editions, Trattner won a "von" to his name, became the court book printer, and had a magnificent apartment building constructed here in 1776. Mozart lived in the house in 1784, and the young students Hermann Bahr (later to become one of the foremost members of Jung Wien, the Viennese impressionist literary movement) and Hugo Wolf shared a tiny room here as well.

We turn right off Graben at **Dorotheergasse**. To the left, at **number 3**, is the **Hotel Graben**, where among the notable guests was a young office worker and sometime writer from Prague, Franz Kafka. Another of the illustrious guests of this hotel was Viennese impressionist writer Peter Altenberg. The bohemian par excellence in slouch hat, cape, and sandals, Altenberg is little translated in other languages because of his very Vienneseness—like the Sacher Torte, this poetic essayist's style examining the minutiae of Viennese life does not travel well. There is a charming story about Altenberg while on the verge of death from his harum-scarum life in 1904. (He was then a ripe old forty-five.) His friends gathered around him and agreed something must be done—some more regular life found for him, or he would indeed go out like a quickly burnt candle. Such heresies, however, were anathema for one of the female friends, who announced she should not want to see Altenberg cheated of "the beauty of his death." Better to let him die in a garret than make a bourgeois of him—whereupon Altenberg, himself present, leaped to his feet from the armchair where he was cozily ensconced and shouted, "You silly goose. I don't want to die; I want to live; I want a warm room with a gas heater, an American rocking chair, a pension, orange marmalade, beef broth, filet mignon: I want to live!"

It was not long after that confab that Altenberg became a permanent guest at this hotel . . . with gas heaters in every room.

The Dorotheergasse is one of those typical side streets to the Graben, narrow and curving, as it well should be, considering its age. Up the street a few paces from the hotel, on the right at **Dorotheergasse 6**, is the **Café Hawelka**, founded in 1939 and once one of the better literary-artistic cafés. Today it is a zoo where people go to see and be seen. The interior is of that warm, cozy, yellow-glowing sort, however, which still beckons.

Two houses from here, at **number 10**, is the former **Dietrichstein Palace**—we saw another of this family's palaces earlier in this walk. This one was originally built in the late seventeenth century, and so got the jump on many of the palaces we have been examining. About two hundred years later, a pastry chef, having grown wealthy on his service to the sweet-toothed Habsburg court, bought the palace and rented it out to Ludwig Doblinger, who began the music publishing house that still occupies the premises. Doblinger was a publisher of Mahler's works as well as of Lehár's. Mahler's wife, Alma, tells a story in her biography of how both Gustav and she were entranced by a song in *The Merry Widow* and wanted to play it together at home. One day Mahler and Alma went to Doblinger's. While Gustav sequestered Herr Doblinger in a corner to discuss sales of his music, Alma slyly picked up a copy of the Lehár score—it would hardly have done for this director of the *Hofoper* and serious composer to buy such a composition—and memorized the passage they were interested in. In addition to being a professional wife, lover, and love object— Klimt, Walter Gropius, Kokoschka, and Franz Werfel were among other better-known conquests—Alma was also a more than adequate musician and composer in her own right.

In the first floor of the music house you can catch a glimpse of a lovely, well-appointed baroque hall, where house concerts have been given for a select few since 1924.

Across the street at **number 9** is the former **Starhemberg Palace**, from 1702. This family also had another palace on Minoritenplatz. Among current lodgers in this palace is a health institute that specializes in those bizarre Central European forms of curing: everything from mud baths to hydrotherapy.

Next door, at **number 11**, is the former **Nákó Palace**, a baroque palace from the late eighteenth century. This one changed hands through almost every noble family of Vienna at one time or another: from the Daun family to Dietrichstein, Esterházy, Harrach, and Kaunitz. It came into the hands of a banking family in the early nineteenth century and then to Count Nákó, who renovated and added the classicist façade. A hundred years later, it was the residence of Chancellor Dollfuss, who created a dictatorship in 1934 and was murdered by Austrian Nazis only months thereafter. In 1936 this palace finally ended up as the fine-arts section of the federally run pawn house, the **Dorotheum**, whose main offices are farther up the street. Auctions of artworks are still held here, open to the public. Check the advertisements outside the palace for times and a list of what is up for auction. There are also times set aside when one may view all that is to be auctioned. Because it is a public building—unlike so many of the other palaces on this walk—take the opportunity for a quick look at its interior.

A brief word about the Dorotheergasse: this street takes its name from a church and cloister of St. Dorothea, which stood up the street about a hundred yards from the fourteenth to the eighteenth centuries. The church and cloister were closed in 1782 as part of the reforms of the Josephinium period, and in 1788 they were turned into a state-run pawnshop. The Viennese have long referred to their periodic visits here as "going to visit Aunt Dorothy." You can get everything from stereos to oil paintings, from minks to cribs. A symbol of the ups and downs that Viennese families have suffered over the years, one man's loss literally turns into another's gain here.

The church to the right, **number 16**, all baroque and magnificently yellow in this dour street, is the oldest Protestant church of Vienna. The building itself dates from 1582 and was a monastic church until its dissolution in 1783 and conversion to a Lutheran church as a result of Josephinium reforms. It is now Vienna's **English Community Church**.

We turn right off Dorotheergasse at this corner, into **Stallburggasse**, one of the most picturesquely romantic streets of Vienna. The picturesqueness comes from the view of the spire of St. Michael's Church over the red-tiled roofs of the church and cloisters behind it.

To the right, at **Stallburggasse 4**, is one of Vienna's better-known Inner City cafés, the **Bräunerhof**, and along both sides of the street are antique and art shops. The street takes its name from the Stallburg, or the former Royal Stables, the back of which you will pass on the left after the Bräunerstrasse intersection. Located in the little island of this same intersection is one of Vienna's smallest secondhand shops.

To the left now is the rather imposing rear end of the

Royal Stables, on an architectural level the most important Renaissance building in Vienna. It has quite a lovely arcaded court. Built as a residence for the Archduke Maximilian in the mid–sixteenth century, later, when he became emperor, it was used to stable the royal stud. It still carries out the same function, though these Lipizzaner horses are no longer royal but federal.

The Lipizzaners, which begin life as black or gray foals and become snow-white as they age, are a Spanish breed, a mixture of Arab and Berber stallions (from the time of the Moorish occupation of the Iberian peninsula) with the native Iberian or Andalusian stock. These horses were the most sought-after breed of the sixteenth century. They have enormous physical strength blended with a grace and lightness that make them superb for dressage. The Renaissance was the heyday of the haute école of horsemanship—a time not only when the practical, military aspects of such horsemanship became apparent (gunpowder put an end to heavy suits of mail, which had made such acrobatics impossible for the horseman) but also when its historical importance for the nobility was recognized. The Habsburgs' recent incorporation of the Spanish realms made the establishment of a Spanish line of stud a simple proposition, and as early as the 1580s the foundations of the stud were being laid at Lipiza, near Trieste (hence the name of the horses). Part military-training school and part imperial show, the Riding School of Vienna developed accordingly from the late sixteenth century. By 1735 the manège had found a permanent home in the Winterreitschule, Winter Riding School, built by Fischer von Erlach father and son. Aficionados of horsemanship will recount the several times the Lipizzaner stud nearly became extinct: running from the French in the Napoleonic wars at the turn of the nineteenth century; barely surviving the poverty that ensued after World War I, the breakup of the Empire, and the subsequent moving of the stud to Pribitz in Styria; the last-minute dash by General Patton into unoccupied

Czechoslovakia (in extreme excess of his orders) to save the horses from falling into the hands of the approaching Russians; and even more recently the epidemic of virus that killed upward of thirty brood mares in the early 1980s and the stables fire of 1992.

At the intersection of **Habsburggasse** we can see the façade of the **Barnabite Cloister** at **number 12**, adjoining the rear of St. Michael's Church. To the left, at the top of the street, is part of the Winter Riding School; notice the high windows of the first floor, which ring this great main performing hall of the horses. Just to the left of that, at the corner of Habsburggasse and Reitschulegasse and also housed in the Stallburg, is the Alte Hofapotheke, Old Court Pharmacy, which dates back to 1564.

We cross **Habsburggasse** and take the *Durchhaus* at **number 14** through Little Michael's House, an eighteenth-century beer house. The interior of this *Durchhaus* continues the romantically picturesque aspect of the Stallburggasse: antique and frame shops, as well as part of the famous Viennese clothing firm of **Loden Plankl**, are found here. About two-thirds of the way through, to the right, is a painted relief of the *Mount of Olives* out of limestone, from 1494. It lies in a little outdoor niche at the back of the church.

We come out onto **Michaelerplatz** between two parts of the Loden Plankl shop, just across the street from the Michaelertor (Michael's Gate), the gate to the Hofburg. From this vantage point we can examine some buildings in the area. To our immediate right is **St. Michael's Church**, at one time the court parish church. According to tradition, it was founded in 1221 by Leopold the Glorious of Babenberg as a thanks for his safe return from the Crusades. This is one of the oldest churches in Vienna, with Romanesque parts from the early thirteenth century. The chancel comes from the early fourteenth

Stallburggasse and the spire of St. Michael's Church

century, as do lower sections of the spire. What you see on the exterior is the final result of renovations in 1792; the interior is a mishmash of styles, yet strangely pleasing to the eye.

Next to the church, at **Michaelerplatz 4** (the same as Kohlmarkt 11) on the corner of Kohlmarkt, is the **Large Michael's House**—as opposed to the little one through which we just walked. Built in 1625 for the Barnabite Order as an apartment house, this building housed young Haydn after his voice broke and he could no longer sing for the court choir. Haydn lived in a garret at the top. He complained that the snow trickled in during winter and the sun turned it into a sauna in summer. These were not the palmiest days for young Haydn. A couple of floors lower, in a much more representative apartment, lived the court poet Metastasio. It was Metastasio who almost single-handedly created the repertoire of Italian opera of the eighteenth century. He wrote twenty-seven *drammi per musica* on ancient history and mythology; these libretti were set to music more than a thousand times, leading to that rote, uninteresting opera that allowed (almost demanded) the singers to engage in ridiculous vocal pyrotechnics and acrobatics. Gluck, living in Vienna at this time, rebelled against this form of opera, and with his *Orfeo ed Euridice* became the first in a long line of Viennese musical revolutionaries.

You might want to pop into the courtyard of this house, since it provides one of those quaint views of Vienna—the Romanesque side of St. Michael's—that are becoming increasingly difficult to find in the modern city.

Almost directly across the street from the Large Michael's House, on the corner of **Michaelerplatz (number 3)** and Herrengasse, is the **Loos House**. This was built in 1910 by the Viennese architect Adolf Loos, a pioneer in modern International style. Up to this point, Loos had been commissioned to do interiors only—and very warm and cozy they were, harkening back to almost a peasant style with their open beams and comfortable nooks, but

The Loos House as seen from the Michaelertor

also incorporating the lines of William Morris. Loos was no friend of *Jugendstil* architecture, finding it overblown and self-important. This building site, directly across from one of the main gates of the Hofburg, was a touchy project. When the scaffolding was taken down, revealing the austere façade, Vienna was scandalized. No façade decoration! The Viennese dubbed it the "eyebrowless house" because of its lack of lintel decoration, and that arbiter of artistic good taste, Archduke Franz Ferdinand, declared he would no longer use the Michaelerplatz gate.

Across the street from the Loos House at **Herrengasse**

1–3 is the former **Herberstein Palace**, the sort of architecture one assumes the Viennese of Loos's day approved. It was built for a bank in 1897 on the site of an older palace that housed the most famous literary café of its time, the Café Griensteidl, which played host to writers such as Peter Altenberg, Hermann Bahr, Hugo von Hofmannsthal, Karl Kraus, Arthur Schnitzler, and Felix Salten (the fin de siècle Austrian writer who gave the world not only *Bambi* but also *The Memoirs of Josephine Mutzenbacher*, one of the raciest books of all times, describing the life and times of a famous courtesan). When this coffeehouse was torn down, Karl Kraus, a sort of Viennese Mencken, decried the "demolished literature" in his journal, *Die Fackel*. Bereft of a meeting place, the writers migrated up the Herrengasse to the Café Central. But the furor over the demolition of the Café Griensteidl, an Austrian tradition, was nothing to that occasioned by Loos's building a decade later. An index of Viennese values.

Next to the Herberstein Palace, at **Herrengasse 5**, is the **Wilczek Palace**, from 1719. One of the last of this Wilczek family wrote a lovely little book about "noble" Vienna entitled *Gentleman of Vienna*. This Count Wilczek was a mountain of a man, an Arctic explorer, and was also noted for his rather curious disdain of stairs. It was not an uncommon sight for this aristocrat to be seen leaping from his first-floor rooms directly down onto Herrengasse and then striding off in evening dress to a soirée at some princess's palace. He was a favorite at court, in the circle of Crown Prince Rudolf, and one can learn more about the aristocratic world of late–nineteenth century Vienna from his memoirs than anywhere else. He knew everybody: the Palffys, Harrachs, Schwarzenbergs, Trauttmanndorfs, Liechtensteins, Schönborns, and Kinskys. He was even a friend of the Rothschilds, being the first to use the familiar *du* with one of the members of this Jewish banking house. He bought and re-created Burg Kreuzenstein, a medieval castle to the north of Vienna that can still be visited today and will deceive the best of authorities—it is pure Disneyland, though, as most of the old castle was already demolished by the time the count took it over.

Of course the building that dominates Michaelerplatz is the **Michaelertrakt** (Michael's Wing) with its gate to the Hofburg, built in the 1890s. The old Court Theater stood in the general area of the Michaelertrakt until 1888; the new theater is on the Ring, built as part of the urban renewal of the mid–nineteenth century. The proximity of the theater and the fact that it was considered a court appendage show the Habsburg penchant for drama and entertainments. It was unusual if the emperor's box was not filled for each performance. Even such a staid and bureaucraticlike worker as Franz Joseph took notice of theater and had a long-standing platonic (?) affair with one of the stars of the Burgtheater, Maria Schratt. Among all the noble villas of Hietzing, the suburb surrounding the Habsburg summer palace at Schönbrunn, one of the loveliest is that of "die Gnädige," the dear Frau Schratt. A gate was added in the wall surrounding the palace of Schönbrunn, which just happened to be across the street from her villa.

But let us not stoop to mere gossipmongering. If Franz Joseph had a vested interest in drama, earlier emperors had no such clear-cut grounds for their attachment. Their love of theater of all sorts—from Punch and Judy shows, to Italian opera, to didactic Jesuitical plays—stemmed from pure joy of theatricals. That the Jesuits adapted their teaching techniques to the stage is indication in itself of not only the Habsburg but also the Viennese love of such performances. It wasn't until the nineteenth century, however, that theater in Vienna became truly German or native Austrian in character. Until that time the repertoire of the court theater, as it was for the opera, was mostly stock Italian and French material. The German players started as bands of strolling players, sort of the *Good Companions* in miniature, and theirs was a hand-to-mouth life. Stranitzky, as we have seen, was really the initiator of German theater in Vienna with his

Hanswurst comedies. Then came the Enlightenment and the importation of German plays by Schiller and Goethe, encouraged by such Austrian statesmen as Sonnenfels. But it was not until the early nineteenth century that Austria developed its own repertoire of plays, with the writings of Nestroy, Bauernfeld, Raimund, and Grillparzer.

To the left on Michaelerplatz, adjoining the Michael-ertrakt, is the **Winter Riding School**. Somehow this Michaelerplatz façade of the school does not really work; the cupola is out of place, as if stuck upon the top as an afterthought. If you think that there is an extraordinarily great resemblance between it and the Michaelertrakt, you are correct. Fischer von Erlach and his son, Joseph Emanuel Fischer von Erlach, drew up plans for the Riding School (as well as other tracts we will be seeing) and also for this monumental entrance on the Michaelerplatz. It took a century and a half, however, for the Habsburgs to scrape up enough funds to finance this last part of the building on the Hofburg (penultimate, actually, as we shall be seeing).

The two fountains with their rather grotesque statuary on either side of the Michaelerplatz entrance symbolize Austrian military power on land and sea—until 1918 the monarchy had a considerable navy in the Adriatic, based at Trieste.

So, cross the Michaelerplatz to enter the Hofburg through the **Michaelertor**. First, we may want to examine some recently uncovered and quite well-displayed parts of the old Roman wall, as well as parts of a nineteenth-century drainage and sewage system in front of the enormous portals to the Hofburg. Notice the double-headed eagle relief on the bricks, symbol of the House of Habsburg. The very mortar of Vienna was *K und K*. Continuing through the portals, we will see that the palace is so large that traffic continues through its precincts. We enter under an enormous imperial cupola, built in 1893. To the right at this point is the entrance to two of the many museums and showrooms of the

A grotesque from the Michaelertor fountains

Hofburg, the **Esperanto Museum** and the **Hoftafel und Silberkammer**, the collection of court silver and porcelain. The former (open Monday and Wednesday, 10:00 A.M. to 4:00 P.M. and Friday, 9:00 A.M. to 4:00 P.M.) is the only Esperanto museum in the world. Through documents and artifacts, it traces the development of this international language, which just never did catch on. The silver and porcelain collection (open daily except Monday and Saturday from 9:00 A.M. to 1:00 P.M.) is an astonishing embarrassment of riches. To call the Habsburg eating utensils "silverware" would be a gross injustice, for most of it was gold. A visit to this collection can be more telling about the lifestyle of the Habsburgs in the eighteenth and nineteenth centuries than is a visit to the **imperial apartments**, just across the road under the cupola (open daily from 8:30 A.M. to 12:00 P.M. and 12:30 P.M. to 4:00 P.M.; mornings only on Sundays). A tour of these apartments takes us through about twenty rooms: private apartments, audience rooms, formal dining rooms, workrooms, smoking salons, bedrooms. On and on you go past Gobelin tapestries and Chinese porcelain and inlaid wood, until your senses are somewhat deadened by the finery. These are mostly the apartments of the Kaiser Franz Joseph and his wife Elisabeth, one of the more reluctant monarchs of her day. A brilliant horsewoman and a startling beauty, Elisabeth cared more for her figure than for Franz. The gym she had set up in her rooms can still be seen, as can Franz Joseph's austere metal bed (several suites of rooms away from his wife's) amid tapestries and oils. Though it would initially seem that you are going through these apartments in the direction of the Winter Riding School, you actually hook around and go through the heart of the Hofburg, ending in the Amalienburg, a Renaissance wing of the palace, at the Alexander Apartments (also used by the last kaiser, Karl, before his forced abdication in 1918). These were named after Tsar Alexander I of Russia, who used them during the Congress of Vienna. A man of rather prolific appetites, he left

Vienna with thousands of crowns outstanding in debts and with more than one lonely "tsarina" bearing a reminder of his visit. But the Alexander Apartments they are, nonetheless. Noblesse oblige? In any case, I'd suggest reserving a visit to these apartments for the end of the walk around the Hofburg so that you have a better idea of its layout (both historically and physically).

Continue through the first huge vestibule into the inner wings of the palace at the courtyard called **In der Burg**. Once there, you can begin to get a feel for the size of this place and realize why the Viennese think of it as a city within a city. In its 18 wings, 54 stairways connect 2,600 rooms. Nineteen courtyards are interspersed between these buildings, which hold 110 apartments (lived in), 45 bureaus, offices, and small businesses, as well as countless cellars and storage areas. About 5,000 people live and work in the Hofburg complex. As a rough indication of the rabbit warren that the Hofburg is, just take a look at the roofline of the wings in the courtyard and try counting the numerous chimneys. A chimney sweep's nightmare.

The pomp of this monarchical city palace now lends itself to republicanism as well; the president of the republic and his staff occupy offices in the Leopold Wing of the palace. Once in this inner courtyard, you will also be able to get an idea of the span of history these buildings represent. There is everything here from Gothic to neo-Gothic; a full circle in the course of European history, from feudalism to republicanism.

Walk to the middle of this courtyard, at the pedestal of the **statue of Francis I or II**. The confusion over his chronology was self-imposed: as Holy Roman Emperor, he was the second Francis. But in 1806 he dissolved that Empire and instead assumed the title of kaiser of Austria, becoming the first Francis (the first anybody) to do so. Francis was the nephew of the reforming Joseph II and as unlike him politically as any two men could be. He was the archconservative, together with Metternich delineating the new Habsburg mission in Europe: as a bastion now against the liberal era, the upholder of the rule by autocracy and aristocracy. Francis's rule epitomized the Biedermeier era, that time of cozy insouciance. But such coziness was brought about only by the machinations of one of the most highly organized police states of its day. Francis walked among his subjects freely, acting the part of the benevolent, fatherly king, even speaking Wiener-isch, the Viennese dialect with them. (In this, however, he had little choice, as it was the only German he could speak; he was raised in the Habsburg duchy in Tuscany and his mother tongue was Italian.) But such chummi-ness was only a façade: meanwhile the censors were ex-amining all books at the border; mail was opened at the post office; newspapers appeared with white holes in them where a story, censored at the last minute, should have appeared. Francis did not outlast the 1848 Revolu-tion—a situation that his policies largely created. But his minister Metternich and his feeble son, Ferdinand I (again, there had been earlier Ferdinands, but not as emperor of Austria), were around to collect payment on the Habs-burg debt of autocracy. Ferdinand was an epileptic and halfwit (he suffered twenty epileptic fits during his hon-eymoon), perhaps as a result of long centuries of Habs-burg inbreeding. The distinctive Habsburg lip was part of this genetic legacy. Actually, it would be more accurate to say the Habsburg jaw rather than lip, for it was a genetic malocclusion of the jaw that caused this jutting, pouty lower lip. That the Habsburgs were mouth-breathers is a certainty: from the looks of their jaws, their mouths were never fully closed. But whether or not they suffered from the usual halitosis of mouth-breathers has never been recorded. Perhaps they chewed the aromatic orris root, just as they and other noble families forced their lackeys to do to cover up the odors of tobacco and garlic.

But even with this weak link in the Habsburg chain of command at the helm, the Viennese were not revolting against the monarchy in 1848 as much as they were against the ministers guiding it. Not until months after the initial fracases with students and workers were more extreme forms of democracy demanded and subsequently suppressed by the imperial troops. As one historian put it, 1848 was the turning point in history at which Europe did not turn. The old order did not bend with the changing times, so some seventy years later it was completely swept away in a radical reversal of a thousand-year tradition.

But all this is getting far away from an overview of the layout of the Hofburg. Standing as we are near the Francis I statue, we can get a good view of the various wings of the palace. The statue is facing the oldest tract of the Hofburg, to your left, the **Schweizerhof**, named after the Swiss Guard, the personal guard of the emperor. Actually this has a Gothic core, difficult to distinguish now, and was begun by Ottokar II, built near the fortress-palace of the Babenbergs. With the defeat of Ottokar by Rudolf I of Habsburg, the Habsburgs took over this seat of power and almost uninterruptedly occupied it and expanded the Hofburg from 1300 to 1918. What you see now in the Schweizerhof is, however, primarily a Renaissance structure, from the mid–sixteenth century. But you can still get an idea of what this medieval fortress looked like, with the four corner towers and the moat, which can still be seen just in front of the wing. This was the residence area for emperors up until the mid–eighteenth century.

The next building phase of the Hofburg, from 1575 to 1577, led to the construction of the **Amalienburg**, which is directly opposite the Schweizerhof. This was started by Maximilian II, who was also responsible for the Stallburg building of the same era. The emperor Rudolf II, however, that strange duck who held court in Prague most of the time, had work finished on the Amalienburg. Reminders of that Prague court can be seen atop the Amalienburg in three timepieces—sundial, baroque clock, and lunar clock showing the phases of the moon.

These measures of time hark back to the work of Tycho Brahe, the astronomer and inventor of the telescope. Brahe was at the Prague court along with Johann Kepler, who developed the Rudolfine Tables (named after their benefactor), which attempted to foretell the movements of the planets to describe a universal order and harmony. We can only hope that Brahe's work was more accurate than this lunar clock is.

The horse-shaped weather vane atop the Amalienburg is trusted by the Viennese more than the television weatherman: when its head points to the west or north, rain is sure to come. This wing takes its name from the widow of Emperor Joseph I, Amalie of Braunschweig, who had her apartments here in the early eighteenth century.

During the next building phase, from 1660 to 1666, the **Leopold Wing** connected the Amalienburg and the Schweizerhof. This is the very simple-looking stretch of building to the left of the Kaiser Francis I statue in the courtyard of In der Burg. Emperor Leopold I, he of the plague year and the Turkish siege, commissioned the building by Italian architects in early baroque style, and Empress Maria Theresa, the first of the Habsburg rulers to move out of the Schweizerhof, had her apartments here with her husband, Francis of Lorraine, and their brood of thirteen children. (There were sixteen in all, three of whom died in infancy.) Her children were to throne much of Europe: her daughter Marie Caroline was married to King Ferdinand of Naples, Marie Antoinette became Queen of France, Leopold became Grand Duke of Tuscany and then Emperor Leopold II, and Joseph succeeded his brother as Emperor Joseph II. But all this siring, as we have seen, did not tire out Francis of Lorraine. He was a womanizer of the first rank and was known to use the Pastry Cooks' Stairs, disguised as a journeyman baker, to sneak away to his rendezvous with

The last remnants of the moat
by the Schweizertor

sweet young things. These Zuckerbäckersteige are still to be seen in the middle of this wing, as are the Lackey Stairs to the far right. In the complicated world of court protocol, the servants were to be, like God, present everywhere but never seen, using back staircases and living in cramped quarters under the eaves. The names of these stairs are themselves indicative of the intricate court structure of the Hofburg.

Opposite the Leopold Wing is the **Reichskanzlei-trakt**, or State Chancellery Wing, which is part of the imperial additions of Charles VI during the early eighteenth century. This period of building activity in the high baroque also saw the construction of the Imperial (now National) Library, Winter Riding School, and Redoutensaal, all on the Josefsplatz (to be seen in a bit). This State Chancellery wing is adorned with statues of the *Labors of Hercules* in all their muscle-straining glory, symbolizing the labors of the Habsburgs on behalf of the Holy Roman Empire, the imperial offices were located here. Later Franz Joseph had his apartments here. The design is a mix of Hildebrandt and Fischer von Erlach— one of the only collaborations of these two rivals in Vienna. Erlach and his son were commissioned for most of the buildings in the baroque extension period of the early to mid–eighteenth century. (You would go through the two wings of the Reichskanzlerei and Amalienburg during a tour of the imperial apartments.)

From this point we follow the course of the road through the buildings out onto the Heldenplatz to the newest sections of the Hofburg, the **Neue Burg**, completed only in the last year before World War I. The Heldenplatz (Heroes' Square—it does sound better in German) was planned as one of the largest squares in the world, to surpass even St. Peter's. To your immediate left as you come out of the passageway is the wing encompassing the Ceremonial Hall—this is an extension, as it were, of the Leopold Wing across the traffic divide. But it is from the next building phase of the Hofburg: although the parts of the Ceremonial Hall not fronting on the square date from the early nineteenth century, the bulk of this wing is from the early twentieth century. This wing now houses the Vienna Congress Center, where, among other activities, the International Atomic Energy Agency has its annual conference. It was also the venue of the SALT talks in the 1970s.

Jutting out perpendicularly to this wing is the Neue Burg, built between 1881 and 1913 by Semper and Hasenauer in the style of copycat historicism—in this case, the design has an ersatz Renaissance form to it. It was from the balcony of this hulking wing that Hitler announced the annexation of Austria on March 15, 1938—to the rejoicing of most Viennese, it must be added. So much for the "conquered nation" status that the Allies awarded Austria. Above the Neue Burg are still the four flagpoles upon which flew the flags of the occupying powers after World War II: the United States, France, Britain, and the former Soviet Union. Today the Neue Burg houses four museums as well as the **National Library** and its reading room. The library here is actually an extension of the old Imperial Library on the Josefsplatz, which we shall be visiting shortly; it is one of eight such divisions of the total National Library system, which includes a printed-matter collection, a handwritten collection, a music collection, a map collection, a papyrus collection, a portrait collection, a photographic collection, and a theater collection. Just one bit of amazing statistics among others: in the printed-matter collection there are almost two million books and periodicals stored in twenty-eight miles of cases. This printed-matter collection is housed in the Neue Burg.

In the same main section of the Neue Burg is the **Ephesus Museum**, ingeniously displaying artifacts from the Austrian digs at Ephesus, Turkey. Above this archaeological collection is the **Collection of Musical Instruments**, where you can browse among the pianos that Beethoven, Haydn, Mahler, and Schumann used. Just opposite this collection is the **Collection of Weapons**, one of the largest in Europe, where you can stroll among crossbows, suits of armor, and early guns—all dating from the Middle Ages to the seventeenth century.

The fourth museum in this wing is reached by an entrance farther to the right, toward the Ring. This is the **Ethnographical Museum**, Museum für Völkerkunde, a rich collection of artifacts from societies the world over. Especially good is the collection from the New World. (Note the work on Montezuma's robe and headdress.) The artifacts gathered here are not just the result of some friendly scientist going out and collecting; rather, they are visible reminders of the length and breadth of the Habsburg Empire. All four museums are open daily, except Tuesday, 10:00 A.M. to 6:00 P.M.

Framing the square on the Ring side is the **Burgtor**, the last remaining part of the old city wall and actually the last part of it to be built, in 1821. This part was left with the razing of the walls. Between the world wars, this bit of wall and gate was turned into a war memorial. A wreath is laid on the grave of the unknown soldier in the first week of November, when the square is peopled by a regiment of the small Bundesheer (a token military force whose number was limited by the State Treaty of 1955, which made Austria a permanently neutral country).

A couple of incidentals mar the otherwise "heroic" aspect of this "Heroes' Square": the original plans called for another wing, mirroring the Neue Burg, to border the Heldenplatz to the northwest, just in front of where the Volksgarten is now located. This wing would serve to tie the entire complex into the twin museums which sit across the Ring, the Natural History Museum to the right and the Museum of Fine Art to the left. (The *Venus of Willendorf*, a Stone Age pinup, is the centerpiece of the former; the Breughels collected by the Prague Rudolf and the Canaletto scenes of Baroque Vienna are my favorite in the latter.) Happily, this monumental plan was never realized. The Hofburg retains its lovely higgledy-piggledy asymmetry, and we are left with the glimpse of the Parliament and Rathaus over the trees of the Volksgarten.

The other blemish on the heroism intended for this square is a result of the sculptor **Fernkorn**, who worked on the two **statues** in its center. Let's proceed to the one on the right, the statue farthest from the Neue Burg. This is of Archduke Karl, brother of Francis I (or II, as you like it) and a man who suffered for this sibling tie. His brother was always a little jealous of the bearing of the militarily minded Karl and was partly responsible for the conspiracies against him at court. That he was subject to fits of depression and epilepsy did not help matters any for Karl, since he would leave the scene at the most urgent of times to retreat into his private shell. But the high point in his phlegmatic career was reached in 1809 at the Battle of Aspern, across the Danube from Vienna, where Archduke Karl dealt Napoleon one of his only defeats. That the archduke's army had allowed Napoleon to take the city in the first place and that Karl was to lose the much more important Battle of Deutsch-Wagram not long after is not mentioned in connection with this statue. Karl, who was a reluctant warrior himself but who had the good grace not to demand of his troops bits of valor of which he himself was not capable, was not safe on some hill viewing the Battle of Aspern from afar. He was in the thick of battle. At one point, when the Austrian lines were sagging against a French cavalry charge, he seized the colors of a regiment of foot soldiers and charged the enemy, rallying the Austrians behind him. This statue depicts this decisive moment, Karl's arm raised high holding the flag. But many years later, when questioned about this deed, Karl—ever a realist—laughed and told his interlocutor: "Do you know how heavy regimental colors are? Do you suppose a little chap like me could go off with them? I simply grasped the regimental staff, not the colors."

Artistic liberties taken or not, this statue works. Fernkorn caught the moment of action and the horse and rider seem to take flight. But Fernkorn ran into problems with the second statue, of Prince Eugene. He worked years on it but could never achieve the dynamism of the earlier statue, especially the fine balancing trick of the steed in midflight. The Prince Eugene statue is heavy and stolid and needs to be balanced by the horse's tail. Fernkorn died insane—many say as a result of this work. And the artist who did the pedestals of both statues, van der Null, who later designed the Opera, committed suicide (though not over these horses; it was over a criticism Franz Joseph leveled at the new Opera). Heroics or histrionics?

From the Archduke Karl statue we turn around and go back to the first courtyard, **In der Burg**. We exit this at the first right, through the **Swiss Gate**, one of the better examples of Renaissance work in Vienna, with a coat of arms over the entrance and its ceiling covered in coats of arms as well as grotesques. The inscription over the entrance gives the date of construction, 1552, and tells us that it was erected at the behest of Emperor Ferdinand I. The moat, as previously mentioned, is still to be seen on either side of this entrance, and the winch for the chains of the drawbridge that stood here until the eighteenth century also still survives. All this defensive posturing reminds us that the Hofburg was actually a fortress-palace and was laid siege to six times through its history, twice by the Viennese themselves, unhappy with the early Habsburgs.

Entering the **Schweizerhof**, we are struck with how compact it is, not much larger than a courtyard of a substantial *bürgerlich* apartment house. This is approximately the size of the original thirteenth-century fortress started by the Babenbergs outside of the then city walls. To the left just upon entering is a covered fountain from 1522, with a relief of the Habsburg *Doppeladler*, the double eagle. This well is a reminder of the difficulties of daily life then, about things that we now take for granted. One of these difficulties was, of course, the water supply. Wells, fancied up into fountains such as this one, served the purpose of communal water supplies. Those lovely rosewood boxes that are often sold in antique shops as shoe boxes or flowerpots once served as commodes; chamber pots had to be emptied daily in those days before central plumbing. As most cities had no sewage system during the years before the advent of central plumbing (Vienna's extensive sewer system, for example, was developed in the nineteenth century), these chamber pots were as often as not simply dumped in the gutter, adding to the other odors of horse dung and rotting vegetables. (There was no garbage man, either, and citizens were responsible for dumping their own garbage at the dump on the present-day Strauchgasse.) As late as the 1880s there was still no plumbing inside the Hofburg; the fastidious Empress Elisabeth was forced to relieve herself on a commode behind lacquered screens in a drafty hallway, protected at a discreet distance by the ever-present palace guard. In those preplumbing days, bathing firms even existed which would bring tubs of hot water to one's house for the weekly or monthly (whether one needed it or not) bath.

However, Vienna is now well served by public utilities. Fresh water is fed into the city primarily from the Rax Alps to the south of the city. Vienna has some of the best drinking water in any European capital—so good, in fact, that the Viennese each consume three hundred quarts of it daily (consume does not mean simply drink, in this case). Garbage is now picked up by a fleet of more than two hundred trucks, making three rounds per day. Some of this garbage is dumped outside of the city and some is treated to become fertilizer, but by far the largest portion is burned in incineration plants (one of whose stacks, recently decorated in gold paint and a pastiche onion dome, can be seen in the northwestern skyline, near Nussdorf) to provide heating for hospitals, public baths, and apartment houses. And the sewage flows along five thousand miles of canals to a central treatment plant in the district of Simmering, before it is released into the Danube Canal.

But this takes us a long way from the realm of the Hofburg. Until Renaissance times, after the first Turkish siege of 1529, the Schweizerhof was still basically the Hofburg. The buildings around you had thus served for more than three hundred years as the total palace; extensions and ad-

ditions over the next four hundred years created the rest of the rabbit warrens making up the entire complex.

Just to the right we can see the flight of stairs across the courtyard that lead up to the **Hofburg Chapel**, built originally in 1296 but renovated in 1449. A later baroque renovation was done away with in 1802, when the chapel was once again renovated, this time to look Gothic. *Plus ça change. . . .* Mass is sung here on Sunday morning, from September to June, by the Vienna Boys' Choir, the remnants of Maximilian I's Hofmusikkapelle, among whom, over the course of the centuries, have numbered the youthful Haydn and Schubert.

Underneath the stairs is the entrance to the **Schatzkammer**, or Imperial Treasury, open daily except Tuesday, 10:00 A.M. to 6:00 P.M. Here are located artifacts—that word hardly encompasses all the gold, silver, and embroidery we will see—covering one thousand years of history. In late 1992 Austria was reminded just how precious this collection is when a fire raged through large tracts of the Hofburg, including the Schatzkammer. Most of the collection was saved, but it was a close call.

A focal point of the collection is the crown of the Holy Roman Emperor, which was fashioned a millennium ago by goldsmiths on the island of Mainau in Lake Constance. There is also the crown of the house of Habsburg, created after Kaiser Francis I shrunk the realm of the Habsburgs to that of hereditary rulers of Austria in the early nineteenth century. Here we can also see the golden cradle of Napoleon's son, the duke of Reichstadt, a child who was the product of yet another Habsburg dynastic marriage, this time of the emperor's daughter, Marie-Louise, to the conqueror of Vienna. The boy lived a rather lonely existence at Schönbrunn, all but a captive of the great powers fearful lest he follow in his father's footsteps. He died at the summer palace, at only twenty-one years of age, of the "Viennese disease," tuberculosis,

Protecting the Schweizertor

and has provided excellent dramatic material for play-wrights and historians ever since.

Also of interest is the Burgundian Treasury, from the duchy of Burgundy, which came into Habsburg domains through the marriage, in the late fifteenth century, of Max-imilian I to Mary of Burgundy. Prominent among this treasury is the Order of the Golden Fleece, a collar of golden links, representing flints, from which was sus-pended the fleece, symbolic of the magic fleece of Greek legend. Maximilian became the head of this order of twenty-four noblemen, the most exclusive of all medieval chivalric orders. This one was pledged to defend the Christian faith, to uphold virtue, to be loyal to their sov-ereign, and to wear the insignia of the order at all times. The Habsburgs were grand masters of this order from the time of Maximilian on; the order still exists today, but in a debased form—just as the Masonic Lodge in the United States is a shadow of the original.

One other thing to see in the treasury is the Holy Lance (in the same room as the crown of the Holy Roman Emperor), which is supposed to be the lance with which the Roman centurion stabbed Jesus on the cross. The lance is supposed to have magic qualities, and one ac-count even has the young bewhiskered Hitler standing forlornly in front of it and experiencing a mystical sen-sation that led to his complete turnabout from a hungry artist to a politician on the make.

We leave the Schweizerhof by the passageway (the Hofburg actually constitutes one monumental *Durchhaus* from the Volksgarten to the Josefsplatz) directly opposite the Schweizertor entrance—that is, between the Burgka-pelle and the Treasury Wing. To the right and left in this passageway are the large and small Redoutensaal (Mas-querade Halls), where in the eighteenth and early nine-teenth centuries the Viennese penchant for masked balls during *Fasching*, or carnival season, was displayed. More than one archduchess and even empress was able to take a turn anonymously on the arm of some young military gallant—something that would normally be beneath her station. It is a credit to the Viennese—and shows their affinities with the south, where such practices are common—that they institutionalized these *Fasching* as a time of licentiousness, as a pressure releaser from their otherwise formalized lives. In a country and city where it is illegal *not* to use one's title on official communication and pieces of personal identification (such professional titles actually become part of one's legal name), these topsy-turvy times are sorely needed. The French have a lovely saying about this Viennese inclination for titles: if you are introduced to a person with the name of Dr. So-and-So, the joke goes, rest assured he is either a medical doctor or a Viennese. Even the form-following, boot-clicking Prussians of our imagination eschew the silliness of a system in which the wives of university doctorates are addressed as "Frau Doktor." Of course the Viennese have managed to make even titles derisive: cabbies and store clerks, if in a cheeky mood, will puff up anybody's supposed title so that the dourest little old lady on a pension of four thousand schillings a month gets a *"Kuss die Hand, Frau Doktor."* More than one multinational has attempted to do away with titles within their ranks (no more Herr Ingenier or Herr Diplom Kaufmann, for example), but the employees became so confused that communication was no longer possible between divisions. A president of Austria (more a titular position, as the real power is wielded by the chancellor) was asked once to do away with all these academic titles—it is clear that they are only substitutes for Herr Graf or Baron of past centuries, titles that were made illegal after the collapse of Austro-Hungary following World War I. But the president was no dummy: he calmly replied that there are far fewer titles for him to remember than there are family names. Eliminating titles would make his job harder.

The passage leads us out onto **Josefsplatz**, named after Joseph II, Maria Theresa's reform-minded son. In the early Middle Ages, this was the churchyard of the **Au-**

gustinerkirche, St. Augustine's Church (which stands opposite from us across the square and to the left). Then the area was used as an outdoor riding school and was replaced in turn by a park. By the late eighteenth century, ancillary buildings to the Hofburg had found their way to this side of the complex as well. Indeed, some of the most beautiful and monumental parts of the Hofburg lie on the Josefsplatz. Maria Theresa's father (a backward way of describing Charles VI, but the daughter is far better known to the world) was, as we have seen already, responsible for much of this Imperial Roman style of architecture that still ornaments Vienna. Charles VI was a better master of symbolism than emperor—he left his daughter an empire diminished by the loss of the Spanish inheritance, an empire in hock up to its eyeballs supporting his monumental building schemes, and an empire that was ready to put the knife to the throat of this first female Habsburg ruler.

Fischer von Erlach was responsible for the design of the **Hofbibliothek** (Court Library) to the right, forming the middle wing of this lovely and most perfect of Viennese squares. The exterior shows Erlach's fascination in the later phase of his career with French baroque. At the top is statuary representing Minerva driving out hunger and ignorance with her four-in-hand chariot.

This former Court Library was eventually completed by Erlach's son, Joseph Emanuel, in 1737. Inside, the Prunksaal, or Grand Hall, is a must for the bookish. This is Europe's largest baroque library room. Here are to be seen in their uniform red-calf bindings, fifteen thousand volumes from Prince Eugene's private collection. The frescoes, masterpieces of trompe l'oeil, are by Daniel Gran. The official name for this library is now the National Library but somehow Hofbibliothek seems much more apposite.

The court librarian for many years was Gerhardt von Swieten, Maria Theresa's personal physician and a noted social reformer. He is buried next door in St. Augustine's Church and is perhaps the first in a long line of Vienna's physician-intellectuals. He reformed the course of medical study at the university, in preparation for that amazing nineteenth-century Viennese medical renaissance which produced such greats as Skoda and Rokitansky, who pioneered in diagnostics; Semmelweis, who founded the practice of antisepsis; Hebra, in dermatology; Dittol, in urology; Nothnagel, who perfected the use of blood pressure and chest percusis in diagnosis; and Billroth, the great surgeon. Like these successors, especially Billroth (who was a great friend of Brahms), von Swieten was an amateur musician and held musical soirées in his home.

Proceed to the middle of the square to the **Joseph II monument**: Joseph would flip in his simple grave if he could see himself in this Roman finery astride a horse. This "simplest" of Habsburg emperors was probably the most complex: a spoiled child wanting to oppose his tough mummy at any cost, even destroying the rights of the aristocracy; or an enlightened monarch, the first and last in Austrian history? Take your pick: historians put him in both camps, and in places in between as well.

Facing the Augustinerstrasse from the statue, the **Winter Riding School Wing of the Hofburg** is on your left. This was built in 1735 by Joseph Emanuel Fischer von Erlach at the bequest of Charles VI. It put the crowning touch to the Josefsplatz and, indeed, made it a square. Inside is the pure white performing hall with its colossal chandeliers, the one spot of color being the portrait of Charles VI on one of the walls. This was the first indoor performing hall for the horses: before that they had performed in the open in the warmer weather. Their morning workout is still an easy and more intimate way to experience this four-centuries-old institution, and you can see the horses training their *Caprioles* and *Levades* in imitation of sixteenth- and seventeenth-century battlefield techniques—the last riding school in the world to practice the classic haute école. On the entryway to the Riding School is a memorial to General Patton, who, as was briefly noted earlier, was responsible for saving the horses from falling into Russian hands at the end of World War II. During the war, the Gauleiter of Vienna ordered the horses shipped to Czechoslovakia, for safety's sake. At the close of the war, the horses were trapped by the advancing Russian forces. Patton, as usual, pushing ahead without orders and completely beyond his authority, decided to move into unoccupied territory to the north and rescue the horses. Which he did. One of those footnotes to history that play a major role in one city's mythology: Patton, that unswerving destroyer of Huns, is all but eulogized for his love of horses. Some would agree that Patton was a better equestrian than general.

To the right in the square (still facing the Augustinerstrasse) is **St. Augustine's Church**, the former court parish church and one of Vienna's loveliest. A Gothic structure, the church suffered the usual renovations in all subsequent architectural styles. And as with other churches near the Hofburg, this one had its baroque interior stripped away in the late eighteenth century and was re-Gothicized. Lovely interior hall and naves: spare, clean lines that force your neck to crane and your eyes to go upward. The Habsburg hearts are stored here in a niche in the Loretto Chapel (guided tours available). There are fifty-four urns—not many for a family that ruled a large part of the world for so many centuries. These hearts include those of nine emperors, eight empresses, two kings, and assorted archdukes and archduchesses. The last heart buried here was that of Archduke Franz Karl, father of Franz Joseph, in 1878. Also in this heart crypt lies that of the duke of Reichstadt, Napoleon's son. For a century his body lay in the Capuchin crypt along with other Habsburgs, until Hitler had it shipped to France as a conciliatory gesture during World War II, where it now lies next to his father's in the Invalides. Hitler forgot, however, to include the heart in the deal.

Just to the right of the entrance of the church is a masterpiece of sculptural work by Canova from 1804: the tomb of Marie Christine, the favorite daughter of Maria Theresa.

Virtue is depicted walking toward the trompe l'oeil grave gate of this pyramid, accompanied by two maidens. When Napoleon occupied Vienna in 1809, he called this tomb "the greatest work of art in Vienna." Thank heavens it was built-in; Napoleon, like the Nazi conquerors of our century, was known to be a great "collector" of art.

Across the Augustinerstrasse at **Josefplatz 5 and 6** are, respectively, the **Pallavicini Palace** and the **Palffy Palace**. The former has had a long and checkered career over its four centuries of life. Symbolic of its fall from aristocratic grace was the fact that it was used as the scene of Orson Welles's character's apartment in the film version of Graham Greene's *The Third Man*, one of the best books—fact or fiction—about the occupation years in Vienna. From the fall of the Axis powers in 1945 to October 25, 1955, when the last of the Soviet troops pulled out, Vienna was occupied by the four Allied powers. Each had its section of dominance in the city, and they shared sovereignty over the First District. These were the "four men in a jeep" years, as the Viennese still refer to them, when an orange was the price of a woman and St. Stephen's and the Opera both lay in ruins. That this was less than two generations ago is a difficult thing to remember in modern, prosperous Vienna.

The Palffy Palace next door has had an equally long history. It began life in the fourteenth century as the first crown chancellery and over the course of centuries belonged to more than one noble family. The current palace was built in the sixteenth century and came into the possession of the powerful Palffy clan a century later. Mozart performed here for private concerts, and the palace is now used for cultural exchanges (readings, chamber concerts, etc.).

Turn right out of the Josefsplatz and continue down the Augustinerstrasse toward the Opera. You will be passing along the length of St. Augustine's Church to the right. To the left, you pass through the intersections first of Dorotheergasse, and then of the **Lobkowitzplatz**, scene in 1401 of the beheading of one of Vienna's first mayors—he had chosen the wrong side in a revolt against the Habsburgs. The square takes its name from the **Lobkowitz Palace** at **number 2**, home of the Austrian Theater Museum. This palace existed in a smaller version before the second Turkish siege, and afterward Fischer von Erlach did some expansion and monumentalizing work on it for its owners, the Dietrichsteins. By 1735 the palace had passed into the hands of Prince Lobkowitz, a patron of the arts, and in particular of Beethoven, whose Third Symphony premiered here in 1803.

Just past the Lobkowitzplatz intersection, we come to the **Albertina** on the right at **Augustinerstrasse 1**. This eighteenth-century palace became the home of Marie Christine (whose tomb we just saw in St. Augustine's Church) and of her husband, Archduke Albert of Sachsen-Teschen. It was here that this art-collecting archduke gathered his collection of graphic works from all over the world, using, for the most part, the enormous dowry that Marie Christine brought with her. Collected here are forty thousand drawings and more than one million engravings from the fourteenth century and on. This is one of the greatest graphic art collections in the world, and Dürer's work (especially the *Praying Hands*) forms a core of the collection. Archduke Karl, the victor of Aspern, was also a collector, in between battles, and he carried on with Albert's collection after the latter's death in 1822. Also in this old palace is the Albertina Film Museum. You can join for a nominal yearly membership fee, which entitles you to purchase inexpensive tickets to showings of retrospective programs by the world's greatest practitioners of a quite different art form, the movies.

Continue along Augustinerstrasse to a ramp that leads you up off street level at the intersection of Augustinerstrasse and Hanuschgasse. Following this ramp, you

*The Burggarten with the spire of
St. Augustine's Church*

mount another one of the remaining city bastions, the **Augustinerbastei**. Atop these fortifications is a statue of Archduke Albert, son of Archduke Karl of Aspern fame. Albert was also a military man, and this statue depicts him as the victor of the 1866 Battle of Custozza. This is a bit of polemic fluff, actually, because that same year witnessed the sacking of the Austrians at Sadowa by the Prussian military machine and the beginning of the end of Austrian pretensions in Western Europe. Bismarck's Germany, for better or worse, became the centralizing influence thereafter of the emerging German nation. Austria was on the downslide after this: The Hungarians forced the *Ausgleich* on Vienna and became co-partners in the realm; the nationalities in the Balkans—where Austria stretched its imperial muscles now—proved a headache for the Habsburgs and the world, as it was the question of the suppressed Balkan nationalities that led to the outbreak of World War I and continues to plague Europe even at the close of the twentieth century.

From our perch on the bastion, with our back to the statue of Albert, we can look to the right over the greenery of the **Burggarten**, one of the first two (along with the Volksgarten) urban renewal projects of the early nineteenth century, which presaged the Ring construction. Napoleon had the old Burg wall razed in 1810, when leaving the city that he had so easily occupied. This was an act of pure venom, as such walls were decorative only in the modern era of artillery warfare. Upon the cleared ground these two parks were erected.

Some other sights: To the left foreground are several stark pieces of modern statuary in the triangular square below. These pieces, created by the sculptor Alfred Hrdlicka, are a memorial to victims of war—in this case, specifically to the tenants of an apartment house that stood here until 1945. It was bombed by the Allies on the same night the Opera was gutted. The victims, trapped in the cellar, perished. Beyond this memorial, at **Philharmonikerstrasse 2–6**, is the **Hotel Sacher**, one of the world's grand old hotels. It was built in the 1870s on the site of the old Kärntnertor

The Hrdlicka war memorial

Theater, the original opera stage in Vienna. The hotel was built by the son of Metternich's pastry chef (and originator of the famed Sacher Torte), who had risen in the world because of his associations with near royalty. This pastry-cook-to-riches road is the Horatio Alger story of Vienna and can be seen also in the Demel shop, which originated from another royal pastry chef, Dehn, as well as with Herr Jahn, Maria Theresa's pastry chef, whom we encountered in Walk 2. The real power behind the Sacher was, however, the daughter-in-law of this pastry chef, Anna Sacher. This cigar-smoking woman turned the Sacher into the meeting place of aristocracy and royalty. The hotel's *Separées* were the scene of more than one royal affair with a "sweet young thing" from the ballet corps of the Opera next door.

And in the middle of our field of vision from atop this bastion, just in front of the Sacher, is the **Vienna State Opera**. With that institution (for it is far more than just a place where opera is performed), we shall begin our last tour.

Walk · 4

Fin de Siècle Vienna

Starting Point: Corner of Kärntnerstrasse and the Opernring

Public Transport: U1, U2, or U4 subways to Karlsplatz stop; T, D, J, or #1, #2 trams to the Opera stop

(Take this walk on Saturday to enjoy the Saturday-only flea market, where the walk ends.)

Franz Joseph was a cautious man. He had much to be cautious about. As a young boy he was in the royal train that hightailed it out of the city after the 1848 Revolution. That was also the year that saw his ascendancy to the throne. Things went downhill from there: the defeats in Italy and Germany confined the Habsburgs to an Austrian and Balkan role; Hungary achieved an equal status with the Austrian realm; nationalities in the far-flung Habsburg Empire were beginning to ferment for independence. Franz Joseph held on fast, despite all this to-do. He was an autocrat in the age of democracy; a ruler with a capital *R* in an age of cultural and social upheaval. He was a walking, breathing anachronism who served out his sixty-eight years on the throne as the voice of reaction in Europe. Personally, too, he walked softly as a result of the tragedies that had come and were to come to him: the

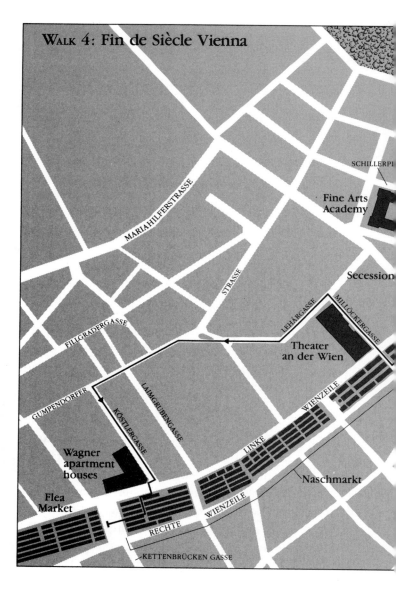

WALK 4: Fin de Siècle Vienna

deaths of brother, son, wife, and nephew—all of them violent and politically (perhaps in the case of Rudolf as well) motivated.

Yes, Franz Joseph had reason to be careful. An inadvertent remark made in 1868 to one of his adjutants would give him even more reason to retire to a shell of politesse in public, for it resulted in the deaths of two

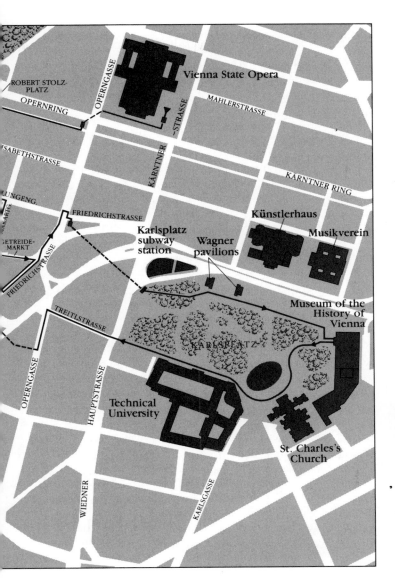

well-known Viennese architects, Eduard van der Null and August Sicard von Sicardsburg. These two men were the architects of the Vienna State Opera, in front of which we are now standing. The Opera was the first building in the gigantic urban renewal project of the *Gründerzeit* (last half of the nineteenth century) which is known as the Ringstrasse. Franz Joseph himself was responsible for this monumental project, the result of the razing of the old town walls and the subsequent building up on the spaces won by the destruction of the walls and of construction on the once-empty glacis. From the outset, however, this project was marred by tragedy and irony. As the boulevard of the Ringstrasse itself was built, its level was raised approximately a yard from original plans. The architects van der Nüll (who also did the Prince Eugene pedestal in the Heldenplatz) and von Sicardsburg could, however, not take such an adjustment into account in their building, which was already well under way. Thus the Ringstrasse side of the building was lower than the street (still observable today). The Viennese of course loved it; they called it the "sunken chest" and the "Königgrätz of architecture," after the defeat of the Austrian troops by the Prussians in 1866. Franz Joseph's remark was innocuous enough: he thought the façade *was* a bit low on the Ring side. But for van der Nüll, this was the crowning blow: he hanged himself a few weeks later. His fellow architect died shortly after, while recuperating from an operation. The Viennese say he died of grief.

So that most careful of men became even more circumspect after learning what his untoward remark had wrought: ever after, the emperor's stock phrase would be, *"Es war sehr schön, es hat mir sehr gefreut."* ("It was very nice, I enjoyed it very much.")

An ominous beginning for our last walk, but more ominous still for the course of development of the Ringstrasse itself and of the Habsburg monarchy. For this was a lavish project: the Opera alone cost six million gulden to build. This in a time when Vienna was suffering under the housing burden caused by a severalfold increase in population in less than a generation. By the turn of the century the population of Vienna stood at 2 million, more than at present. (At 1.7 million inhabitants, Vienna is one of the few Western cities to have *lost* population in the last century.) Thousands of these newcomers were roofless and depended on public charities, warming rooms, park benches, and the sewers for a place to sleep at night.

Thousands more lived in cramped quarters with other families. Thus the lavish building on the Ringstrasse, a feeble symbolic attempt at shoring up flagging Habsburg power, was a slap in the face to the poor and dispossessed. The results of this architectural extravaganza also left something to be desired. In their fervor to work in all the "neo" styles they could think of, at tying form to symbol rather than to function, these architects made some howlers. The Viennese had, of course, the apposite quip: "In the Parliament one could hear nothing, in the Rathaus one could see nothing, while in the Burgtheater one could neither see nor hear."

The theaters, in neo-Renaissance style to symbolize the arts, had problems, especially the Burgtheater. Its original auditorium was lyre-shaped to salute Greece as the home of drama. (Yet even in symbolism the architects were wrong, for it is the reed pipe *aulos*, not the lyre, that is connected with the beginnings of Greek drama.) All very well, but the acoustics were so bad that the auditorium had to be redesigned. The twin Museum of Fine Art and Natural History Museum make splendid backdrops for the square that they inhabit, but their interiors are meant for self-display rather than the display of art and science. The windowless façade of the neo-Gothic Rathaus might have been true to style, but it played hell on the eyes of weary bureaucrats in the age before electricity.

The State Opera is actually one of the better achievements (outside the façade-level question) of the Ring. (And, to be fair, the above criticism loses weight as the years pass. In the twentieth century, out of their historical context, the buildings of the Ring take on real stature and give Vienna that flavor of Europeanness that travelers here always remark on. Thus a new art maxim: Kitsch plus age equals beauty.) For me the biggest drawback is its situation: so snuggled into the crowd of buildings is the Opera that one cannot really get a full picture of the building, as one can with the Paris Opera, which tops the broad avenue of approach to it.

Some facts: This house, one of the largest in Europe,

holds 2,209 people; 567 of these are standing room sold at reduced prices of under two dollars. The daily budget for this state-subsidized luxury (under the Ministry of Education, which gives you a good idea of the importance of music and musical prestige to the Viennese) is more than half a million Austrian schillings, or about $50,000 a day, year-round, even during the almost four months when the Opera is closed in the summer. The singers and dancers of the State Opera are on the same salary and pension scheme as any other bureaucrat in the bureaucratically run city: artistic civil servants, if you will. The Vienna State Opera is accompanied by one of the finest symphonies in the world, the Vienna Philharmonic, and over the course of the years the directors of this house have been some of the finest conductors and composers around: Gustav Mahler, Felix Weingartner, Bruno Walter, Franz Schalk, Richard Strauss, Clemens Krauss, Wilhem Fürtwangler, Karl Böhm, Herbert von Karajan, and Lorin Maazel. Most if not all of these men have suffered from the form of Byzantine court intrigue in which Vienna specializes, even without a court. The most famous of these cases were Mahler, who left for the Met in New York in 1907 rather than have to battle the court chamberlain, Prince Montenuovo, any longer; and von Karajan, who left for Berlin after being hounded for his jet-set ways at the State Opera.

The Vienna Opera is as much a symbol to the Viennese as is the *Steffl*. It has been the subject of entire books; I will not attempt to compete with those. If you have the chance, however, go on a guided tour (originating on the Operngasse side) of the auditorium and behind stage to get the feeling of how a theater of this size and importance operates. Indeed, that the Opera functions so smoothly in this capital of *fortwursteln*, or muddling through, is a wonder. It is one of the few institutions that does. Once a year the house is used for nonoperatic entertainment: the Opera Ball, which is the culmination of the carnival season. More numbers: Fourteen thousand carnations are flown in for the occasion, six thousand guests clamor for tickets, and one thousand employees serve them. It is one of those anachronistic holdovers from another time that are almost more interesting in an anthropological way than they are as a participatory event.

The low point of the Opera was reached on March 12, 1945, when Allied bombers destroyed the roof and much of the interior of the house. The helpless Viennese could only stand and watch as the place went up in flames, for the Municipal Fire Department (where water was available) was fighting fires all over the city. It took more than ten years for the Opera to open again, shortly after the pullout of the last of the occupying forces. The opening program was Beethoven's *Fidelio*, and people were paying upward of four hundred dollars in poverty-stricken Vienna to be present at the performance, while thousands of others braved a drizzle outside to listen to the opera on loudspeakers. The last program to play in the old house before it was closed on June 30, 1944, was, ironically enough, Wagner's *Götterdammerung*.

As we stand at the corner of Opernring and Kärntnerstrasse, a few quick notes before we proceed: To your left as you face the Ring, you will see the Hotel Bristol at the corner of Kärntnerstrasse and Kärntner Ring. Along with the Sacher and Imperial, this is one of the grand hotels of Vienna, where five o'clock tea is still a tradition. Back down Kärntnerstrasse to your left at the corner of Mahlerstrasse is the new Café Sirk, built on the same location as its famous predecessor, a nineteenth-century meeting spot for the smart set.

So, with our backs to the Opera, we turn right and follow Opernring to Operngasse where there is an **underground passage**. Go down and cross diagonally under the Ring, taking the far right stairs or escalator up aboveground once again, in front of Aida's, one of a chain of fast-food cafés spread throughout Vienna and the provinces. No need, however, to get your dander up at yet another American import (though McDonald's does, unfortunately, exist in a dozen locations, which I refuse to divulge). In the case of Aida, it is Austrian ingenuity at work, and as fast-food cake goes, theirs is more than adequate. The quality, in fact, is not an issue with such *Konditorei*, as these pastry shops are called. At Aida's you can stand at the zinc bar and wolf down a Sacher Torte mit Schlag that may be every bit as good as that served at the Hotel Sacher (perhaps even fresher) but with none of the grace of the latter establishment.

One short comment about Viennese categories of coffee shops: There are three main types of establishments where one may indulge in sucrose and caffeine intake. In the first category come the *Konditorei* such as Aida (the famous Demel's on the Kohlmarkt is also labeled a *Konditorei* but is in a class by itself), which serve all types of coffee and cakes and pastries. There is usually a stand-up section where tipping is not obligatory, and a seating section, usually with uncomfortable furniture that looks as if it might have been imported from a bowling alley, where prices are a trifle higher than at the bar and tipping (10 percent) is expected.

A middle range of establishments also exists: the *Espressos*. Their name tells the story. These are not really specialty pastry shops like the *Konditorei*, though they will surely have some pastries as well as snacks, such as toasted cheese sandwiches. They will have a stand-up and seating section as well.

These *Espressos* and *Konditorei* are the perfect places for a quick cup of coffee at theater intermissions or for a cup of strong black coffee laced with brandy on a cold winter's morning.

And third, there are the more formal, proper cafés, concentrated mostly in the Inner City (although there are sprinklings in each of the outer districts as well). These are not for the quick cup of coffee or the fast snack. Prices are higher in these opulent old establishments, which are holdovers from a more leisurely way of life. Here a cup of coffee is meant to be dawdled over; the newspapers,

A typical Viennese Konditorei

both foreign and domestic, are intended to be pored over; the cheesy illustrated magazines to be happily thumbed through. At these old-time cafés, the waiter is always dressed in a tuxedo and serves your coffee on a tiny silver tray, along with a sparkling glass of water fresh from the Rax Alps south of the city. This water glass will be refilled periodically in the best of the real cafés, just to make you feel at home. The Viennese call this custom of refilling the water glass a cloudburst. You are not expected to order another cup of coffee or another pastry in order to retain your seat; nor should you expect a refill of the coffee.

The great cafés of Vienna (and we will visit two of them during the course of this walk) have chessboards, billiard tables, playing cards, and felt-covered card tables available for their customers. At one time, the best of the cafés were truly homes away from home for a multitude of writers, artists and intellectuals. Something on the order of the British men's club, these cafés were mailing addresses, libraries (complete with standard reference works), and debating societies all in one. Some still marginally retain this intellectual tradition, and there are cafés, for example, where the theater crowd hangs out or the writers congregate or the painters meet. But it is an uphill battle for these dinosaurs in the age of profit over quality.

Let's hope you have taken advantage of this discourse for a quick cup of coffee. From the corner of Operngasse and the Opernring, facing Aida's, you turn to the right, walking away from the Opera. The second store past the *Konditorei* is a stationery shop. From the display window, with its large sampling of personal cards and print styles, you can get an idea of the level of formality that still exists in this once-imperial city. The tradition of carrying one's card (not necessarily for business) is still very much alive here. In fact, new automats are sprinkled along the city streets where you can print your own calling card any time of the night or day—desktop publishing at its most unique.

A few buildings along you will pass Maxim's, not to be confused with the one in Paris of infinitely better quality. Upstairs in this same building, **Opernring 11**, is one of the city's better elite small hotels, indeed called the Opernring, where many of the guest stars of the Opera put up.

Continue to your left to Robert Stolz-Platz (hardly a square itself), which opens onto **Schillerplatz**, with the **Akademie der bildenden Kunst** (Fine Arts Academy) directly behind it. A few things quickly, however, before proceeding to the left. Across Opernring, to your right, you can see a statue of Goethe. He sits quite languidly on his bronze chair looking awfully self-satisfied, except when the occasional pigeon decides to roost on his head. And straight ahead, on our side of the Ringstrasse and across Robert Stolz-Platz just past the art shop on the corner, is the Burg Kino, one of the local movie houses that shows English-language films. You might want to check the coming attractions while in the neighborhood.

But for now, turn left on Robert Stolz-Platz and head across the Elisabethstrasse toward Schillerplatz. The house to your right at the corner of Elisabethstrasse and Schillerplatz (**Elisabethstrasse 16**) is where the Austrian composer Robert Stolz lived for forty years of his life. He died in 1975, occasioning some street-name changes. Continue on through the center of Schillerplatz past the statue of the poet and playwright Schiller. Look back from this point to the Goethe statue across the Ring, and you will see how at one time those two statues were intended to bind contiguous squares on either side of the Ringstrasse.

On either side of the Schiller statue, set back into the greenery of the square, are statues of two Austrian poets of the Biedermeier or *Vormärz* era: Lenau and Grün. Both were aristocrats using pen names. Lenau was a naturalist, and Anastasius Grün (to the right) criticized the Metternich system in subtle political lyrics.

From the Schiller statue, proceed across the square to the entrance of the **Fine Arts Academy** at **Schillerplatz 3**. This building was part of the Ringstrasse program, built between 1872 and 1876 by the Danish architect Theophil Hansen. He was a very busy man. From 1850 through the building of the academy, he was responsible for the Army History Museum (1850); the Musikverein (1868), which we will view later in this tour; the Parliament (1873–1883); the Vienna Stock Exchange, or Börse (1874); as well as the police headquarters building and a fine apartment house that was destroyed in World War II.

The Hellenic pastiches that you see in this building (and that are much more prevalent in the Parliament) are the result of Hansen's studies in Greece. But on the whole this building was designed in the Italianate Renaissance style, of which the architect was particularly fond.

Hansen was one of the favorite architects of no less scrupulous a judge of the art than Adolf Hitler. Hitler was filled with high hopes and respect for the architecture of the place when he entered the doors of the Fine Arts Academy in the fall of 1907 at the age of eighteen to sit for the entrance exam. A few hours later he was straggling down these steps in a daze. He had failed to gain admission. He would fail the next year as well. The opinion of the judging commission was final: "Too few heads." Hitler, while he had a flair for architectural renderings, had not the slightest talent for rendering the human form. I'll leave the implications of that to the psychologists.

The building itself, aside from its rather shocking pink terra-cotta façade, is nothing spectacular in this city of monumental architecture. But the academy *was* (its influence has since faded) more than just a building. It was a symbol of acceptance into the Viennese art world. Without an academy degree, the painter in Vienna at the turn of the century was a fish out of water. Hence Hitler's disappointment at rejection.

All signs from Hitler's test drawings—they still exist, by the way, and show a more than adequate talent for line and detail, given the pressures of time and theme imposed on the applicants—pointed toward an architectural career for this youngster from the provinces. He was advised to follow such a course by the director of the academy, to whom he applied for advice; and he duly applied to the architecture school in the academy. It fell to Otto Wagner, then director of that school, to reject the application out of hand. Hitler did not have the requisite degree, a *Matura* (high school degree), to be considered for admission.

So much for Hitler's formal art training. The world may have been saved a lot of bother had he been admitted to the academy. Ironically, the painter Egon Schiele, just Hitler's age, was desperately trying that fall of 1907 to *get out* of this academy that Hitler wanted so desperately to enter. Schiele had had enough of the conservative training the school offered. He went on to become one of the new generation of Viennese painters in the years just before and during World War I who broke away from nineteenth-century painterly ideals. He shocked the Viennese with the extreme eroticism of his nubile and angularly sketched nudes. Schiele would make an expressionist breakthrough in Vienna during the next years, years in which Hitler sank to the lowest depths of poverty, for a time living the life of a *clochard*, sleeping on park benches and begging his food from cloisters. Later Hitler would earn a tenuous living painting sentimental scenes of Vienna sold to Jewish frame dealers for cheap fillers to help advertise their frames. The six years Hitler spent in Vienna changed not only his life but also the course of world history. Not only did he suffer the hard knocks of rejection here, but he also learned from the German nationalism and anti-Semitism that was in the fin de siècle Viennese air, as promoted by such diverse personalities as the charismatic mayor Karl Lueger, the German nationalist Schönerer, and the crank defrocked monk with his bizarre race theories, Adolf Josef Lanz, alias Lanz von Liebenfels.

The Fine Arts Academy and its nearby exhibition hall, the Künstlerhaus, would reflect the battle between conservative, academic painters and the new school of painters in Vienna known as the Secessionists. All over fin de siècle Europe a revolution was happening in art: in France, Belgium, Great Britain, and Germany. Known as art nouveau elsewhere, this new, flowing, sensual style was known as *Jugendstil* in German-speaking lands. Its early Viennese proponents were men such as the painters Gustav Klimt and Kolo Moser and the architects Otto Wagner, Josef Hoffmann, and Olbrich.

Fin de siècle Vienna is the emphasis of this walk. Though the effects of that age are visible throughout the city, nowhere else in Vienna are they so concentrated as in this southwest section. The French gave us the phrase fin de siècle. It is at once a product of Gallic love of drama and of pessimism. But the more prosaic, neutral German *Jahrhundertswende* (turn of the century) would be closer to describing events in Vienna 1900. Fin de siècle is too decadent in connotation, too much a statement of the end of the road rather than of the possibility of new beginnings in the new century. And in Vienna 1900 both of these impulses were at work. There was the literal decadence of the moribund Habsburg state, on its last legs. But countering this political stagnation was a cultural renaissance unparalleled in the modern world. It would not be stretching the facts to say that in another hundred years, given the proper Burckhardt to chronicle it, this Viennese renaissance may well equal the Italian Renaissance in depth and influence on later generations.

Both sides of Vienna 1900 still affect the world we live in. While men such as Hitler, Trotsky, and Tito took their political lessons from the incompetent Habsburgs, there were others, such as Freud, Mahler, Schoenberg, Wittgenstein, von Hofmannsthal, Schnitzler, Otto Wagner, Adolf Loos, Karl Kraus, Martin Buber, Theodor Herzl, Egon Schiele, Oskar Kokoschka, and Gustav Klimt, who have changed forever the manner in which we can perceive the world.

As the historian Edward Crankshaw puts it, these men and women in this city at this time created the "modern sensibility" in music, thought, painting, and letters. It is impossible for us even to think in pre-Freudian framework.

Yet at the same time, no city was so decisive in the development of a tyrant as Vienna was for the young Hitler, who lived here from 1907 to 1913 as a struggling "artist." (Trotsky lived in Vienna during the same period, as did Tito from 1910 to 1913.) A city and an age that could produce both a Freud and a Hitler were chameleon ones.

There is always something romantic about self-proclaimed artistic rebels and the Secessionists were no exception. Klimt scandalized bourgeois Vienna in his flowing robes and paternal beard, painting canvases alive with sensuality unrelieved by historic or mythic content. Wagner, a fusty old professor, writing daily letters to his long-dead wife when the Secessionist movement embraced him, outraged the Viennese with his functional building styles, which put ornament second to practical considerations of utility. For the Viennese who found neoclassicism the last word in architectural good taste,

Wagner's dictum that "form follows function" sounded like the basest form of jabberwocky.

The composer Gustav Mahler led the musical arm of the Secession and was as reviled in the press as his painterly and literary opposites were. Though Mahler was, as we have seen, director of the prestigious Vienna State Opera (Hof Oper, or Court Opera in his day) and conductor of the world-renowned Philharmonic, still none of his symphonies premiered in Vienna during his lifetime.

"The line in love with itself" is perhaps the best description ever given to *Jugendstil* art. You will be meeting up with quite a lot of it, both architectural and acrylic, in the course of this walk.

But first, there is some of that "staid, conservative" art that the Secessionists were revolting against to be seen inside the Fine Arts Academy in the Painting Gallery (open Tuesday, Thursday, and Friday from 10:00 A.M. to 2:00 P.M.; Wednesday from 10:00 A.M. to 1:00 P.M. and from 3:00 to 6:00 P.M.; and Saturday and Sunday from 9:00 A.M. to 1:00 P.M.). With the passing years, *Jugendstil* itself looks fairly staid and conservative. (The best gallery for *Jugendstil* is to be found in the Oberes Belvedere in the Fourth District.) Here there are paintings by such masters as Bosch, Veronese, Titian, Botticelli, Lucas Cranach the Elder, Guardi, Rubens, and Rembrandt. Though most guidebooks, in their interminable star wars, rate this at the bottom of the galaxy, you should still be sure to see at least Bosch's amazing, agonizing polyptych *The Last Judgment*, which seems somehow to anticipate the Holocaust.

Just inside the building, before coming to the Gallery, you will pass through the *Aula*, or main covered court. The ceiling here was painted by Anselm Feuerbach, nephew of the German materialist philosopher Ludwig Feuerbach. (You will find there are wheels within wheels in Central European history and especially in Vienna, akin to the chronicles of some remote Alpine valley where everyone is related to everyone else.) The ceiling painting depicts *The Fall of the Titans*, a rather ironic theme in light of the subsequent fall of the house of Habsburg, which had commissioned the work. Feuerbach worked primarily in Italy, but was a professor here when the academy first opened.

After a visit inside and returning to the entrance facing Schillerplatz, you turn to the right to continue the tour. Proceed to the corner of Makartgasse and turn right into this street, following now along the length of the academy.

Makartgasse was named after Hans Makart, the personification of all the sham artistry of the Künstlerhaus that the Secessionists wanted to leave behind. Handsome Hans was the most beloved painter in late–nineteenth century Vienna. He painted huge and hugely flawed canvases designed on the Rubens model to fit into large drawing rooms and reception halls. Makart depicted great moments in Habsburg history in these canvas murals and became a favorite of society and the court alike. Supplied with a studio just behind the Karlskirche by no one less than Kaiser Franz Joseph himself, Makart became a trendsetter not only painting famous society women into his huge canvases (it became a game in Vienna to guess which nude body belonged to which society belle), but also advising these women on their toilette. He popularized everything from large, flowing hats to bouquets of dried flowers named after him. He was the Johann Strauss of acrylics, staging festive parades around the Ringstrasse for the twenty-fifth wedding anniversary of Franz Joseph and Elisabeth in 1879 and attracting a crowd of thirty-four thousand to view his *Charles V's Entry in Antwerp*. (Klimt would later attract as large a crowd of jeering, dumbfounded Viennese to see his university pictures, painted for the *Aula* of the new university. So great was the scandal that resulted from these series of pictures, on themes such as *Medicine* and *Jurisprudence* in which less-than-noble man was depicted, that Klimt withdrew his paintings, returned the commission, and vowed that it

The Secession

was a mistake to paint for the public; to please oneself was most important.)

Makart was a handsome, charming dandy with a mediocre talent. And the young Hitler, among others, idolized him. Anselm Feuerbach called Makart a tailor who painted clothes into which no one could fit.

Whatever his talents, Makart was the center of Vienna's pretentious art world in the late nineteenth century—his paintings are still to be seen on display at the Museum of Fine Art on the Ring. Every day at four his studio was opened to the public, transforming itself from workshop to salon. It was the destination of every important visitor to the city, of all society. The young Gustav Klimt, later to become an enfant terrible, was even among Makart's admirers, and once sneaked into the painter's studio during siesta time to catch a glimpse of the latest work-in-progress.

Makart the womanizer lost prestige after marrying a ballet dancer. Ballet dancers were suitable for dalliances in those days, but not for marriage. He died at forty-four, the victim of a dandy's disease: syphilis.

273

Following Makartgasse you can see directly ahead of you atop a cuboid building a strange bronze ball of laurel leaves—actually an open filigree leaf pattern as a cupola to a geometric box of a building beneath. There are three thousand bronze laurel leaves in the cupola and seven hundred berries as big as a lightweight's fist. This building is the **Secession**, the exhibition hall of the Secessionists built by Olbrich in 1898. It was an accident that this building was located so close to the Fine Arts Academy. But it was no accident that its design was calculated to lend the highest possible contrast to the traditionalists as expressed in their school, the academy, and in their exhibition hall, the Künstlerhaus.

To be fair to those faceless legions of bourgeois Viennese about whom the Secessionists caviled so heartily, it was they at first who supported the Secessionists. At the Secessionists' first showing in 1898, fifty-seven thousand curious Viennese flocked to the temporary exhibition rooms near the Parkring and bought 218 of the exhibited works. (Among the exhibitors were not only Viennese but also artists from abroad such as Whistler and artisans of the Glasgow School of Charles Rennie Mackintosh, which had so influenced *Jugendstil*.) These purchases enabled the Secessionists to build their own exhibition hall on land donated by the city of Vienna, another strange example of the schizoid nature of this city, which beckons with one hand and reprimands with the other.

But with the erection of the Secession, the Viennese were no longer so sure they thought Secessionists playful and amusing rebels. The Viennese are ever ready with a nickname and alternately dubbed this building the "Mahdi's Tomb," because of its severe cubic lines, and the "Gilded Cabbage," because of its cupola.

From the laying of the first stone onward the Viennese, ever anxious for a *Hetz*, or public scandal, turned their wrath on this affront to their sensibilities. Hermann Bahr, a literary exponent of *Jugendstil* artists, describes the building site in the summer of 1898:

You can see a crowd of people standing around the new building. On their way to work . . . they stare, they interrogate each other, they discuss the "thing." They think it is strange, they have never seen anything of the kind, they don't like it, it repels them. Filled with serious reflections, they pass on their way, and then turn around yet again, cast another look backward, do not want to depart, hesitate to hurry off about their business. And this goes on the whole day!

To viewers of the late twentieth century, accustomed as we are to box architecture, the lines of this building are no longer shocking. But at the time, the Secession was revolutionary indeed. The outside was as simple and unadorned as possible—no unnecessary frills, a restraint to be expected from a man who had worked in Otto Wagner's studio for five years. And inside, horror of horrors! There were no magnificent murals and gilding and no massive marble staircases or columns, as one would expect from a gallery. Instead, Olbrich created a building in which to display art, not which displays itself. Bare walls, movable panels, natural lighting from skylights—all these were innovations at the turn of the century.

To arrive at the Secession you must continue along the short Makartgasse. About a hundred yards ahead you will come to the intersection with Getreidemarkt (Grain Market), with its hectic traffic pouring past you to disguise totally its medieval function. You turn left at Getreidemarkt and walk another thirty yards to the crosswalk and intersection with Friedrichstrasse. The Secession building stands just to your right at this point. Cross the pedestrian walk and go toward the **Secession** at **Friedrichstrasse 12**, past the statue of Marcus Aurelius in his chariot to the immediate right. This statue is a great example of Viennese mentality: it was put in this spot more than eighty years ago as a temporary solution for what to do with both the space and the statue. It will probably be standing here eighty years from now as well.

A detail of the Secession façade

In Viennese parlance, adverbs of time just do not mean the same thing they mean elsewhere. Thus, "temporary" really means "forever." At a shop, if you order something and are told that it will come "soon," forget it or at least do not hold your breath.

The Secession building has not withstood the years very well, as you will see for yourself by the chipped and unloved façade. The small bit of ornament Olbrich allowed himself—wreaths and scrollwork in gilding and owls at the corner—is no longer in very good condition. Over the door can still be read the motto of the Secessionists:

> Jeder Zeit sein Kunst
> Jeder Kunst sein Freiheit.
>
> To every age its art
> To every art its freedom.

The building, in spite of its sad condition, does still engender respect: its near whiteness in contrast to the dull gray of the buildings around it can give you a rough idea of how it must have stood out in its day.

The Secession is still the home of private exhibitions, which change frequently. Placards announcing the current exhibition are displayed at the entrance.

From this point on the steps of the Secession and facing out to Friedrichstrasse, you can see the small forest of wooden huts to the right on Wienzeile that constitute Vienna's several-blocks-long outdoor market, the Naschmarkt.

We will give more than a cursory view to that market later in this tour, but for now, turn left and go back up Friedrichstrasse, retracing your steps and crossing the Getreidemarkt intersection. Continue along Friedrichstrasse for another hundred yards to the intersection with Nibelungengasse, which you then cross. On the **corner of Nibelungengasse and Operngasse**, to your left, is the pharmacy **"Zum heiligen Geist,"** "At the Sign of the Holy Ghost." Take a look at the elegantly appointed interior of this *Apotheke*: fine ceiling moldings and shining ceramic canisters holding herbs that line an eye-level shelf. Traditionally, since the time of Maria Theresa, such pharmacies have assumed this very elegant appearance, an offshoot of their pseudo-court status—they have been protected by law for two centuries against encroachment of competition into their "sales territory." This is a very broad prohibition against the founding of a new *Apotheke*, creating in effect a monopoly situation, for the *Apotheken* themselves determine if a new pharmacy is needed or not.

To your right you will be facing **Operngasse** once again, and across the street from here is the **Café Museum**, one of those old-time cafés I promised you we would encounter. The building sits on a corner, with good light exposure through its banks of windows on both the Operngasse and Friedrichstrasse sides. The very location of cafés such as this one is now working against them, however. With the relaxation of incorporation and interest laws in 1979, banks have begun sprouting up all over the city like so many mushrooms. Corner locations are their favorite spots, and they have made large inroads in the last few years into café territory, buying up these marginally profitable establishments and ripping out lovely old interiors to make way for tellers' cages and other such paraphernalia of the banking trade. But the Viennese—not all of them at any rate—do not suffer fools gladly. Out in the Thirteenth District of Hietzing, the local citizenry banded together and forced the bank that had purchased the building housing the local café into a compromise: instead of closing down the café completely, it now inhabits the back of the bank and part of the first floor, proving to be a winning combination for both concerns.

The Café Museum is not of the faded-elegance type one comes to expect from the grand old cafés: this one underwent a face lift in the 1950s, which unfortunately destroyed the interior Adolf Loos had designed in 1899. But by now, even 1950s' kitsch begins to look good.

Ever since the Turks left behind bags of the strange brown beans after their unsuccessful siege of 1683, the Viennese have been coffee-happy. There are as many ways to brew the drink as there are drinkers of it—one writer has calculated fourteen different ways to drink coffee. The basic three ways to order coffee are: *Mokka*, which refers to the mocha bean, a dark and strong brew akin to but far more pungent than plain black coffee; *Brauner*, coffee with a little milk; and *Melange*, which is half coffee and half milk served frothy in large cups. When ordering either a *Mokka* or *Brauner*, you should ask for either a *kleine* (small) or a *grosse* (large).

The Café Museum is spacious and comfortable and has a wide supply of periodicals and English-language newspapers, such as the *Observer* and *International Herald Tribune*.

From the Café Museum we descend once again into the **subway pedestrian underground** by the stairs directly in front of the café doors. We turn sharply to the

The Wagner Stadtbahn pavilion on Karlsplatz

left at the bottom of these stairs and follow the subway signs as well as the Wiedner Hauptstrasse sign along a football-field-long corridor (which should, by the way, give you some idea of the enormity of this subway project). This corridor then opens onto a large subterranean hall, where you turn right, again following the signs for Wiedner Hauptstrasse. By this time you will be seeing daylight from out on Karlsplatz directly ahead. From the windows to your left, you can see the hustle and bustle of commuter traffic on the subway platforms below. This is the U4 line, which travels between the suburbs of Hütteldorf in the southwest and Heiligenstadt in the north. Work on this system (there are at present five lines in operation: the U2 and U1 also stop at Karlsplatz, but on different levels) took place only in the last two decades, and the Inner City looked like a combat zone all through the 1970s and 1980s. Construction in Central Europe takes on a very different look from what we are accustomed to in other Western countries. Lots of manual pick-and-shovel work by southern laborers in tattered sports jackets. One feels training for such work as construction is at an absolute minimum. Heavy reliance on manual labor indicates how the Viennese in general feel about the technological age: distrustful.

Continue on out to **Karlsplatz**. Once aboveground, you take the wide stone steps to your immediate left up to street level out of the bowl of Karlsplatz. Proceed from here then another hundred yards toward the two elegant little white buildings trimmed in green and gilding, which sit on a promontory over the Karlsplatz. These are the old station buildings or **pavilions of Otto Wagner's Stadtbahn**, the metropolitan railway built in 1898. The modern subway system uses many of the lines laid down by Wagner for this Stadtbahn, and some of the old red cars of this system are still in use around the Gürtel. It was while constructing the Stadtbahn that Wagner controlled the River Wien and covered it over along the Wienzeile where the Naschmarkt is now located. Formerly that market was in the Karlsplatz.

Wagner became something of an engineering and architectural legend: he was responsible for the total planning of this extensive Stadtbahn system and finished these labors in the amazingly short time of seven years.

There is now a small café housed in the old station house, as well as a small museum with exhibitions that usually detail some aspect of turn-of-the-century Viennese life. The building technique employed with these stations was an interesting one for its day, using corrugated copper roofing (which happily corrodes to such a pretty shade of green) to contrast the curving lines of *Jugendstil* art transformed into architecture. Notice the rosette pattern on the cast-iron railings around the top of the building. These are repeated in railings used on *K und K* railways as far afield as Dubrovnik, in Croatia, and are still to be seen throughout other lands that were once part of the Habsburg Empire. These Karlsplatz stations formed the model for other stations of the Stadtbahn lines and missed demolition only by a hairbreadth. They won a last-minute reprieve in the 1970s and were refurbished instead to their current mint condition. It was simply a happy coincidence that artistic fashion and the city fathers had begun to take an interest in times other than baroque and Biedermeier.

Go to the little square between the pavilions for a good look at Karlsplatz, which Otto Wagner once lamented could never be more than an "area." Too large really to be called a square and too small to be termed a park, the Karlsplatz has stumped city planners since its development over a hundred years ago. Turn your back to the pavilions and you can see the fanciful, baroque Karlskirche (St. Charles's Church) with its twin marble columns and copper dome greening with oxidation. In the pond just in front of the church is a Henry Moore sculpture, and to the right of Karlskirche is the Technische Hochschule (Technical University) at Karlsplatz 13. To the right of this long university building is an outdoor café in a parklike setting, where kids play soccer in the fine weather and throw snowballs in winter.

We'll be visiting those sights in a bit, but for now turn around so that you face out onto the busy Friedrichstrasse. Looking across the road, you will be confronted with a massive wall of buildings à la Ringstrasse style, two of which I would like you to note. At **Friedrichstrasse 5**, a bit to your right, is the **Künstlerhaus**. You will recognize this light yellow building (and its film and theater appendages to either side) because it usually has large banners hanging from the front proclaiming its current exhibition. This was the official exhibition hall of the academy artists, and though architecturally it is not terribly noteworthy, historically it is.

The word *Künstlerhaus* at the turn of the century was synonymous with conservative art. Today it is less easy to make such sweeping generalizations. It is interesting to note, however, how quickly the nineteenth-century art movements came in and out of style: the Künstlerhaus itself was completed only in 1868. Three decades later the style it promoted was already considered old hat. Secession style suffered the same fate, only more quickly.

Already in the early 1900s, Adolf Loos was blasting the tyranny of this "self-indulgent" style.

To the right of the Künstlerhaus is the **Musikverein**, the concert house of Vienna's Society of the Friends of Music. It is here that the traditional Sunday morning concerts of the Vienna Philharmonic are held. The musicians of that symphony orchestra traditionally had no other time for concerts, employed as they were with opera performances. These Sunday morning performances started as a way to augment their meager incomes. Even today very few get rich playing music in Vienna. There are currently about 800 professional musicians in the city (not counting the more than 1,000 singer hopefuls looking for a position), and 150 of these are Philharmonic members, paid by the state, as are the singers and performers at other state-run theaters. The Sunday-morning subscription concerts have been held at the Musikverein since 1870. The subscription holders fill the hall, and some have had their yearly tickets for more than half a century. Generally, the only way for one of these subscriptions to open up is for the holder to die. (They cannot be passed down through the family.)

The Musikverein was built by that busy-as-a-beaver architect Theophil Hansen, who built the Fine Arts Academy and the Parliament. This building is from 1867 to 1869, and once again Hansen dipped his revivalist hand into his bag of tricks and came up with a Renaissance building. The interior here is really quite pleasing, however, especially the main hall, where the Philharmonic often performs.

Compare these two buildings with Wagner's Stadtbahn stations, however, and with Olbrich's Secession across Karlsplatz and you will be able to see the huge difference inherent in the styles. Though separated by less than a generation, these buildings are worlds apart stylistically and philosophically. The Musikverein and the Künstlerhaus are products of Ringstrasse Vienna, of the pomp and masquerade of the last half of the nineteenth century. Loos was no friend of historicism, just as he was a critic of Secession style. He criticized historicism especially as it was applied to the Ringstrasse project, likening it to a Potemkin city. (Loos was referring to the papier-mâché town that Count Potemkin had constructed to convince Catherine the Great as she passed by in her carriage that this area of the Ukraine was thriving.) And Bahr, the literary spokesman of *Jugendstil*, once said: "When one crosses the Ring, one gets the feeling that one has suddenly stumbled into the middle of a carnival. Everything is masked. Everything is disguised."

Jugendstil art and architecture reacted to that overornamentation and put the scalpel to the disguised façades of Vienna.

So, back to our tour of Karlsplatz. Before heading for Karlskirche, however, we'll make a short detour to the **Historisches Museum der Stadt Wien** (Museum of the History of Vienna). Go out of the little square between the pavilions, down the steps, and turn immediately to the left, following the little asphalt path through Karlsplatz to the museum building to the far left of Karlskirche (**Karlsplatz 8**; open daily except Monday, 9:00 A.M. to 12:15 P.M. and 1:00 P.M. to 4:30 P.M.). About halfway to the museum from the pavilions you will pass a statue to the German composer Johannes Brahms on your right. Brahms was one of that long list of foreign composers who settled in Vienna. Gruff and crusty as an old miner, he had beneath this exterior the traditional heart of gold. A favorite apocryphal story tells of his usual statement upon leaving any gathering: "If there is anyone here I have not insulted, I apologize."

But Brahms could also be terribly human. Hidden in the deep pockets of that cloak which is sculpted as draped about his legs were handfuls of sweets he would distribute to urchins during his walks about Vienna. Through the intercessions of the powerful Viennese music critic Eduard Hanslick, Brahms became to the late–nineteenth century world the great upholder of classicism, the "foe" of Wagner and "new" music. But Brahms himself was

Karlskirche with a Henry Moore sculpture in front

too simple a soul to go for such self-selling. It is strange, looking at the figure of this short, burly German-cum-Viennese, to realize that he was the creator of all the passion and depth of the First Symphony and of the romantic longings to be heard in the piano concerti. Critics—other than Hanslick—of his day said his music would not last. So much for critics.

So, on we go to the Museum of the History of Vienna. Actually, this book could well have started with a visit to this museum; but perhaps it is just as well to have waited. Now the insides of this living "history book" will have some real meaning to you. As with all the municipally operated (as opposed to federal) museums, this one has a nominal charge. There is always some exhibition going on in the lower rooms and the regular exhibitions are to be seen all the time. Here are Roman gravestones, the missing stained-glass windows from St. Stephen's, electric-train-sized models of Vienna in the Middle Ages and in the nineteenth century, weaponry, heraldic devices, porcelain, paintings—even two mock-up rooms, one of Grillparzer's and one of Loos's. In short, all the panoply of more than two thousand years of Viennese history under one roof. If you have made it through this book to this point, you owe it to yourself to visit this museum and see how all the component parts of Vienna knit together in a *civitas*.

To the right of the museum—you need no address for this green-domed giant—is **Karlskirche**, or St. Charles's Church, which gives its name to this square, as well—Karlsplatz. One immediately assumes that both church and square were named after Charles VI, the Holy Roman Emperor so building-minded at the turn of the eighteenth century. It was he who, having lost the Spanish inheritance in the War of the Spanish Succession, set about to right this "most grievous" wrong by turning Vienna into even more of an imperial Roman capital than it already was, by commissioning Fischer von Erlach to extend the Hofburg in the grand imperial style. His was an ever-shrinking empire—the result of badly planned wars and neglect of foreign policy to the life of a sumptuous court. The Habsburg domains were thus in desperate straits by the time that his daughter, Maria Theresa, came to the throne. Charles's great pastimes were music and the hunt. He paid his court musicians more than a colonel in the imperial army. He had musical chairs built for his court that played a flute solo when sat upon. It was as if, with the loss of the Spanish domain, the court of Charles VI steeped itself ever further in Spanish court etiquette. Though not quite as bad as his father Leopold and *his* court, where all manner of prestige mattered—from how many times a courtier must bow when leaving his imperial majesty to how many steps forward the emperor would make greeting guests of different ranks—still, Charles had his favorite quirks. It is said that on his deathbed he arose with a start upon seeing that only four candles had been lit instead of the six due to an emperor—he pointed this out to his startled physicians. Father Leopold of course one-upped him here also: when being examined by his physicians it is said that he chided them with *"Eheu! hoc est nostrum membrum imperiale sacrum-caesareum!"* ("Careful! That is our imperial sacred Caesarian member!")

At any rate, the name of the church and the square actually come from St. Charles Borromeo, a sixteenth-century bishop of Milan canonized for his service to the people of Milan during a plague epidemic. But the confusion was deliberate: part of the gimmick of dedicating this church to St. Charles was this name similarity. In 1713 Vienna was suffering from its seventh plague epidemic in a century. Emperor Charles VI promised to dedicate a church to his name saint if he would intercede in this latest visitation of the plague. This seems to have worked, or the plague simply wore itself out and went away, for building was started on the Karlskirche three years later.

For Fischer von Erlach the senior, who was commissioned for this project, the Karlskirche provided one of the great projects of his life, the one for which he is best remembered by the rest of the world. The site chosen for this magnificent church was at that time outside of the city walls, on a small hill on the banks of the river Wien. In those days, long before the Ringstrasse project, the church faced the Hofburg, and it was clearly visible from the Herrengasse and Augustinerstrasse. So we get the idea: this was to be an imperial adjunct for which there was no room within the walls. The church has always served the twofold function of votive church and monument of imperial greatness. This double function can be seen immediately in the twin columns that front the church. Spun out on these columns like an anachronistic filmstrip are

scenes from the life and miraculous times of Charles Borromeo. (His "intercession" in Vienna's plague is reserved
for a more prominent spot on the tympanum of the
porch.) But at the same time these double columns are
reproductions of Trajan's column in Rome—signs of imperial power as well as symbols of the Pillars of Hercules,
which would suggest the Habsburgs' right to the Spanish
dominions that Charles VI had been forced to renounce.
The columns are out of place with the high baroque of
the total church—but the symbolic function of the church
had to be appeased. Borromeo himself is shown in statuary at the apex of the pediment over the entrance, and
his apotheosis is represented in the soaring dome—for
which three hundred oak trees were felled. No less a
personage than the philosopher Leibniz detailed the complex symbolic program that is embodied in this church.
Actually the church did have a historical forerunner in
the Temple of Jerusalem, which mannerist prints and
paintings of an earlier time represented as a domed building with porch flanked by two huge columns. But for all
the symbolic hoopla contingent upon its building, the
Karlskirche (ultimately finished by the younger Erlach)
has, as the architectural wallahs say, harmony. The
dome, side towers, and columns all tie together; their
dimensions work with one another; there is a sort of
tension as a result of these component parts that works
like a glue rather than as a divisiveness. Inside, the church
is surprisingly simple, as baroque goes. The eye is led
insistently upward into the curve of the dome, where
Rottmayr's frescoes show St. Charles's apotheosis.

In front of the church is the fountain pond, which
was a parking lot not that long ago. A sculpture by **Henry
Moore**, **Hill Arches**, is placed off center in the fountain.
Moore made a gift of this statue to the city in 1978.

The third of the large buildings ringing Karlsplatz is
the **Technical University**, built in 1816. Of the important lodgers of this university, perhaps the foremost was
the mayor of Vienna at the turn of the century, Karl Lue-

ger, a name we have already come across in Walk 2. But Lueger was no student here; his father was a janitor and later caretaker of the university building, and this is where Lueger was born. During his first four years of life, this future haranguing near-demagogue did not speak at all. He made up for this in later years. Out in his men's hostel in the working-class district of Brigittenau, Hitler later studied the municipal socialism of Lueger as well as his scapegoating use of anti-Semitism.

Two of the Strauss brothers—Josef and Johann (the waltz king)—were students at this school. Their father Johann Strauss senior, though making himself a good living from the waltz craze, wore himself out with continual tours. He wanted a better life for his sons, but they "failed" him terribly, all becoming musicians. Johann became *the* famous Johann Strauss, usurping that position from his father. The other brothers, Josef and Eduard, were no slouches either, each having his own orchestra and composing waltzes prolifically, touring all over Europe as had their father. The last survivor, Eduard, died in 1916, the same year as Franz Joseph. Taken together, the amazing Strauss family, father and sons, encompassed nearly a century of musical life in Vienna and around the world. They became symbols and synonymous with Vienna and the merry life one could lead here, though they were themselves a melancholy brood. Hitler, by the way, later did them the great "service" of Aryanizing them by having father Johann's birth certificate forged and thus wiping out the tint of Jewishness blemishing their otherwise "clean" pedigree.

Karlskirche and the Technical University are separated by Karlgasse, past which you will walk, continuing this tour. First, at **Karlgasse 4**, to your left, is a plaque stating that this addition of the Technical University was built on the site of the apartment house where Brahms died in 1897.

Continue along the front of the Technical University, with a rogue's gallery of busts of architects, engineers, and professors fronting the building. To your right is the Ressel Park, named after the Austrian inventor of the propeller. Other monuments and statues to Austrian inventors are to be found here as well: to Josef Madersperger, the inventor of the sewing machine. Madersperger was a poor apprentice tailor from Tyrol when he built his first sewing machine in 1815. He was so poor, in fact, that he did not have sufficient capital to develop his invention and died in poverty, a nobody, while Mr. Singer raked in millions. Included in the statues here is one of inventor Siegfried Marcus, who invented the first gasoline-powered automobile in 1864.

Austria has supplied an amazing number of inventors and innovators of world rank. Josef Weineck, a soap maker from just north of Vienna, discovered a method for solidifying fats and thus laid the foundation for our modern cosmetics industry, with its toothpaste, creams, and soaps. Ernst Mach, whose name is still recalled in connection with the speed of sound, did his work in Vienna.

And we have already mentioned the medical community—whose crowning achievement (debacle, some Viennese might say) was Sigmund Freud, whose work appeared concomitantly with the Secessionists and which earned him the title of a dirty old man to most Viennese. Most historians agree that Freud's work would have been impossible without the aid of the neurosis-laden Viennese public to observe and learn from. Whether one agrees with psychoanalytic theory or not, one must agree that Freud's conquistadorial breakthrough into the formerly unmapped unconscious has changed the way in which humankind perceives the world.

Continue on between the Technical University and the park, past the outdoor café on your right and, on your left, the brick building of the **Schule der Evangelische Gemeinde**, a private Protestant school built by the Ringstrasse architect Theophil Hansen in 1861.

Ahead of us, across the intersection and to the left, we see a new tract of the Technical University, with its rather fantastic façade statuary. This intersection is called

the Wiedner Haupstrasse, the medieval road leading to the south, to Venice and Trieste. Though today it does not have the appearance of age, actually this area to your left is one of the oldest *Vorstädte*, or suburban fringes, of Vienna outside the wall. Known as Wieden since 1211, this district has by now lost most of its antique character. One reason for this was the destruction of the Freihaus, an enormous building complex that stemmed from the seventeenth century and encompassed several square blocks between the Karlsplatz and the Wienzeile (where the Naschmarkt is located). The original buildings in this complex were destroyed during the 1683 Turkish siege and were rebuilt on a monumental scale, becoming one of the largest housing tracts in Europe at that time. By 1769 the entire Freihaus was finished and had no less than one thousand residents in it on thirty-one different stairwells. The old Theater auf der Wieden was opened in a wing of the complex in 1782, and Mozart's *The Magic Flute* premiered there. During the nineteenth century, the Freihaus began to deteriorate and became one enormous tenement to house the ever more crowded population of the city. By the end of the nineteenth century, plans were afoot to raze the building, and just before World War I part of it was demolished. Between the wars more of the building complex was razed and new buildings were put in its stead—by the looks of these, the city might have been better off keeping the old Freihaus intact. There was heavy bomb damage in this area during World War II. More building space was gained and more questionable buildings were thrown up in the hectic days of postwar Vienna. Parts of the old Freihaus area that are not yet rebuilt still exist as vacant lots here and there.

Let's cross over Wiender Hauptstrasse and continue on Treitlstrasse toward Operngasse. There is a small park to our right, **Girardi Park**, named after the nineteenth-century actor who initiated the star system. Girardi was

Façade statuary on the new Technical University

such a popular actor in this city of theater lovers that a whole generation began to imitate the way in which he held a cigarette in his mouth and wore his straw boater cocked to the side of his head. Beyond the park to the right you will see the roofline of the Inner City. Your vision may or may not be blocked at this point by a glass and corrugated metal structure to our immediate right. This, if it is still standing, is the **Kunsthalle** (Art Hall), a showcase for avant-garde art, and the building itself is avant-garde with its pipe-bridge pedestrian walkway going over its top and its bright colors in the midst of the sedate Karlsplatz. I speak tentatively about its presence because as of this writing Karlsplatz is considered a provisional site, until the Kunsthalle's real home is completed in the Messepalast. (See the "Other Sights of Interest" section in the introduction of this book.) But as with so many things in Vienna, provisional or temporary solutions often take on permanency. This sight is open daily, except Tuesday, 10:00 A.M. to 6:00 P.M.

In a hundred yards or so you will come to the intersection with Operngasse, where you turn left. Again, there are new, unimaginative buildings all over this oldest core of the old villages. The Freihaus was an enormously huge complex for its day (Operngasse was created on land it once occupied), quite like what later urban architects would develop during the interwar years under "Red Vienna," the first of the socialist governments. Those huge tracts of fortresslike buildings such as the Karl Marx-Hof created a new, symbolic feudal structure—this time with the proletariat on top. (During the Civil War of 1934 between the Right and Left, the Karl Marx-Hof did in fact become a fortress. It was here that the Leftists made their last stand before being quelled, leading to the establishment of the Dollfuss dictatorship. Governed by a Habsburg paterfamilias for so many centuries, the Austrians were hardly prepared for the test of democracy.) Proceed up Operngasse for thirty yards to the first traffic lights, where you can cross the street to the right-hand side.

Bounteous produce at the Naschmarkt

Then take the *Durchhaus* at **Operngasse 25a** through this apartment house to Rechte Wienzeile, just across the street from the **Naschmarkt** and with the Secession in plain view to your right. Cross at the traffic lights to the island between Rechte ("Right") and Linke ("Left") Wienzeile (the island was created with the controlling of the waters of the river Wien, which once flowed here), and go to the left down the center alleyway of this huge outdoor central market. Unlike many other major urban cities—obvious examples being London and Paris—Vienna has retained its central market, and it is alive and well.

The name of the Naschmarkt is another one of those Viennese etymological mysteries. *Naschen* means to secretly nibble away—the midnight raider of the fridge. So it would seem that a simple joining of this verb with market is responsible for the name of the Naschmarkt, "Nibbler's Market." But nothing is so simple in Vienna. Actually the name stems from the word *Asch*, which no longer means what it once did. *Asch* now means ash, as in the tree or in cinders. But *Asch* once had a meaning close to milk bucket. This was formerly the Aschenmarkt describing part of its country aspect, where farmers brought their fresh milk—among other things—into the city. The Viennese dialect played with this word (as with so many others) and turned it into Naschmarkt, with its double meaning. This several-blocks-long outdoor market is not only one of the best places in town to shop (there are other outdoor markets in the outer districts, but none quite with this panache) but also a feast for the eye and ear. As with Les Halles in its heyday, the area around the Naschmarkt has become one of those late-night slumming regions (I use that word in the positive, not perjorative, sense), full of cafés and *Beisln*, where you can get a late-night bite to eat and drink without having to pay nightclub prices. And, as with all other markets of all times, the women (they are still mainly women selling here) who run the stands are feisty and full of humorous venom. Woe be to the unsuspecting who tries to buy less than a half kilo of potatoes, for example. Even if one does not understand the caustic remark shot his way by the shopkeeper, the other customers' laughing will be enough. These women hand down the stalls as the Naschmarkt from generation to generation, as other families might favor the military or law. Some of the slang bandied about here has been refined over generations as a result.

The Naschmarkt is organized, roughly, in the following manner: The top of the market—that is, the end where we are starting—has the more expensive specialty shops. Here are the Italian and French delicatessens (the word itself comes from the German), the fish shops, specialty vegetable stands, and the like. Then as you near the middle there are the everyday shops—vegetables, butchers, bakers, wooden kitchenware, herbs, and spices. Everything you need to make your life more redeeming. Scattered about are *Wurstl* stands with their tempting smells. One can easily make a walking picnic of a visit to this market, some *Wurst* here,

The Papageno door at the Theater an der Wien

some beer there, a little fruit thrown in for good measure, and a pastry or cake at one of the bakeries.

Continue through the first quarter of the market to the first intersecting street, **Millöckergasse**, where you turn right and leave the market, crossing the street now to Linke Wienzeile—obviously the corresponding sides of Wienzeile were determined by a trip cityward. Millöckergasse, by the way, was named after the Austrian operetta composer Karl Millöcker, who lived from 1842 to 1899. To your immediate right on the corner of Millöckergasse and Linke Wienzeile is a delicatessen landmark in Vienna, a very good Italian food and wine importer. This may seem a silly thing to mention just a few pages distant from Brahms and the Karlskirche, but, if you had known Vienna before the 1970s, you would wholeheartedly agree to the inclusion of such trivia. Up until that time in conservative, sausage-eating Vienna, a specialty restaurant meant either Chinese or Hungarian. The location of a shop where one might find, for example, cold-pressed virgin olive oil was no small cultural-culinary achievement. You can still go into neighborhood grocery shops in the outer districts and befuddle the shop-keepers by asking for such exotica as oregano and zucchini.

But enough of food for a time. To the left at this point, just up the **Linke Wienzeile** at **number 6** is the **Theater**

an der Wien, Vienna's oldest existing theatrical establishment. The theater, with its modern façade, is now run
by the city of Vienna, which purchased it after World
War II to save it from destruction. This theater is almost
two centuries old, but you cannot see this from the
Wienzeile façade, where the main entrance is, for this
portion of the building was destroyed in 1900 and rebuilt
into a four-story apartment house. To get a true feeling
of the history of this fabulous institution, you have to
proceed up Millöckergasse to the old **Papagenotor** at
number 8, now the stage door. Over the ornamental
doorway to the left we see, as Papageno in Mozart's *The
Magic Flute*, a likeness of no less than Emanuel Schikaneder, the originator of that role and the librettist of the
opera. As we earlier saw, this opera premiered in the
theater in the Freihaus. Schikaneder was director of that
theater at the time and later, in 1801, won an imperial
patent to open this new theater. To the left of the Papageno door is a plaque commemorating the fact that
Beethoven lived in the theater from 1803 to 1804 and
composed parts of the Third Symphony here as well as
the *Kreutzer* Sonata. His *Fidelio* premiered here—quite un-
successfully, it must be added. It wasn't until a decade
later that Beethoven reworked the opera and won the
Viennese over to it.

The theater itself has had a long and colorful dram-
aturgical history, the stage for everything from comedy,
to high opera, to operetta. Grillparzer and Nestroy both
had plays produced here, and by the late nineteenth century the theater was the showplace of operetta, with
Strauss and Millöcker pieces being played to packed
houses. Under the direction of Wilhelm Karczag from
1900 to 1935, the theater hit the golden age of operetta.
It was during the winter of 1910–1911 that a bedraggled-
looking down-and-outer showed up for auditions for the
chorus at the Theater an der Wien. This young man sang
the tenor part of the opening song to Lehár's *The Merry
Widow*—all the rage in Vienna at the time. Karczag was

surprised at the quality of the voice that came out of this emaciated tramp and offered him a place in the chorus. But the young man had to turn the offer down when he discovered that members of the chorus had to supply their own tuxedos and costumes. Adolf Hitler found it difficult enough at this time to rub two groschen together in his pocket, let alone buy a tuxedo.

The theater was closed down during World War II and used as a storehouse for German military equipment. After the bombing of the Opera, the Theater an der Wien became *the* theater of Vienna for the next decade, taking over the role of both opera and dramatic theater during the occupation.

Today mostly musicals play here, and during the spring *Festwochen* (festival weeks) it is used for everything from drama to ballet. The perfect time to visit the Millöckergasse entrance is near twilight, when the actors and actresses can be seen bustling around inside getting their makeup on and going through their lines one last time.

Continue along the Millöckergasse and turn left in back of the theater onto Lehárgasse, whose name is intimately (as is Strauss's) bound up with the Belle Epoque of Vienna. To the right immediately behind the theater is the gray, somber, hulking façade of an extension of the Technical University. Continue on **Lehárgasse** to **number 9–11** on the left-hand side of the street, just as it curves to the right. Here we have two buildings bound together by a sort of Greek classical gate house in front of an open courtyard. Max Fabiani, whose work we saw at Kohlmarkt 9, was the architect for this building constructed from 1909 to 1911. It is a far cry from his other truly Secessionist work, but novel, nonetheless. Interestingly, this building was constructed to house one of Vienna's first rubber industries and was later taken over by one of Austria's biggest lingerie manufacturers.

The Lehárgasse is, even on the sunniest of days, rather oppressive, with its large buildings lurking around unrelieved by a fresh coat of paint. Follow it to its intersection with Gumpendorfer Strasse, where on the right you will find one of the best coffeehouses in Vienna, the **Café Sperl**, at **Gumpendorfer Strasse 11–13**. If you do not like this café, you simply do not like cafés at all. This one has it all: a century old, with pool tables, felt-covered card tables, brass fittings, oils on the walls, lots of marble, discreet service, magazines, and peace. Ever since its opening it has been the meeting place of actors and artists. It was here that the Haagengesellschaft, one of the precursors of the Secession, had their *Stammtisch*, or permanently reserved table. Restauranteurs once had their eye on something besides money, it seems.

Look just across the street from the Sperl at **Gumpendorfer Strasse 14** to a house with lovely rounded corner bay windows from 1891—one of a series of representative apartment houses in this lower part of Gumpendorfer Strasse. This street name must be one of the less noble in Vienna—it comes from the name of one of the earliest of medieval *Vororte*, or first ring of villages outside the city gates, Gumpendorf. The name comes from the old German word *Gumpe* (with much different meaning from its modern variant of the same spelling) and is closest in meaning to a slough or puddle. One can see how this area might have fostered such toad-friendly spots: it's midway between the fall of the land from Mariahilferstrasse and the banks of the River Wien. The question is, however, how it came to pass that people would actually settle in such a region. The village of Gumpendorf was incorporated into Vienna's Sixth Municipal District in 1850. There are twenty-three such districts in all, and the character of this seven-hundred-year-old village was so cannibalized by incorporation that the district to which it belongs is named after another village that stood nearby, Mariahilf (itself a name used only since 1650 to rename a yet earlier village in the same location—it's the layers of Troy all over again here). All these old suburbs

Interior of the Café Sperl

(faubourg, in the French meaning, is probably a better translation of *Vorort*) created what became the first ring of districts outside the old wall: numbers two through nine. Then come the even more removed villages, outside the old Line Wall built by Prince Eugene at the beginning of the eighteenth century. They form the districts outside the present-day Gürtel, or second concentric ring of the city. By and large it is safe to say that the districts between the Ring and Gürtel have more character, in the architectural sense of the word, than those outside the Gürtel. There are, of course, exceptions to such a sweeping generalization, and the wine villages that are at the very outer ring of building in these outer districts are only one instance. But much of the building in the other districts—between the Gürtel and the villages at the foot of the Vienna Woods—took place in the mid– to late–nineteenth century, not a time when the speculators gave much of a hoot for the aesthetics of day-to-day living.

Each district does have its own flavor, however, no matter where it is. And there is always some old village center that still plays the role of town square even in the bleakest of the worker districts. The Viennese have a most careful pattern of personal gradation for each of the districts, and one must only look at a *Postleitzahl*, the zip code that has the number of the district in it, to know where one is approximately on the socioeconomic ladder. For example, 1010 is pretty hot stuff—that is the First District. You have arrived. Some others mean the same: 1130, 1180, or 1190, being the Thirteenth, Eighteenth, and Nineteenth districts in the "green" or "cottage" area on the fringes of the city near the Vienna Woods. The Viennese also have names for all these districts, most stemming from old villages that were incorporated as the city grew and encompassed them. And there are even districts within districts, as we can see here. Someone who lives near the Sperl, for example, does not live in Mariahilf, the name of the district, but in Gumpendorf. Like most things European, the geography of Vienna is also on the micromodel. The Viennese pride themselves on knowing all the ins and outs of their city more than any other urban inhabitants that I know of. Nevertheless, they are easily stumped by the districts within districts, where even streets become a "region" that old school chums wax nostalgically about over a glass of wine at the *Heurigen.*

At the intersection of Lehárgasse and **Gumpendorfer Strasse** we turn left into the latter street and head away from the city center. Ahead to the left, at **number 17**, stands a newer house on the site of the house where Karl Millöcker, the operetta composer, was born in 1842. Millöcker left the world some very hummable melodies, especially those from *Der Bettelstudent.* Along with Strauss the younger and Suppé, Millöcker was one of the most prominent of operetta composers in that golden age of operetta in the late nineteenth century that was discussed earlier.

Continue up Gumpendorfer Strasse, keeping your eyes open for the first intersection to the right, Fillgradergasse, about fifty yards from the Millöcker house. At the top of this street you will see the *Jugendstil* **Fillgrader Steps**. These should give you an idea of the hills and dales aspect of Vienna. There was really quite a steep drop into the small valley of the Wien River before houses were built upon its banks and the waters were diverted. And don't forget to notice the striking caryatid on the second floor at **Fillgradergasse 2**, just on the right-hand corner of Gumpendorfer Strasse.

Continue along Gumpendorfer Strasse across the intersection with Laimgrubengasse, Laimgrube being another of the medieval villages or settlements that later incorporated into the Sixth District. And no, the Viennese do not say they live in Laimgrube. The building on the corner to your left, number 25, was built on the site of "Zum Blauen Strauss," a well-known nineteenth-century *Gasthaus* where the Albrecht-Dürer-Verein had its *Stammtisch.* This group was the precursor to the group that formed the Künstlerhaus in 1861. How typically Vi-

ennese again that within two blocks were the seats of the two opposing artistic communities of the city.

All along the Gumpendorfer Strasse at this point are fine Ringstrasse-style buildings, some looking overly cumbersome with all their glops of façade decoration, but many look dignified for all that. Next door to the site of "Zum Blauen Strauss" is a butcher shop that could stand as the archetypal Viennese butchers: lots of immaculate white tiling with *Wursts* and smoked meats hanging from metal hooks over glass display cases. In an age when vegetarian and low-fat diets are the norm, meat is still king in Vienna. And pork is the main meat, with more names for it than can be translated into English. Each different cut is given all the pride and discrimination that good beef is in Iowa.

We turn at the next left onto **Köstlergasse** (*not* named after the Hungarian-British writer Arthur Koestler who was a student in Vienna, by the way, but after a municipal councillor from the Mariahilf District in the late nineteenth century). This street is an interesting one in that it is wide without being heavily trafficked, giving it a feeling of sudden spaciousness in this crowded district (there are more than 33,000 inhabitants in the one square mile encompassing Mariahilf). Several of the apartment buildings have courtyards giving off to the street, increasing this feeling of openness. Most of these houses are in the Ringstrasse style, even the one to the left midway down the block at **number 6–8**, which is actually from 1910 in some kind of bizarre mix of Secession and historicism. Across the street from this building, at **number 3**, is the first of three **Otto Wagner buildings** that go right round the corner of Köstlergasse and back out onto Linke Wienzeile. This one is *so* Wagner, with its projecting roof and simplified, almost geometrically patterned façade. This building, the one next to it (which goes around the corner), and the third house

Projecting bay windows with caryatid

(next to that on Linke Wienzeile) mark the turning point in Wagner's career. He was just finishing up with the monumental Stadtbahn project and was the darling architect of Vienna (a rather facetious way to describe a sixty-year-old architect, but true nonetheless). We have seen Wagner buildings already on the Graben (Walk 3). The works on the Graben were early, heavily influenced by historicism, by symbolic representation at the cost of the form following function. Intellectuals (in the perjorative sense of the word) make much ado about the intellectual content of Wagner's work. He did so himself, actually, in his treatise on architecture. But one must separate the intellectual chaff from the wheat of what exists in the buildings he left. It is not as if Wagner suddenly invented the dome. His houses, to the untrained eye, follow traditional architectural principles—they are square and large and tall. Maybe a little less decoration here, a little more there. They do stand out from the ones around them, it is true (and in the smaller buildings of the villas on Hüttelbergstrasse 26 and 28, in the Fourteenth District, this is even more noticeable). But from the vantage point of the late twentieth century, it is hard to see how innovative they really were. For us, the principle that form follows function is only *too* obvious—we have been bombarded by the products of that dogma-as-rationale-for-lack-of-imagination for the last two generations. Give me a little façade decoration, please, rather than sterile concrete and steel.

But Wagner was a revolutionary for his time. His work on the Stadtbahn had taught him about new building materials and how one might get away with using structural bits and pieces as decoration in themselves. No need then, as can be seen in the Postsparkasse, the Post Office Savings Bank on Coch-Platz in the First District, to hide the ventilation system: better to use these pipes as decoration than to try to hide them. A brave idea for the turn of the century.

Move on to **Köstlergasse 1**, where you can take a

peek into the foyer. It is excellent: human-sized, it curves to the left around the corner of the street and leads to an elevator of such amazing *Jugendstil* completeness that it looks almost kitsch. Right down to the hinges and push buttons inside the cage, every centimeter is *Jugendstil*. Wagner had a bit of a fixation on the *Gesamtkunstwerk* (total art work), as you will see if visiting his church Am Steinhof. (It's on Baumgartner Höhe 1, in the Fourteenth District. Guided tours are available from the main gate every Saturday at 3:00 P.M. Since it lies inside the grounds of a functioning mental institution, the guided tours are necessary. This church is almost painfully *Jugendstil*, right down to the chalice.)

Look at the excellent doors and lights in this hallway on Köstlergasse. Once you're back on the street, notice that the façade of this building is fairly plain: go round the corner to the continuation of the building and you will see the amazing amount of façade detail added there on the upper stories. This and the next house up **Linke Wienzeile, number 40 (the Majolikahaus)**, "fit" together as it were by this façade decoration in the upper stories, which have flats. The bottom stories of both of these buildings are all but sealed off by the railing above the ground floor from the residential floors. Again—so what? We are all accustomed now to the mixed-use theory of architecture. And indeed Vienna always had such a mixed use: even in the noble town houses there would be an artisan or two stuck away in the upper stories, or perhaps a vegetable shop at the back. But Wagner "officialized" such practice and actually divided the parts by means of architectural articulations such as the railing and the decoration in the upper stories. At number 40 the tiles are laid out to form a giant rose tree in the façade of these residential stories; to the right at **number 38** (also Köstlergasse 1), the upper stories are covered in rather gaudy gilded decoration: swags, wreaths, and medallions cover the façade. The artist Kolo Moser, also a big gun in the Secession, was responsible for the façade decoration here; Moser also did the stained-glass windows of Wagner's Am Steinhof church.

It must be obvious to you by now that I am not quite sure how I feel about Wagner: whether he was an innovative genius or a theorizer who, along with Loos and Gropius, saddled us with the excesses of Bauhaus. Wagner was the first to define officially the twofold function of buildings: both business and domicile. But as with his structure-as-decoration, this new idea was soon corrupted into the apartment building as office-cum-rabbit warren. In the end, Wagner will probably be remembered in world history not as the functionalist master, but as the man who refused Hitler admittance to architectural school at the Fine Arts Academy.

Wagner died in 1918: a prophetic year for Vienna and the rest of the world. In that same year Klimt and Schiele also died, as well as the socialist leader Viktor Adler—so too did the Habsburg Empire. By this time expressionism had taken the place of *Jugendstil* as the motive force in the world of art: Kokoschka and Schoenberg and their protégés now held sway. The interwar years were not kind to Vienna: as elsewhere, inflation ruined the economy; private armies were built up by the Catholic and Socialist parties. Putsch followed counterputsch. And all the while the Nazis, banned from Austria, were biding their time. The fledgling Republic of Austria fell in a swoon into the arms of someone who promised the fatherlike guidance that the Habsburgs had, at least figuratively, so carefully provided all those centuries. Then followed World War II, the occupation, the shoeless 1950s, the rebuilding 1960s, the prosperous early 1970s. Vienna once again made itself an international city by using one of the clauses imposed on it by the occupying powers—that of permanent neutrality. It built itself into an international center for United Nations agencies on the banks of the Danube and is now beginning to rival Geneva as the premier international city of

Wagner's Linke Wienzeile architecture

Europe. Recent renovations and face lifts in the 1980s and 1990s have created one of the loveliest cities in Europe as well. And with the collapse of communism, Vienna has become a mecca for Central and Eastern European immigrants looking for a new life of great promise and challenge.

Over the course of these four tours we have seen myriad buildings, paintings, parks, and great palaces. I have bombarded you with a plethora of facts, figures, and anecdotes about Vienna and the Viennese character. I have tried to paint, in terms of words and deeds, the history of this metropolis, and I have tried to present it as a living and breathing phenomenon, not some museum piece through which we must gingerly proceed. And I can think of no more fitting way of finishing this all off—that is, outside of sitting down together over a glass of this year's best—than by visiting the mercantile "museum" of Vienna's past and present, the Flohmarkt, or Flea Market. We cross Linke Wienzeile back into the Naschmarkt and go to the right, away from the city center, by crossing Kettenbrücken Gasse to the U-Bahn station. The flea market lies just to the rear and side of this Wagner station building.

The **Vienna Flea Market** is not the most gemütlich place in the world. It is hectic and crowded and the meeting place for every young Viennese trying to be cool and wanting to watch others who think likewise. But over the several square blocks of this open market, the living history of Vienna is spread out before us on tables, on crude cloths on the asphalt, and in bins and boxes. Here is that chipped teapot from Tante Emmie who got it as a wedding present from Great-uncle Hans. There is the garnet brooch that Frau Dr. Novotny always meant to wear to her son's graduation—she sold it off after he committed suicide. Over in that old bucket is a collection of medals and war decorations (who would put a price on a wound or valor? who could buy one?), and next to these are some finely etched wine-

glasses. There are chamber pots, wobbly chairs, paintings, and collarless shirts in search of owners and a
starched collar. But this flea market is more than a museum of memorabilia on sale to the highest price. It is
also a metaphor for a city at work creating its own
mythos; it is a new generation finding meaning and continuity with the older generations; it is a bridge from
the past to the present—as I hope this book has been
for you.

Restaurants, Cafés, and Shops

RESTAURANTS

The following lists include both simple *Gasthäuser* and *Beisln*, with more of a publike atmosphere, as well as the more traditional sorts of restaurant. The distinction is made with each listing, as it does usually imply a price difference. As most are located in the busy First District, go early or late for lunch—before noon or after 1:30 P.M. These are listed in the order you will find them in the walks.

Walk 1

Salut, Wildpretmarkt 3. French style. Definitely for those tired of *Knödeln*. With sidewalk restaurant for the warmer months. Expensive.

Alte Rathauskeller, Wipplingerstrasse 4. Traditional Viennese fare in cozy atmosphere. Garden. Moderate.

Panther-Bräu Gasthaus, Judenplatz 10. Very *bürger-*

lich inn with good food and excellent sidewalk garden for the summer months. Moderate.

Gösser Bierklinik, Steindlgasse 4. A bit kitsch and probably not worth the money, but very gemütlich in the lower *Stube* for a beer. Moderate.

Dobinger Weinstube, Drahtgasse 2. Newish but handy. Typical Austrian fare. Moderate.

Urbani Keller, Am Hof 12. Elegant wine cellar; touristy but should be visited just for the scene. Moderate to expensive.

Esterházy Keller, Haarhof 1. Middle-class wine cellar. Huge subterranean halls with simple fare. Cheap.

Stadtbeisl, Naglergasse 21. Newly renovated but still gemütlich and central. Garden. Moderate.

Walk 2

Griechenbeisl, Fleischmarkt 11. Very cozy atmosphere, ancient inn. Food okay. Moderate to expensive.

Restaurant Marhold, Fleischmarkt 9. Nothing special, but adequate. Expensive restaurant upstairs and moderate inn down.

Siddartha, Fleischmarkt 16. Vegetarian restaurant, one of the few in carnivorous Vienna. Expensive.

Gaststätte zur Hauptpost, Postgasse 15. Neighborhood joint with simple, wholesome food. Inexpensive.

Thomas Keller, Dr. Karl Lueger-Platz 2. Adequate wine cellar though nothing special. Moderate.

Gaststätte Pfudl, Bäckerstrasse 22. Good food in a nicely appointed *Gasthaus*. Some game served. Moderate.

Zwölf-Apostelkeller, Sonnenfelsgasse 3. Kitschy but okay. Moderate.

Zum Figlmüller, Wollzeile 5. Original type of city winehouse. Famous for their *Schnitzel*. Moderate.

Dom Beisl, Schulerstrasse 4. Simple *Beisl* frequented by the fiacre drivers, in back of St. Stephen's. Moderate.

Zum Grünen Anker, Grünangergasse 10. Italian res-

taurant with Viennese gemütlich overlays. Garden. Moderate.

Zu den 3 Hacken, Singerstrasse 28. Good middle-class joint with fine lunch *Menü*. Get there early. Moderate.

Josef Mnozil's Gastwirtschaft, Seilerstätte 13. Old Vienna cooking. Neighborhood pub. Moderate.

Walk 3

Zimmer's Groschen Küchl (formerly the Schubert Stüberl), Schreyvogelgasse 4. Restaurant outlet of the cooking school. Expensive.

Johann Gossinger Gastwirtschaft, Schreyvogelgasse 3. Old-time Vienna *Gasthaus*. Moderate.

Melker Stiftskeller, Schottengasse 3. Roomy wine cellar. Specializes in baked ham hock. Moderate.

Restaurant Kern, Wallnerstrasse 3. Rather fusty eatery, but centrally located with a good lunch *Menü*. Reasonable.

Augustiner Keller, Augustinerstrasse 1. Not belowground at all, but the same atmosphere as a wine cellar. Moderate.

Gasthaus Reinthaler, *"Zum Dorotheum,"* Gluckgasse 5. Cheery and bustling neighborhood joint. Simple fare. Inexpensive.

Walk 4

Gösser Bier Keller, Elisabethstrasse 3. Large cellar type of atmosphere for a beer house. Food is not great but location is, near the Opera. Moderate.

Smutny's, Elisabethstrasse 8. Lots of tile; orchestra members come here for parched throats after concerts. Expensive.

Naschmarkt Beisl, Linke Wienzeile 14. *Beisl* frequented by shoppers and workers from the market. Inexpensive.

Gasthaus zur Eisener Zeit, in the Naschmarkt, opposite Linke Wienzeile 14. The regulars of the market hang out here. Simple food. Cheap.

Café-Restaurant Resselpark, in the park in Karlsplatz. More eatery than café. Very nice. Moderate.

CAFÉS

Walk 1

Café Altstadt, Judenplatz 2. Not of the classic variety, but it has a good garden. Moderate.

Walk 2

Café Pruckel, corner of Stubenring and Dr. Karl Lueger-Platz. Cavernous coffeehouse with immense card room in back. Moderate.

Café Huber, in Stadtpark. Nice terrace setting over the all-but-defunct Wien River. Good sun spot in the summer. Moderate.

Café Diglas, Wollzeile 10. Again, not of the classic variety, but nice enough and with good small things to eat. Moderate.

Café Ball, Ballgasse 5. New and good-looking. Moderate.

Café Frauenhuber, Himmelpfortgasse 6. Old-time elegance. Moderate.

Walk 3

Café Landtmann, corner of Dr. Karl Lueger-Ring and Löwelstrasse next to the Burgtheater. Freud's favorite, and snooty as hell. But outside seating makes it bearable. Moderate.

Café Haag, Schottengasse 2. Central, of the classic variety and terrific pastries. Moderate.

Demel's Café-Konditorei, Kohlmarkt 14. More the latter than the former, specializing in pastries for generations. Moderate to expensive.

Café Hawelka, Dorotheergasse 6. Terribly overrated as some kind of intellectual hangout, but a charming interior nonetheless and bearable only in the early-morning hours before the people crawl out from under their rocks. Moderate.

Café Bräunerhof, Stallburggase 4. Fine old café with lots of reading material and awfully good lunch fare as well. Moderate to pricey for food.

Café Mozart, Albertinaplatz 2. Just in back of the Opera, this is a bit ritzy, but a cup of coffee is a cup of coffee at the same price almost all over Vienna. Moderate to expensive.

Café Sacher, Philharmonikerstrasse 4–6. Just because you have to have chocolate cake at the "Sach" once in your life. Expensive.

Café Tirolerhof, Tegetthoffstrasse and Führichgasse. Good reading matter, busy, and a great mélange to be had. Moderate.

Walk 4

Café Museum, Operngasse 7. Cavernous and of the old school, though renovated in the 1950s. Moderate.

Café Sperl, corner of Gumpendorfer Strasse and Lehárgasse. Until very recent renovations, one of the most authentic cafés in the classic style. For those who didn't know it before, it won't be apparent. But the guts were taken out of it. Pool tables, card tables, and fin de siècle atmosphere. Moderate.

Café Wienzeile, Linke Wienzeile 36. Fake opulent, but okay. Moderate.

SHOPS

Walk 1

Knopfkönig, Freisingergasse 1. All sorts of buttons for the fetishists among you. Across the street is another part of the shop, which specializes in petit point.

Ono Deco, Brandstätte 7. One of the few shops specializing in deco, a very short-lived style in Vienna.

Shakespeare and Company, Sterngasse 2. Great English-language bookshop.

The Second Hand Shop, Judengasse 4. Good Inner City *Altwaren* shop, where you can pick through all sorts of things from old tweeds to old oils.

Nefertiti, Judengasse 7. The magicianlike proprietor turns old brocades and carpets into hats and bags. Very clever.

Galerie Image, Judengasse 16. Poster art from around the world. Great assortment of exhibition posters.

Ferdinand Masserl, Schlossermeister, Wipplingerstrasse 6. Wrought-iron handiwork at its best.

Bourcy and Paulusch Antiquariat, Schultergasse 5. Old books, maps, and lithographs of Vienna and Austria-related subjects.

Kunst Stil, Kurrentgasse 4. Antique shop of the classier style, specializing in porcelain and glass.

Kühner, Drahtgasse 3. Chic-rustic houseware and furnishings. Pricey but lovely.

Walk 2

Herbert Born, Köllnerhofgasse 4. Unique shop specializing in brass fittings and elegant parchment lampshades.

Hans Schwanda Jagd und Camping, Bäckerstrasse 7. Good selection of outdoor clothing and equipment. Everything from knickers to hiking boots.

Gustav Friedrich Leder, Bäckerstrasse 4. Huge assortment of leather sold by the hide or to measure.

Galerie Ambiente, Lugeck 1. *Jugendstil* and deco furnishings and paintings. They usually have great ad posters for sale.

E. Metzger, Stephansplatz 7. Excellent assortment of *Lebkuchen* (gingerbread) and beeswax candles.

Keramik aus Gmünden, Seilergasse 7. Excellent selection of this very rustic ceramic ware.

Schönbichler Teehandlung, Wollzeile 4. Large assortment of teas, liquors, and liqueurs.

Grams and Co., Singerstrasse 26. Wine merchants par excellence. Try their house dry *Sekt*. Fine assortment of Austrian and international wines.

Antiquariät-Bücher-Curiösitäten, Weihburggasse 16. The name tells it all. Good section of Viennese books, in German. Great and arty postcard selection.

The British Bookshop, Blumenstockgasse 3. Another quite excellent English-language bookshop. Strong on teaching materials (at Singerstrasse branch).

Backhausen und Söhne, Kärntnerstrasse 33. Elegant household fabrics: curtains, tablecloths, and carpets.

Buchhandlung Prachner, Karntnerstrasse 30. Fine old Viennese bookshop with select collection of English-language books.

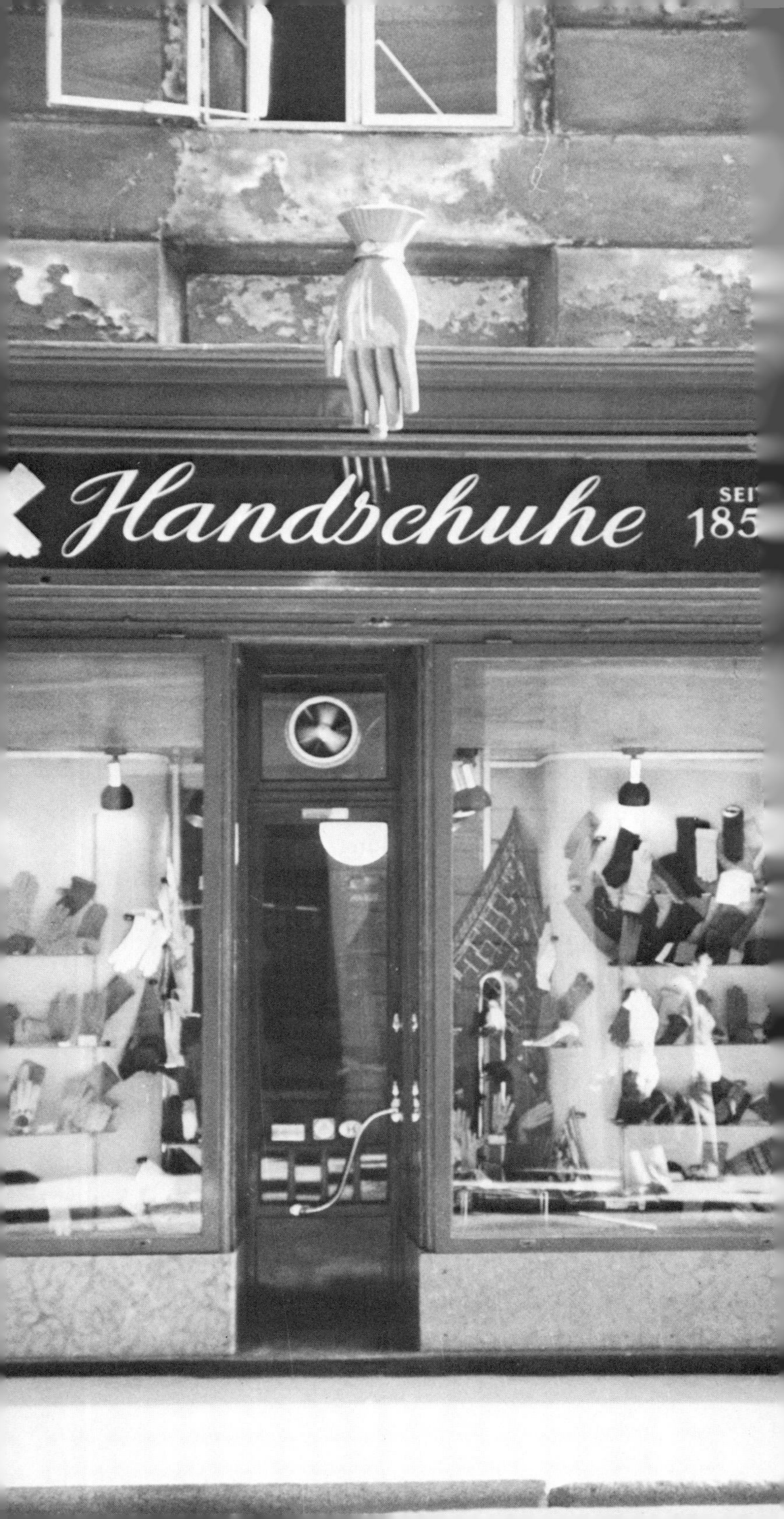
Handschuhe
SEIT
185

Walk 3

Trachten Tostmann, Mölker Steig and Schottengasse 3a. The first address is for children's *Trachten* and all sorts of folkloric gift items. The latter is the adult clothing section of this classic Viennese institution.

Niederoesterreichisches Heimwerk, Herrengasse 6–8. More folk art and *Trachten* accessories. Fine rag rugs, handmade.

Loden Plankl, Michaelerplatz 6. Another Viennese clothing institution for traditional wear and for fine coats and capes. Tailoring is still an excellent buy here, as it is all over Vienna.

Frick Books, Graben 27. Some English-language books.

Musikhaus Doblinger, Dorotheergasse 10. Everything musical available here, from instruments to sheet music to CDs.

Dorotheum, Dorotheergasse 11 (fine art) and Dorotheergasse 17 (everything else). This is the state-run pawn shop with auctions weekly. You can browse both sections and see the *Rufpreis*, or call price, and maybe go to the auctions. But be sure to keep your hand down if not bidding.

Wolfrum, Augustinerstrasse 10. Excellent selection of prints and art postcards.

Walk 4

Antiquitäten Helmut Heinzl, Gumpendorferstrasse 20. Turn-of-the-century collectibles moderately priced.

Flohmarkt, Kettenbrücken Gasse U4 station. The central Vienna Flea Market, at the end of the Naschmarkt, or central outdoor market. Open Saturday only.

Selected

Bibliography

"Selected" means exactly that: I have avoided the esoteric in this list as well as the German-language contributions and have chosen only books that are still in print or that are easily obtainable from libraries.

Barea, Ilse. *Vienna, Legend and Reality.* New York: Alfred A. Knopf, 1966.

Barker, Elisabeth. *Austria 1918–1942.* London: Macmillan London Ltd., 1973.

Brion, Marcel. *Daily Life in the Vienna of Mozart and Schubert.* New York: The Macmillan Company, 1962.

Brook-Shepard, Gordon. *The Austrian Odyssey.* London: Macmillan London Ltd., 1957.

Clare, George. *Last Waltz in Vienna.* New York: Henry Holt, 1989.

Crankshaw, Edward. *The Habsburgs: Portrait of a Dynasty.* New York: Viking Press, 1971.

———. *Maria Theresa.* New York: Viking Press, 1969.

———. *Vienna,* 2d ed. London: Macmillan London Ltd., 1976.

Giroud, Francoise. *Alma Mahler, or the Art of Being Loved.* New York: Oxford University Press, 1991.

Gruber, Helmut. *Red Vienna.* New York: Oxford University Press, 1991.

Grunfeld, Frederick V. *Vienna.* New York: Newsweek Book Division, 1981.

Henderson, Nicholas. *Prince Eugene of Savoy.* London: Weidenfeld and Nicolson, 1964.

Hofmann, Paul. *The Viennese: Splendor, Twilight, and Exile.* New York: Anchor Press, 1988.

Janik, Allen, and Toulmin, S. *Wittgenstein's Vienna.* London: Weidenfeld and Nicolson, 1973.

Johnson, Lonnie. *Introducing Austria.* Vienna: Österreichischer Bundesverlag, 1987.

Johnston, William M. *The Austrian Mind.* Berkeley: University of California Press, 1972.

———. *Vienna, Vienna: The Golden Age 1815–1914.* New York: Clarkson N. Potter, Inc., 1980.

Jones, J. Sydney. *Hitler in Vienna 1907–1913.* New York: Stein and Day, 1983.

Landon, H. C. Robbins. *Mozart and Vienna.* New York: Schirmer Books, 1991.

Lehne, Inge, and Johnson, Lonnie. *Vienna, The Past in the Present.* Vienna: Österreichischer Bundesverlag, 1985.

Leitich, Ann Tizia. *The Spanish Riding School in Vienna.* Munich: Nymphenburger Verlag, 1956.

Macartney, C. A. *The Habsburg Monarchy 1790–1918.* London: Weidenfeld and Nicolson, 1968.

McGuigan, Dorothy Gies. *The Habsburgs.* Garden City, N.Y.: Doubleday, 1966.

Morton, Frederic. *A Nervous Splendor: Vienna 1888–89.* New York: Penguin Books, 1980.

———. *Thunder at Twilight: Vienna 1913–1914.* New York: Scribner, 1989.

Musil, Robert. *The Man Without Qualities.* London: Pan Books, Limited, 1979.

Musulin, Stella. *Vienna in the Age of Metternich.* London: Faber and Faber, 1975.

Nebehay, Christian Michael. *Vienna 1900: Architecture and Painting*. Vienna: Verlag Christian Brandstätter, 1983.

Osborne, Charles. *Schubert and His Vienna*. New York: Knopf, 1985.

Pick, Robert. *The Last Days of Imperial Vienna*. New York: Dial Press, 1976.

Powell, Nicholas. *The Sacred Spring*. London: Studio Vista, 1974.

Prawy, Marcel. *The Vienna Opera*. New York: Praeger, 1970.

Pryce-Jones, David. *Vienna*. Amsterdam: Time Books, 1978.

Rath, R. John. *The Vienna Revolution of 1848*. Austin: University of Texas Press, 1957.

Schnitzler, Arthur. *My Youth in Vienna*. New York: Holt, Rinehart and Winston, 1970.

Schonberg, Harold C. *The Lives of the Great Composers*. New York: W. W. Norton and Company, 1970.

Schorske, Carl E. *Fin-de-Siècle Vienna: Politics and Culture*. New York: Vintage Books, 1981.

Stoye, J. W. *The Siege of Vienna*. New York: Holt, Rinehart and Winston, 1965.

Taylor, A. J. P. *The Habsburg Monarchy, 1809–1918*. London: Macmillan and Company, 1941.

Vergo, Peter. *Art in Vienna*. London: Phaidon Press Ltd., 1975.

Vienna Tourist Board. *Vienna Present and Past*. Vienna: Jugend und Volk Verlag, 1974.

Wechsberg, Joseph. *The Waltz Emperors: The Life and Times and Music of the Strauss Family*. New York: G. P. Putnam's Sons, 1973.

Wolff, Larry. *Postcards from the End of the World: Child Abuse in Freud's Vienna*. New York: Atheneum, 1988.

Zweig, Stefan. *The World of Yesterday*. Lincoln: University of Nebraska Press, 1964.

Index

Index

Index

Index

THE HENRY HOLT WALKS SERIES

For people who want to *learn* when they travel, not just see.

Look for these other exciting volumes in Henry Holt's best-selling Walks series:

PARISWALKS, Revised Edition, by Alison and Sonia Landes
Five intimate walking tours through the most historic quarters of the City of Light.
288 pages, photos, maps $12.95 Paper

LONDONWALKS, Revised Edition, by Anton Powell
Five historic walks through old London, one brand-new for this edition.
272 pages, photos, maps $12.95 Paper

VENICEWALKS by Chas Carner and Alessandro Giannatasio
Four enchanting tours through one of the most perfect walking environments the world has to offer.
240 pages, photos, maps $12.95 Paper

ROMEWALKS by Anya M. Shetterly
Four walking tours through the most historically and culturally rich neighborhoods of Rome.
256 pages, photos, maps $14.95 Paper

FLORENCEWALKS, Revised Edition, by Anne Holler
Four intimate walks through this exquisite medieval city, exploring its world-famous art and architecture.
240 pages, photos, maps $14.95 Paper

VIENNAWALKS, Revised Edition, by J. Sydney Jones
Four walking tours that reveal the homes of Beethoven, Freud, and the Habsburg monarchy.
304 pages, photos, maps $14.95 Paper

RUSSIAWALKS by David and Valeria Matlock
Seven intimate tours—four in Moscow and three in St. Petersburg—
that explore the hidden treasures of these enigmatic cities.
304 pages, photos, maps $12.95 Paper

NEW YORKWALKS by The 92nd Street Y, edited by Batia
Plotch
One of the city's most visible cultural and literary institutions
guides you through six historic neighborhoods in New York.
336 pages, photos, maps $12.95 Paper

BARCELONAWALKS by George Semler
Five walking tours through Spain's cultural and artistic center—
synonymous with such names as Gaudí, Miró, and Picasso.
272 pages, photos, maps $12.95 Paper

JERUSALEMWALKS, Revised Edition, by Nitza Rosovsky
Six intimate walks that allow the mystery and magic of this
city to unfold.
304 pages, photos, maps $14.95 Paper

BEIJINGWALKS by Don J. Cohn and Zhang Jingqing
Six intimate walking tours of the most historic quarters of this
politically and culturally complex city.
272 pages, photos, maps $15.95 Paper

MADRIDWALKS by George Semler
Five intimate walking tours through the cultural and geograph-
ical center of Spain.
272 pages, photos, maps $14.95 Paper

BERLINWALKS by Peter Fritzsche and Karen Hewitt
Four intimate walking tours of Berlin's most enchanting quarters.
288 pages, photos, maps $14.95

PRAGUEWALKS by Ivana Edwards
Five walking tours through this ancient and beautiful city that
has been described as a museum.
256 pages, photos, maps $14.95

Available at your local bookseller or from Special Sales Department, Henry Holt and Company, 115 West 18th Street,
New York, New York 10011, (212) 886-9200. Please add
$2.00 for postage and handling, plus $.50 for each additional
item ordered. (New York residents, please add applicable state
and local sales tax.) Please allow 4–6 weeks for delivery. Prices
and availability are subject to change.